Isn't This Fun?

Isn't This Fun?

Investigating the Serious Business of
Enjoying Ourselves

Michael Foley

SIMON &
SCHUSTER

London · New York · Sydney · Toronto · New Delhi

A CBS COMPANY

First published in Great Britain by Simon & Schuster UK Ltd, 2016
A CBS COMPANY

1 3 5 7 9 10 8 6 4 2

Simon & Schuster UK Ltd
1st Floor
222 Gray's Inn Road
London WC1X 8HB

www.simonandschuster.co.uk

Simon & Schuster Australia, Sydney
Simon & Schuster India, New Delhi

The author and publishers have made all reasonable efforts to contact
copyright-holders for permission, and apologise for any omissions or errors in
the form of credits given. Corrections may be made to future printings.

A CIP catalogue record for this book
is available from the British Library

Paperback ISBN: 978-1-4711-5482-9
eBook ISBN: 978-1-4711-5483-6

Typeset in the UK by M Rules
Printed and bound by CPI Group (UK) Ltd, Croydon, CR0 4YY

Simon & Schuster UK Ltd are committed to sourcing paper that is made from
wood grown in sustainable forests and support the Forest Stewardship Council, the
leading international forest certification organisation. Our books displaying
the FSC logo are printed on FSC certified paper.

For my Zen Masters, Mia and Conor

Contents

Part IV – Assessing Fun

PART I

Defining Fun

1

Isn't this Fun?

In its close crowding and clutter the scene resembled a school hall converted into a dormitory for the victims of a disaster – except that these people were all in dark glasses and swimwear. This was a New England beach in high summer, so packed that movement in any direction was as tricky as crossing a stream on widely spaced, very small, slippery stones. The proximity encouraged conversation and the benign old lady in the neighbouring group ('Everyone calls me Grammy') befriended our daughter – and then my wife and me. She was, she explained, a piano teacher who specialised in tutoring unmusical adults and had just converted a retired dentist into an accomplished boogie-woogie performer.

'You can teach *anyone* to play jazz piano?' I asked.

'Shuhwuh.'

'But to play jazz piano *like Thelonious Monk*?'

'Shuhwuh.'

Immediately I saw myself in a dark club, hunched over the keyboard, deep in a broodingly intense rendering of 'Round Midnight'.

'What a shame we don't live here.'

Grammy, moved by my disappointment, laid a consoling hand

on my arm and suggested that, as an alternative, her son would take me sailing. Obviously it had not occurred to her that lovers of 'Round Midnight' are unlikely to be sailing enthusiasts. I made demurring noises ... couldn't possibly ... too much trouble etc. .... and the loved ones, aware of my profound aversion to small boats, also added fervent protests. But Grammy had already turned: '*Rich!*'

The son Rich was an Americanised Viking, tall, strikingly blond, with a substantial unit filling tight swimming trunks and one of those evenly golden tans that look absolutely natural but also absolutely non-genetic. It was as though King Midas, forbearing to touch such a splendid creature, had instead breathed gently all over Rich and aurified only his hair and skin.

The only consolation was Rich's American-size belly. *Check out my thirty-inch waist, blubber gut.* Instead he looked lower down, at my chinos. 'You'll need a swimsuit, Mike. You'll get wet.'

'Ah,' I sighed, in apparent rue but secret joy, the chinos being my limited but final concession to beachwear. 'I don't have a swimsuit.'

This lack of trunks should have been decisive – but not in can-do America.

'Get a pair up in town,' commanded Rich.

This was a classy New England town, with none of the usual cheap, trashy resort shops and only one menswear outlet, whose window displayed a single polo shirt on a pedestal, like a sculpture, and whose interior had a polished wood floor with, here and there, a few tables bearing a few items each. Many of these garments were embellished with discreet anchors and dolphins, and on the side wall two long, highly polished oars were fixed in a crisscross with an old ship's wheel at their junction. Beneath the wheel stood an unsmiling middle-aged woman who may well have been a descendant of the puritans on the *Mayflower*.

I brought to her what seemed like the cheapest pair of trunks – there were no price tags – but still experienced a moment of vertigo when the amount appeared on the till. This holiday was already well over budget.

Then came the misery of appearing in public in swimming trunks, revealing a terminal-invalid pallor and legs luridly scarred from mosquito bites gone bad. And since it was still early in the day, I had yet to apply insect repellent, leaving me exposed and defenceless before the enemy, surprisingly and shockingly numerous in upmarket New England. Rich glanced at my legs – and looked quickly away.

Could there have been a less likely sailor? But sailing enthusiasts are among the most evangelical believers. Certain of making a convert, Rich led me to his dinghy and soon had me flinging myself from side to side under the boom as he explained each manoeuvre. The destination was a tiny sandbank, where we disembarked and stood side by side, looking back at the beach and its restless, densely packed crowd, at this range like some sort of dark insect swarm.

'Now, Mike,' cried Rich, with a wild expression of visionary triumph, 'isn't this fun?'

His rhetorical question was depressingly familiar. On many occasions, in a variety of environments, with a variety of companions, I have been assured that an experience will be fun, asked while it's going on to agree that it's fun, and after it's over prompted frequently to acknowledge that it was indeed fun. The environments have included other beaches, where I lay among holiday paraphernalia, propped uncomfortably on an elbow and squinting against the sun, clubs at 2 a.m., where I held a glass of wine priced like Bollinger but tasting like vinegar, hoarse from shouting banal short sentences, and trying to close out the painful noise that probed eardrums for a weak spot to pierce, and football terraces, where I could see only a corner of the pitch now and then and nothing whatever at the exciting moments, while trying to keep my balance against the unnerving sways of the crowd.

I have often pretended to be having fun and wondered if the enthusiasts were genuinely enjoying what felt like torture to me. If so, why am I different? If not, why would they pretend? What is fun and why do so many value it so highly and seek it so fervently? But I have rarely asked such questions aloud. In the modern era fun has become an unchallenged good, a key desideratum, the quality that can redeem any form of activity. It has even become a duty. In the premodern era the duty was saving your immortal soul, in the modern age it was making money, and in the postmodern world it's having fun.

So work aspires to be fun. Education aspires to be fun. Religion aspires to be fun. Political protest aspires to be fun. Even war would like to be fun. I was shocked by a documentary on the Falklands war, when a young English officer admitted to shouting, 'This is fun', moments before a chunk of his brain was shot away – and again by a news report, when an English Islamist fighting in Afghanistan described his experience as 'quite fun actually'. The idea that anyone could find war fun was grotesque – but while I was wondering if I had heard these people correctly, a headline jumped out of the evening paper: 'The hidden awful truth about war is how much fun it is'.[1] This was the title of an interview with a war reporter and a quote from his book on the experience of reporting the Arab revolutions and civil wars across the Middle East and North Africa.[2] The demand to have fun seems often to become a need to interpret whatever is happening as fun, an insistence that *everything* has to be fun.

Imagine rejecting, or even being sceptical about, fun, and becoming known as the man who hates fun. Nowadays refusing to believe in fun is the equivalent of professing atheism in the early Middle Ages and is likely to be punished as severely, with eternal banishment from social networks the equivalent of burning at the stake. No one openly sceptical about fun is ever likely to get a date or even to be invited out for a drink. My wife and daughter have always suspected me of being a secret afunist and I have always refused to admit, even to myself, an abiding aversion to nightclubs, discos, DJs, beaches, rock concerts, festivals, carnivals, fancy dress, weddings, parties, barbecues, charades, Monopoly, Scrabble, football matches, charismatic religion and carnivalesque street protest. But the prevalence of fun got me thinking, and an early thought was that the problem may not be in the fun activities but in me. As an intellectual snob, I shudder at fun because it's vulgar and frivolous, and as a goal-driven puritan I despise it as hedonistic and feckless. Of course fun is frequently all of these – but it also offers much else.

So what is fun and why is it valued so highly? One consequence of its value is that the word is used so frequently and generally it defies definition. Originally a noun, it's now also an adjective to describe anything enjoyable in an undemanding way – a fun event, a fun person, a fun thing. Even when used as a noun it's difficult to define. Another problem is that fun is assumed to be a simple, obvious phenomenon that requires no explanation or even consideration and so has received none. When people say, as they constantly do, 'It was fun', few ever ask, 'What do you mean exactly?' If someone does ask, the questioning often goes in a circle. Why do you do these things? Because they're fun. But what is fun? Doing fun things. And such questions often provoke irritation because they seem so superfluous. Yet fun has many forms and functions and is far from simple.

In many ways fun is like happiness – an experience everyone wants but no one can define, elusive and nebulous, available only unconsciously and intermittently, likely to disappear if consciously pursued.

Fun is certainly more complex than the term it has replaced, leisure, which was simply defined as the opposite of work. Where work was tiring, leisure was restful, where work created tension, leisure compensated with relaxation, where work was active, leisure was passive, where work was important, leisure was trivial. However, fun is not the opposite of work, nor even an alternative to it. Work can be fun and fun can be work, and often work is more fun than fun while fun is more work than work.

The first definite fact is that fun is a recent phenomenon. For all but the last few centuries of over 200,000 years on earth *Homo sapiens* had no fun at all. This is not just because life was hard, although that was certainly the case, but because there was no such thing as fun. The word in its modern meaning did not appear until the eighteenth century and is thought to derive from the old English word *fon*, meaning cheat or hoax, which is wonderfully appropriate because fun is, in a way, artificial, and the response to it is often a lie, as when I responded with a rousing affirmative to Rich's question, 'Isn't this fun?'

The timing of the earliest appearance of the word suggests that it is connected to the emergence of the modern world in eighteenth-century Europe. The key development was the erosion of a feudal, hierarchical society where *what* you were determined *who* you were, and the human, natural and divine were combined in a unified whole. Everything in life, from the natural world to the social order and the primacy of the family, was a given – inevitable, fitting, divinely sanctioned, and beyond question, never mind change. But then everything *did* become questioned and everything *did* change, with the rise of the concept of individual freedom, the blessing and curse of the modern age.

This concept was, and remains, terrifically exciting – but freedom came with a price. There is always a price. The problem with rejecting the ready-made is that you now have to make everything yourself. All that had so far been taken for granted, so much so that often it had not been given a name, had now to be made anew, self-consciously, artificially – and named. And the many novel experiences and expressions of individual freedom also had to be named. So there came into the language new terms such as fun, boredom, identity, authenticity, interestingness, the sublime, beauty (in the aesthetic sense), celebrity and genius – and familiar terms such as childhood and play acquired a new significance.

Historians argue about the origins of individual freedom but two important factors in the modern era were the glorification of reason by Enlightenment thinkers such as Descartes – who claimed that the individual could and should establish everything of importance by rational calculation alone – and the growth of commerce and the emergence of a middle class of merchants, prosperous farmers and urban craftsmen, who believed in private property and unhindered individual wealth accumulation. This was a partnership of ideas and business, such as contemporary universities dream of, and it replaced the feudal world with capitalism. Fun then emerged as a range of activities to respond to these developments.

The purpose of fun as pleasure was nothing new, but the rejection of religious control opened up the possibility of hedonism, of the individual living exclusively for pleasure. With the old prohibitions revealed as invalid, why not indulge to the full? And indeed Enlightenment thinkers developed philosophies of hedonism, while many have been happy to practise it without the support of theory. However, even pleasure turns out not to be simple. Among other complications, the pursuit of pleasure is like the pursuit of happiness – often self-defeating. Though fun shares with hedonism a belief in pleasure, it is much more than personal pleasure seeking.

Fun is not individualistic but social. The free individual rejects the old divinely ordained embedding in family, social structure and nature, and relishes liberty, but misses the warmth of the connections, the certainty of the fixed role and the reassurance of the rituals. Fun compensates for this loss with a new sense of belonging and new sanctioned routines – in other words an alternative set of group rituals. Fun is essentially communal. It's possible to have pleasure alone but not fun. (This is another reason for my afunist tendency – as a product of modern individualism, I have an instinctive aversion to any form of group endeavour.)

Fun was also a response to the modern belief that the guiding principle in life is reason, which will rationally establish goals and the most efficient way of achieving them. This in turn encouraged the belief that nature was to be dominated and used, rather than venerated, and resulted in a new tyranny of the project. Fun counters this with the concept of play, activity enjoyed for its own sake.

Fun even has a role in replacing religion. The loss of both a connection with nature and belief in a divine plan brought about the well-known modern feeling of disenchantment, the view of the world as a dreary piece of clockwork, and the idea that life might be futile, which brought in turn the modern affliction of boredom. The terms 'fun' and 'bore', in the sense of diversion or its lack, entered the language around the same time, in the eighteenth century, and the two are intimately connected, opposite sides of the same coin or, rather, opposite ends of a new scale for evaluating experience, with 'great fun' at one end and 'deadly boring' at the other. Fun can provide an antidote to boredom by offering re-enchantment, the possibility of a personal transcendence in secular group rituals. Hence fun has a quasi-religious function as a light of the world, an answer to the hunger for meaning. As religion confers divine grace, fun confers profane grace. And fun is like religion in that many believers feel it necessary to cry hallelujah even when they have experienced little benefit from the rituals. (Did Rich really believe that sailing to a sandbank to look back at a crowded beach was a terrifically meaningful and rewarding experience?) Appearing to have fun is as important as the genuine experience because fun, like religion, is a mark of superiority. Fun is coveted and those having fun are the secular saved. In the endless struggle for distinction, fun snobbery is an important new stratagem, especially for those without status or money. A major function of social media is to show the fun-rich enjoying their fun wealth, in those millions of group photos with arms around shoulders, heads leaning in together, and faces wearing the fun smile, which is not just radiant but also beatific, to demonstrate the religious nature of the experience. The Holy Spirit has descended and entered the funists.

All these factors, the weakening of divine, social and familial connections, the surrender to instrumental reason and the feeling of disenchantment, have created the modern fear of a loss of authenticity, the feeling that much of what was genuine and valuable has gone missing somewhere along the way. So another function of fun is to restore this lost sense of the authentic.

Then there is the recent shift in capitalist culture from the desire to possess to the desire to experience (a trend obvious in bookshops cluttered with books on 'decluttering'). This discovery that doing is more fulfilling than owning has been hailed as progress, though experiences are also commodities that can be manufactured and marketed in the same ways as goods, and spending a large sum of money to climb Everest may be every bit as unsatisfactory as using it to buy a sports car. However, experiences do not yet have the stigma of possessions – and fun is not only pure experience but one of the most valued forms of experience.

Finally, there is the fun of transgression that flouts the conventions and social order, and the fun of humour that mocks the pretentious, the hypocritical, the greedy and the powerful. These kinds of fun have also emerged as alternatives to violence in political protest, a way to bamboozle and undermine authority.

All this can be put together in a tentative definition. Fun is a set of group rituals designed to provide a range of experiences that banish boredom and give pleasure, through the comfort of belonging and sometimes the euphoria of transcendence, and that restore the delight of re-enchantment and sometimes the reassurance of authenticity, as well as the insouciance of play and sometimes the defiance of humour and transgression.

But any definition makes fun appear static whereas it must constantly mutate to meet the changing demands of the times. The story of life on earth can be seen as an incessant splitting, branching and mutating into ever greater diversification and complexity, until the original cell division has produced over 30 million species and one of these, *Homo sapiens*, has spread and filled the earth with a multiplicity of cultures that continue to split, branch and mutate with the manic energy of cancer cells. Understanding fun involves seeking its sources in cultural history and following its adaptations to cultural change. When I was young I believed that history could have no bearing on that brilliant autonomous creation, my free life, but the older I get the more I realise that this supposedly free life has been culturally determined. We are all at sea but believe ourselves to be swimming purposefully when in fact we are largely at the mercy of the prevailing cultural currents.

Fun is not only complex but paradoxical. It's an entirely modern concept, and yet investigation will reveal that it often involves a return to the oldest rituals of pre-history. It's the most profane of activities and yet it can also be religious. It's a way of achieving individual transcendence, yet it works only by immersing the individual in the social. It's frequently destructive and yet also redemptive, frequently frivolous and yet also crucial, a sedative encouraging passivity and yet often also an agent of radical change. It pervades every aspect of contemporary Western culture, and is constantly and universally invoked, yet it's never analysed or even considered worthy of analysis. The only unequivocal fact is that it has a multitude of difficult tasks to accomplish. No wonder fun often seems more work than work.

PART II

Understanding Fun

2

Fun and Ritual

'I really *hate* rituals,' I proclaimed to a group of friends over an aperitif, almost spilling my Pouilly-Fumé in a sweeping gesture of emphasis – but instead of nodding in solemn agreement they burst into helplessly gleeful, and even slightly malicious, laughter. It took a while for them to regain sufficient composure to explain that I was rejecting ritual not just while gladly participating in a ritual but in *a ritual that I myself had devised and established.* This was the ritual of the aperitif, in fact a ritual so sacred it's more like a sacrament. Did I not insist, they pointed out, that an hour be set aside for this ritual and that food preparation be suspended so that everyone could gather in a room solemnised by subdued light, the removal of daily detritus and the distribution of little Chinese bowls of macadamia nuts, Bombay mix and hand-crafted sea salt and balsamic vinegar potato crisps? And did I not also insist that everyone attend solemnly to the solemn pouring, then solemnly rise to clink glasses and solemnly sit down to drink as one? Did I not recall giving this ritual the special name, A-time, and even its own sacred music – Duke Ellington's *Take the A Train*?

In fact what I hated was *religious* ritual, the multitude of Catholic observances that had dominated my childhood and always seemed an absurd relic of archaic superstition with no place in the rational modern world. To ensure that their children passed examinations and got prestigious jobs, my mother and aunts would oblige God to be merciful by making a pilgrimage to an island on Lough Derg in Donegal, where for three days they walked barefoot on jagged rocks sustained only by black tea. And to supplement the magical coercion of the three days of mortification they also observed the four mysteries of the rosary, the seven sacraments of the Church, the nine Tuesdays of St Anthony and the fourteen stations of the cross.

I evaded most of this but had to endure the annual mortification of abstaining from confectionery during Lent (my attempt to continue eating potato crisps on the grounds that they were savouries rather than sweets was angrily rejected by my mother as typical of my smart-alec casuistry and arrogant refusal to submit to the sacred). Then the privations of Lent were followed by the most excruciating boredom I have ever had to endure – the ritual Holy Week ceremonies.

There were many other observances throughout the year and many magical objects to be carried on the person. Children went forth into an evil world protected by the full spiritual body armour of Holy Water on the face, scapulars round the neck, a miraculous medal pinned to the vest and blessed rosary beads in the pocket. As a consequence of these absurdities, I rejected all ritual, not realising that ritual was my joy as well as my grief. My escape from ritual was itself a ritual, and what seemed so thrillingly new was actually as archaic as could be.

The new temple was a dance hall and the new priests were the Irish showbands of the time with names like Big Tom and the

Mainliners, Pat and the Gay Dons, Patricia and the Crackaways, Dermot and the Philosophers, Deirdre and the Defenders, and Teresa Conlon and the Yukons. I can still remember experiencing for the first time live rhythmical music driven by a drummer joyously pounding a kit that rattled, shook and rang under the impact of the sticks. This was Butch Moore and the Capitol Showband doing a Beatles number, 'I Saw Her Standing There' – but it was nothing like the weak, tinny sound of transistor radios that entered feebly through the ears. Instead something ancient, primal and powerful had seized the entire tawdry building, and was shaking it in triumph and jubilation, as King Kong shook Faye Wray, the walls and floor vibrating and its message coming up from the boards through the legs to possess the body and make it its creature. 'Well she was just seventeen,' Butch yelled, 'you know what I mean,' and the drummer exuberantly crashed a cymbal to indicate that he understood exactly. I too understood. From the depths of a time long before the Nazarene, Dionysus, in the form of this paunchy drummer, was issuing a summons to an ancient ritual, and immediately, renouncing fifteen years of relentless indoctrination, I surrendered my body and soul.

Everything in the dancehall was as tightly ritualised as in church. Outside the ladies' toilet, girls clustered in a dense, heaving array of white arms and throats, and it was astounding to know that most of them would agree to dance if asked, would move forward to offer a hand to be held and permit my other hand to rest on a waist, overwhelming me with the dual intoxication of scent and the sense of a warm body moving beneath the clothes. A dance was actually three dances, three numbers in the same tempo, usually fast but if you were lucky, slow, and if you were really lucky, on a slow dance the girl would allow you to press your lower body against her and experience an intimation of an ancient unity that was at once a new realm and a sublime coming home.

Before I swoon let me get to the point, which is that ritual is unavoidable, a form of communal activity as important in the secular world as it is in religion. When I believed I was renouncing ritual, both as adolescent and adult, I was actually embracing it in a new, profane form (or, in the dancehall, a form which seemed profane but was actually a modern form of the ancient religious rituals of dancing to rhythm).

Ritual, which likes to present itself as unchanging tradition, is constantly changing, with practices mutating, evolving and growing, or going out of fashion and being replaced, or coming back into fashion in new forms. As fun has become increasingly important in the West, rituals which encourage group fun have flourished and become more elaborate, for instance the calendrical rituals of Christmas and the summer holiday, and some life rituals, especially christenings, birthdays and weddings. In the UK non-religious naming ceremonies for newborn children are a growth area, though often parents borrow churches for their incomparable solemnity. Churches generally seem to have accepted this, though no officially recognised church agreed to host the naming ritual devised by the footballer David Beckham and his wife, possibly due to Beckham's shop-around approach ('I definitely want Brooklyn to be christened, but I don't know into what religion yet'[1]). Undeterred, the Beckhams built their own pick 'n' mix church, a traditional building with an arched entrance surmounted by an angel but flanked on either side by Buddhist shrines.

But the most astonishing development has been the growth

of wedding ritual, ever more elaborate and extensive. A wedding celebration used to be merely a meal after the ceremony. Then it became necessary to have an evening session, with a band and dancing, for those not invited to the meal, and now the ritual extends over several days, with the official rites including an evening-before rehearsal dinner (which is never a rehearsal) and a day-after barbecue (usually a hog roast), and, preceding all this, the increasingly elaborate hen and stag nights, often involving extended holidays in Eastern Europe or the Baltic States, or, if you are unlucky enough to be friends with a banker, a trip to Miami, Vegas or the Caribbean.

There is a tendency for ritual to turn into spectacle in the course of time, to become a performance intended to impress rather than a group activity intended to involve. Lovers now like to propose on television, if possible, or at least in public, and the weddings, accompanied by fireworks, boats shooting water cannon or planes dragging banners, are performed in hot-air balloons, on cranes, mountain tops, beaches, in caves and underwater (the world's largest underwater wedding was in a flooded open-pit mine in Southern Poland in August 2011), on a parade float, in a cage in a shark tank, in a Metro station, a branch of Starbucks or the queue for tickets for a *Star Wars* premiere, with the happy couple sky diving, bungee jumping, cycling in the city, walking in the woods, swimming in the sea, or working through an assault course, such as the 20-obstacle Tough Mudder. Wedding wear is as various, with the couple nude, or with the groom wearing a clown costume or an animal head, while the bride can be in a dress made from bubble wrap and packing foam, or decorated with 3,000 real cow nipples, or sporting a 600-yard-long train or a 1.8-mile-long veil. It's only a matter of time before the first wedding in a space station, with the happy couple floating weightlessly, though if a guest overdoes the champagne, there could be a permanent confetti of half-digested canapé particles.

Naming ceremonies, birthdays and weddings are increasingly extravagant – but the initiation rite, an essential ritual for young men in many cultures and near universal in early societies, has disappeared from the West. This could be because it's not fun, even involving pain (though the ritual wounding is often merely symbolic) and is performed to ensure acceptance of adult responsibility, which nowadays can be even more painful than the physical wounding.

To remain popular, the initiation rite would have had to drop the emphasis on wounding and pain – as the festival of Halloween has prospered by dropping its association with death, and in the West is now second only to Christmas as a seasonal celebration. Halloween is a good example of a ritual that has changed constantly with the times – first pagan, then Christian, and now secular. If Halloween was a corporation, it would be used as a shining example by every business school in the world.

Originally the Celtic festival of Samhain (which marked the end of summer by lighting bonfires to strengthen by magic the waning sun), it quickly understood that paganism was so over and converted to Christianity, changing its name to All Hallow Even, the evening before All Souls' Day, when the faithful were expected to pray for the souls of the dead.[2] However, the ritual also soon realised that the focus on death was a bummer (no one in the modern world wishes to hear about death, not even once a year) and so it lightened up with an abbreviated name, Halloween, that weakened the connection to All Souls' Day by concentrating on the evening before the day, when participants mocked death by putting candles in human skulls, dressing as ghosts, and playing goofy games, such as trying to bite a swinging apple without using hands.

But, as in all inspirational success stories, Halloween had to endure major setbacks, long wilderness years of neglect and persecution, when it must have wondered if it could survive. In England, the Protestant Reformation made a serious attempt to stamp it out and largely succeeded, and in North America the Puritans made an equally determined attempt to prevent it from taking root in the New World. The latter failed because not even the Puritans could control the Irish immigrants who insisted on the old ways. Halloween established itself on the east coast of the USA, became in the late nineteenth century more of an urban, youth-oriented ritual, and in the twentieth century spread out of the Irish communities and expanded north and west (and even south across the border by establishing a tactical alliance with the Mexican Day of the Dead, *El Dia de los Muertos*).

By the mid-twentieth century it was an established American ritual but now with a middle-class family orientation that made it begin to seem boring. There was a need to re-energise the brand, and in 1978 the film *Halloween* and its many sequels made a bracing change of association from bourgeois child in witch's hat to psychopath with butcher's knife. Fear always captures the attention and the first film was especially effective by using handheld camera and heavy breathing on the soundtrack to give the viewpoint of the hidden psycho. The third in the series, *Halloween 3*, acknowledged the Celtic and Druidic roots with an Irish maniac called Conal Cochran who uses his Silver Shamrock Toy Factory to manufacture Halloween masks designed to kill children by exploding at 9.00 p.m. on the evening and delivering shrapnel made of chips from Stonehenge's Blue Stone.

But the crucial master stroke was to capitalise on the new fun ritual of dressing up and rebrand as the main fancy dress festival of the year. Halloween went global and, just as French vines were reintroduced from the New World after they succumbed to disease in France, the festival has been reimported to England and now threatens to supplant the Guy Fawkes celebration of November 5th.

In a pleasing example of a ritual travelling round the world before returning home in triumph, though much changed by its experience, Halloween has even returned to its Irish roots. I was astounded to see in the travel section of a newspaper an ad for a package holiday to 'Halloween in Derry'. Apparently my home town, which once seemed to me terminally sunk in apathy and torpor, has adopted the Halloween franchise so successfully that it now boasts of hosting the biggest Halloween Carnival in Europe, a 'spooktacular' lasting several days. The cunning move was to precede the Halloween evening with a free rock concert, offering young people the irresistible combination of fancy dress and live music, and to extend the event into a three-day 'carnival' (a much more exciting term than 'festival').

When I asked my Derry friends about this they all agreed that the phenomenon was now 'huge', even 'massive', but were unable to explain exactly when, where, how or why it got started, other than that it was at some point in the early 1980s. Eventually the local council came in with a firework display, and then the rock concert was added – but it seems to have started spontaneously, with a few more people than usual deciding to dress up and then a few more, until it became a local ritual. But why Derry? A reaction to the troubles of the previous decade? A need to escape the constraints of the Catholic and Protestant religious identities that drove the two communities apart and gave the town two names – Derry (Catholic) and Londonderry (Protestant), now combined in the unwieldy Derry/Londonderry?

The novel concept of the Halloween package holiday is also taking hold (no doubt encouraged by the realisation that Halloween falls conveniently in the middle of the slackest period in the holiday calendar). An enterprising hotel in the Thorpe Park amusement complex offers a two-night deal including a Fright Night, when guests will be locked into the Park until 2.00 a.m., before being 'kidnapped and bagged' and brought to the hotel to be 'terrorised' for the rest of the night. All that Halloween lacked was dancing and this has now been addressed by the staging in Covent Garden of an attempt to break the world record for the highest number of zombies dancing simultaneously.

These regular innovations have enabled Halloween to evolve continuously for a thousand years and now to develop fun appeal by replacing the rituals of prayers to the sun and for the souls of the dead with tourism, fancy dress, Hollywood movies, rock music and parties. Like the psycho in the first *Halloween* movie, who seems to have been killed off but keeps springing back to re-energised life, Halloween is a good example of ritual's refusal to die.

The Protestant Reformation, which believed it had suppressed the October festival, was probably the most concerted, determined and prolonged attempt to eliminate ritual from social life, and from religion in particular, with its churches stripped of symbols and its ceremonies reduced to sermons based on readings from the Bible. But the concentration on the Bible turned the book itself into the ultimate symbol and totem, leading to the nineteenth century claim that its stories are not myths but literal truth. And the Protestant communities in Scotland and Ireland have created in the Orange Order a secular organisation with rituals and symbols as numerous, diverse and arcane as those of their Catholic neighbours. To the outsider the rituals of a group can seem meaningless, often outlandish, and even laughable, but to the group members the rituals are the very essence of meaning, so necessary that they are worth fighting, and even dying, for. Some of the worst eruptions of violence in Northern Ireland have been due to the Orange Order's insistence on marching through Catholic areas in full regalia, wearing bowler hats and sashes, carrying swords and banners and pounding drums. Then there were riots in Protestant areas after the decision to stop flying the Union Jack over City Hall in Belfast. And, neatly complementing this, one of the concessions demanded by Catholics was the right to fly the Republican flag in their own areas. What matters to many on both sides are not their religious beliefs but their rituals and symbols.

The French and Soviet Revolutions made the most concerted, determined and prolonged attempts to suppress religion itself, along with its rituals, but soon had to replace these with secular versions.[3] It seems that rituals are always needed and, when suppressed or no longer resonant, must be revised or replaced. And often new rituals are created not as replacements but to sanction nations, institutions and elites by giving them an aura of *mysterium tremendum*, numen, inevitability and permanence. The rituals of the British Royal Family, for instance, which appear to preserve venerable tradition, were mostly invented in the nineteenth century.[4] And that suppos-edly traditional garment of Scotland's highland clans, the kilt, was created by an eighteenth-century English factory owner, Thomas Rawlinson, to provide suitable clothing for the Scottish workers in his iron-ore smelting plant in Invergarry.[5]

As the French, Soviet and other authorities have discovered, ritual is more effective than precept and prescription because it replaces the cerebral with the physical, concentrating solely on symbols and ceremony, and operating subconsciously, below the level of language, awareness, explanation and choice. Just as convention is rarely recognised by its practitioners as convention, ritual is rarely understood to be ritual. It rejects definition and justification. It is just what is necessary. It is what is done.

This suggestion of inevitability makes ritual a potent resource for the powerful, and to the powerless it can offer the consolations of a community of the faithful without the need to practise values. The stronger the emphasis on a religion's rituals, the weaker the emphasis on its teachings. In the extreme case, ritual makes the teachings redundant, which is why my aunts could so fervently profess their faith while having no interest whatever in the message of its founder, and in general why religion can continue to flourish in a sceptical age. Often the attraction is not the beliefs but the identity and rituals of the group.

Ritual is also effective at alleviating anxiety. It is an adult version of the repetition that reassures and comforts children, but with a sacralising of the routine, so that habit's changelessness is enhanced by the sense of a connection to some greater changelessness, which does not have to be specified. By assigning a special time and space (or by temporarily sacralising familiar space), and by using special objects and actions, ritual suspends everyday life and establishes an atmosphere of mystical significance, which authenticates and ratifies, without recourse to argument. Ritual provides a sense of community to dispel the fear of isolation, a sense of participation to dispel the fear of powerlessness, a sense of permanence and continuity to dispel the fear of change and mortality, and a sense of sacred purpose to dispel the fear that life is arbitrary, random and meaningless.

But ritual's most important role may be in creating and preserving group unity, a contemporary version of the original unity of clan or tribe. There are of course comforting solitary rituals, but group ritual performs the social function of initiating and integrating group members, establishing consensus, creating and preserving solidarity and strengthening allegiance.

This communal spirit depends on a suspension of everyday attitudes, either by religious solemnity or its opposite, carnival exuberance, as in many new rituals of group fun. A few months ago I was in central London, mooching between bookshops and becoming increasingly conscious that there were more people around than usual and in unusually animated groups. It was only when I returned home that I discovered I had missed two new fun rituals – a little to one side of me there had been a Gay Pride March, and a little to the other side the World Naked Bike Ride (WNBR), an annual event held in mid-June, when thousands of nude or semi-nude cyclists (official motto: as bare as you dare) ride together through the streets of a city.

According to the official WNBR website, 'creative expression is encouraged to generate a fun and immersive atmosphere during the ride', and such expression can take the forms of 'body art, such as body painting, as well as costumes, art bikes, portable sound reinforcement systems (public address systems, bull horns and boom boxes) and musical instruments or other types of noisemaker'. As with archaic ritual, the crucial elements are music, costumes and body painting. The other archaic element, drumming, would surely also be encouraged if it were not for the practical difficulty of wielding drumsticks while riding a bicycle. Note the telling adjective, 'immersive', a new term of praise because it suggests active participation rather than passive spectating. The WNBR has certainly struck a chord, for there are now naked bike rides in more than seventy cities all over the world, with the number still rising and participation increasing.

It was disappointing to have been so near to two exciting fun rituals and missed both. But on another occasion I was lucky. This was in Paris at dusk, as the beloved and I were seeking a suitably sacred venue for our own solemn aperitif ritual. Suddenly the search was interrupted by a distant rumble, like thunder, but coming from the ground rather than the sky. As it grew louder and nearer other passers-by also stopped in consternation. And there was some other eeriness that was at first hard to identify. But of course – there was no more traffic, though this was a city during rush hour. Then the rumble became overwhelming and from round a corner came a thunderous phalanx of rollerbladers. This was entirely different from a parade in that they were moving at speed and there was no attempt to impress, amuse or in any way interact with the spectators. Instead they powered silently and purposefully forward. And neither did the spectators make any attempt to communicate, looking on in awed silence. It was like a visitation from another world. And then towards the end, where the phalanx began to thin out, there came a septuagenarian, serenely driving forward with long graceful thrusts of each leg in turn, long curling grey locks sustained out behind him – both solemn *and* carnivalesque, God on skates.

3

Fun and Transcendence

Group ritual was ubiquitous in the earliest days of pre-history and took everywhere the remarkably similar form of drinking, feasting, communal dancing and chanting at prescribed times in sacred places to loud, rhythmic music wearing headdresses, costumes and masks, with bodies and faces painted or tattooed, and finishing in group sex. Evidence of such dancing has been found in prehistoric art on every continent. Even the dance structures and forms of individual expression were similar, with line and circle dances common, and individual dancers expressing themselves with vigorous head movement and hair flinging. In a chastening example of the transformative effect of knowledge, discovering this has made me less contemptuous of the party people of my childhood finishing the night with a hokey-cokey and conga, and headbangers going wild at heavy metal concerts. These apparent vulgarians are actually in touch with their ancient roots and I am the frigid aberration.

Far from being spontaneous wildness, the rituals were carefully planned, taking place only at appointed times, in headgear, costumes and masks prepared in advance and with choreographed dance moves. All this required considerable time and energy and so must have had profound meaning. In fact the ecstatic dancing was an expression of worship for a variety of deities, at first goddesses[1] and, later, gods like Dionysus – androgynous, with long curling hair, irresistibly attractive to women and inspired with a divine madness expressed through intoxication and dancing.[2]

The religious experience was achieved through what the French sociologist Emile Durkheim defined as 'collective effervescence',[3] an intoxicated trance state involving not just loss of self but the merging of self with the group. Prolonged dancing to rhythm provided the intoxication; costumes, masks and body painting encouraged a loss of personal identity; and choreographed movement aided the sense of immersion in a single being. The reward was an experience of oneness and belonging, which many believe to be one of the deepest and most necessary satisfactions for the conscious creature, and one of the most difficult to experience in the modern world.

The crucial feature at the heart of the ritual is rhythmic drumming. The drum preceded the dance and rhythm preceded the drum. Rhythm is the central process of life. Pacemaker cells in the heart generate an electrical rhythm that regulates the beating, the human gut pulses rhythmically, and oscillator cells in the brain make waves that have characteristic rhythms for wakefulness and sleep. The human body is a rhythm orchestra that not only performs perfectly without a conductor but also matches its rhythms to the 24-hour day – a circadian rhythm orchestra.

Unsurprisingly, neuroscientists have discovered that the human sense of rhythm can be detected even in babies and is universal. Aniruddh Patel, an authority on the neuroscience of music, has established that, 'In every culture there is some form of music with a regular beat, a periodic pulse that affords temporal coordination between performers, and elicits synchronised motor response from listeners.[4] He believes that this rhythmic sense evolved too early to date, and certainly long before the development of language. Beat, Patel explains, 'is an aspect of rhythm that appears to be unique to music ... and cannot be explained as a by-product of linguistic rhythm'. And, as other neuroscientists have pointed out, our sense of beat is so strong that we impose a beat – a rhythmic pattern – on sounds without a pattern, interpreting the ticking of a clock not as it is, 'tick, tick, tick, tick', but as 'tick, tock, tick, tock'. Indeed, the rhythmic sense may have become strong before we had language because it facilitated mimesis, communication by gesture, movement and sound ('Rhythm is ... the quintessential mimetic skill'[5]) – and because of its synchronous ability to unify people in a group.

It seems that rhythm and synchrony are fundamental to life. To have a poor sense of rhythm is as grievous a loss as having a poor sense of taste or smell, and I would never wish to trade my poor taste and smell for rhythm deficiency, even though God has softened this blow by making the arhythmic unaware of their lack, so that one of the most painful aspects of wedding ritual is the sight of the dance floor. Indeed, rhythm-deficient men may have difficulty in finding a partner. Women like men who can move in rhythm and my beloved has confessed that what first attracted her to me was my neo-shamanic freestyle dance (though good taste in shoes was also important). Rhythm deficiency also makes it hard to appreciate poetry because poetry *is* rhythm. This is why poetry preceded prose and is as common in early cultures as alcohol and dance, why only poets can successfully translate poetry (poets must have a strong feel for rhythm in language) and why so much contemporary poetry seems like chopped-up prose (what is missing is not rhyme but rhythm).

The urge to express rhythm is as basic and powerful as the sex urge and indeed linked to it (the trick seems to be to let the woman dictate the rhythm, at least until very close to the end). Whacking things with a stick is as old as whacking creatures with clubs, but much safer. The drumstick was born with the club and has largely outlived it, though part of the attraction of drumming is that it retains the primeval violence of hitting and so combines celebration with aggression. Whenever I handle anything that could be used as a drumstick I have an overpowering urge to look for a surface to drum on. I love getting chopsticks in oriental restaurants, though not for eating (I have never mastered this skill) but to play a percussion solo on the glasses and finish with a rimshot on the table edge.

When I had nothing that could serve as sticks and no surface to drum on I would tap rhythmically on one hand with the thumb of the other – or drum on my skull. This was until the beloved discouraged what she assured me looked neurotic and mad. I did give up using myself as a drum kit – but was astounded to discover subsequently that tapping the hand and head has been discovered to have a therapeutic effect and may even be adopted by the National Health Service to treat anxiety and depression, the suggestion not of some new age guru but a research team at Staffordshire University led by Professor Tony Stewart. Of course 'tapping' is a feeble name, entirely without resonance, so it has been given the much more impressive title of Emotional Freedom Technique or EFT.[6]

And I once had a spiritual experience with a full-sized rock drum kit. This was during a dinner visit to the country home of a wealthy dentist. His spoilt teenage son had the kit assembled in the foyer and I was irresistibly drawn to sit down and thrash away with the Dionysian abandon of Keith Moon, much to the consternation of my hosts, who had taken me for a reserved intellectual, and the beloved, who was hoping I would impress the company with urbane sophistication. It was worth the disapproval, more intoxicating than any of the cocktails – and probably beneficial too. If tapping your head can be therapeutic then thrashing a drum kit must be as good as a decade of analysis with Freud.

Even the most scholarly intellectuals love drumming. The immensely erudite critic James Wood, chorister child of Evangelical Christian parents in a provincial Cathedral town, and the author of deep essays on the spiritual torments of Herman Melville and Matthew Arnold, has also stated bluntly that 'everyone secretly wants to play the drums'.[7] One reason is that drumming is so intimately connected to dance. Wood: 'Music makes us want to dance, to register rhythm on and with our bodies. So the drummer and the conductor are the luckiest of all musicians, because they are closest to dancing. And in drumming, how childishly close the connection is between the dancer and the dance!' Another attraction is becoming one with the instrument. 'When you play the drums you *are* the drums. "Le tom-tom, c'est moi", as Wallace Stevens put it.' And the return to childishness and primeval rhythm offers unique release from the burden of self, the curse of modernity. 'Drumming has always represented for me that dream of escape, when the body forgets itself, surrenders its awful self-consciousness.' Finally, drumming, and especially rock drumming, has the thrill of rebellion. Wood's favourite drummer is Keith Moon, who '*was* the drums, not because he was the most technically accomplished of drummers, but because his many-armed, joyous, semaphoring lunacy suggested a man possessed by the antic spirit of drumming'.

Drumming is so fundamental that animals do it. Kangaroo rats drum on the ground with their paws, many primates chest beat or hand clap, and macaque monkeys drum on objects to demonstrate social dominance. This monkey drumming is processed in their brains in the same way as vocalisation in humans, leading to a theory that drumming was an early form of communication. And animals who do not normally drum can be taught to do so. Aniruddh Patel investigated The Thai Elephant Orchestra, made up of elephants trained to play elephant-sized drums, and after recording and analysing performances, concluded that elephants can indeed 'play a percussion instrument with a highly stable tempo'.[8] It would be wonderful if the Orchestra could go on a world tour but, as with famous rock groups, providing appropriate dressing room facilities could be difficult.

Patricia Gray, a professor of the new research area of biomusic at the University of North Carolina, has had even greater success with bonobos by designing special big bonobo drums that can withstand being regularly jumped on, peed and shat over, rolled and chewed. These apes like to play with, as well as on, their drums, but when in the Keith Moon mood can maintain a regular 280 beats per minute (twice as fast as most pop music).[9]

Evidence for early human drumming is hard to find because drums made of wood and skin rarely survive – but alligator-skin drums dated to the Neolithic era, 5000 BCE, have been found in China and drums dated to 3000 BCE have been found in Mesopotamia. As soon as writing emerged there were records of drumming, and, though this is thought to be as quintessentially male an activity as barbecuing hamburgers, the first recorded drummer was a woman, a Mesopotamian priestess called Lipushiau who laid down the beat on a drum known as a *balag-di* in Ur in 2380 BCE, making a noise 'not conducive to sleep'.[10] This was not an exception because it is thought that all the earliest drummers were priestesses. The Sumerian goddess Inanna is credited with inventing the frame drum, precursor of the tambourine, in the third millennium BCE, and the Old Testament mentions a woman leading a dance with such a drum, a timbrel. 'And Miriam, the prophetess, sister of Aaron and Moses, took a timbrel in her hand, then the women went out after her with timbrels and with dances.'[11]

So the drum compelled a listener to move to the beat and the sight of a dancer compelled others to join in and synchronise, an urge that seems to be as basic as the urge to beat out a rhythm. Many living creatures unconsciously synchronise. Crickets chorus together, frogs croak in unison, mothers playing with babies bring their brain rhythms into sync, female friends or colleagues find their menstrual cycles coinciding, and audiences applauding a performance first clap in chaotic rapidity but then coordinate in rhythmic clapping at a slower tempo. However, the most spectacular example, which baffled scientists for most of the twentieth century, is the light show performed at evening along the rivers of Asia, when, for miles at a time, thousands upon thousands of fireflies not only flash together but flash in rhythm to a constant beat. These are nature's disco lights, encouraging all of God's creatures to get on down.

Even inanimate things have a tendency to come into sync. The first recorded example was in 1665 when the Dutch physicist Christian Huygens observed that two pendulums set swinging in the same room would eventually oscillate in step, an effect he described as 'miraculous'. Soon after, it was discovered that many heavenly bodies move in sync – the moon has coordinated its turning to match its orbit to that of the earth. And in the twentieth century the invention of lasers was due to the discovery that trillions of atoms can synchronise their light emission to produce a thin beam. As the mathematician Steven Strogatz, an expert on synchrony, has put it: 'For reasons we don't yet understand, the tendency to synchronize is one of the most pervasive drives in the universe, extending from atoms to animals, from people to planets.'[12]

It's hardly surprising that the synchrony of group rituals is deeply satisfying, especially if physical activity is synchronised. This explains why singing in choirs, long dismissed by non-believers as a purely religious activity, has broken away from religion and is increasingly enjoyed as a secular pleasure. In London choirs seem to be springing up everywhere. Nick Stewart, a psychologist at Oxford Brookes University, has investigated this phenomenon and found that choristers reported higher levels of mental wellbeing than those who sing alone or play a team sport: 'These findings suggest that the experience of using your voice to make music may be enhanced when you feel part of a cohesive social group. Further research could look at how moving and breathing in synchrony with others might be responsible for creating a unique well-being effect.'[13]

The historian William McNeill has reported similar exhilaration from an entirely different form of physical synchrony – military drill. 'Words are inadequate to describe the emotion aroused by the prolonged movement in unison that drilling involved. A sense of personal well-being is what I recall; more specifically, a strange sense of personal enlargement; a sort of swelling out, becoming bigger than life, thanks to participation in collective ritual.'[14] Drill may seem the opposite of dance but Busby Berkeley, famous as the choreographer of elaborately synchronised routines with dozens of elaborately costumed female dancers in the musicals of the thirties (such as *Dames*, *42nd Street* and *Footlight Parade*), once revealed that the 'best apprenticeship' for his future career was devising parade drills during his time as an army lieutenant in the First World War.[15] And, as William McNeill points out, dance and drill were often combined in the ritual of the war dance. McNeill also notes that rhythmic synchrony has been common in work – in the USA slave gangs hoed cotton by chanting and keeping in time with a 'lead hoe'. In England the clog dancing often dismissed by urban cosmopolitans as rural nostalgia was actually invented by factory girls who wore wooden clogs for safety, then discovered that they made a wonderful drumming sound on the floor and began to tap dance together in time to the bobbins and shuttles.

Even rebellious, anarchic youth, which abhors most forms of group discipline and would laugh in contempt at singing in choirs or military drill, has developed a way to enjoy rhythmic synchrony in the contemporary ritual of 'moshing'. At live music gigs, where bands play at manic tempos, young men next to the stage become a 'mosh pit', a densely packed seething mass dancing with a frenzy and abandon that would have alarmed even Dionysus. The ingenuity of this ritual is that it does not seem like a ritual. Each mosher seems to be involved in purely personal, antisocial, violent and even aggressive movement, while actually in the closest possible contact with others. Moshing permits both individual wild rebellion and total immersive surrender to the group. The more possessed moshers even cede all personal control to body surf on top of the mosh pit, recklessly indifferent to the fate of wallets, keys and change, borne aloft and along by the willing hands of fellow moshers.

The early Dionysian revels continued virtually unchanged for millennia, often orchestrated by a shaman in a distinctive, often outlandish costume, and often with a painted face or mask, and beating a drum, chanting rhythmically and demonstrating frenzied dance moves to generate an ecstatic trance state so extreme that it feels like a journey out of this world. And in fact the key gift claimed by the shaman was magical flight to the spirit realm, facilitated by the drum, which, as historian of religion Mircea Eliade explains, has 'magical functions many and various' and is 'indispensable in conducting the shamanic séance, whether it carries the shaman to the "Center of the World" or enables him to fly through the air'.[16]

The shrewdness of the shaman was in understanding the advantages of claiming responsibility for group transcendence. The magical ability to transport to a spirit world can bring many benefits in the flesh-and-blood world. As the anthropologist I. M. Lewis noted, shamans not qualified by birth for the role were often originally of low social status, or had suffered affliction, privation or trauma, and like many contemporary comedians borne up on flights of fancy, made use of spirit flights to 'rise to fame and fortune'.[17] And no doubt part of the fortune was an even more magical transportation to women's beds.

It's not surprising that there has been renewed interest in shamanism since the sixties, beginning with the hugely popular writings of Carlos Castaneda, an anthropologist who claimed to have been initiated by a Yaqui Indian shaman capable of flying from mountain peak to mountain peak, and who, in the familiar manner of cult leaders, withdrew from the world to live with several women, obliging them to sever all connections with family and friends.

There are now many self-professed neo-shamans offering courses, workshops and manuals on how to attain SSC (the Shamanic State of Consciousness). But those seeking this state might be better off listening to Keith Moon, who would certainly have qualified as a neo-shaman, not only because of the Dionysian drumming but also his obsession with costumes and clowning and prodigious consumption of all forms of intoxicant. He frequently dressed as Adolf Hitler or Noel Coward and much of his play-acting was not just the mindless destructiveness of the rock star (though he vandalised his share of hotel rooms) but required forethought, imagination and humour. A favourite prank was to take a can of Campbell's chicken soup onto a plane, surreptitiously empty it into a sick bag, then ostentatiously and noisily pretend to vomit into the bag before lifting it to pour the contents into his mouth, sighing in apparent contentment and, with an expression of bewildered innocence, turning to ask his fellow passengers why they looked so disgusted.

As far as I know, humour has not been cited as an element of shamanism and while most shamans may have been deadly serious, many others must have been chancers, performers who would have found it useful to include clowning in their acts. The Dutch historian and philosopher Johan Huizinga argues that many of the early rituals had an element of play and are at once entirely serious and a kind of made-up game played according to strict rules, with a 'unity and indivisibility of belief and unbelief', an 'indissoluble connection between sacred earnest and "make-believe" or "fun"'.[18] And the shaman was frequently play-acting: 'The behaviour of those to whom the savage community attributes "supernatural powers" can often be best expressed by "acting up to the part".' Certainly the shaman is the first to be able to stand outside the community while still belonging to it, a key characteristic of the comedian.

Humour was definitely a key characteristic of the trickster, not a real person like the shaman but a character in the oral mythology of many disparate cultures – Hermes in Greece, Eshu in West Africa, Krishna in India, Loki in Scandinavia, Coyote in North America. Probably a later development than the shaman, the trickster represents a shift in emphasis from the superheroes and magic of the spirit realm to the follies of fallible, desirous, deluded, mortal human flesh and blood, and introduces a new kind of transcendent fun, mockery. As the anthropologist Mac Linscott Ricketts has shown, many trickster tales actually ridicule the beliefs and practice of the shaman, as when the trickster tries to fly like a bird and ignominiously falls to earth, or, in one of the Coyote tales, attempts prophecy by reading his own excrement, produced with much effortful grunting.[19] The trickster character demonstrates the new possibility of worldly transcendence, of escaping from the community and the self by making fun of them, and is often an outsider, loner, traveller, wanderer, always questioning community beliefs and codes, amoral, witty, mischievous, disruptive, greedy, opportunistic, sometimes a liar and a thief, indeed a sort of con man, though one who is himself often duped.[20] The short trickster tales, with their weird twists and mysterious punch lines, are early versions of the joke, and the trickster is an early ancestor of that crucial fun figure, the comedian.

But laughter goes back beyond trickster and shaman and even beyond *Homo sapiens* to the primates. Chimpanzees and bonobos laugh, but only separately, as individuals, not together as humans do. The evolutionary anthropologist Robin Dunbar has suggested that social laughter preceded language and may have evolved in *Homo erectus* as much as a million years ago. 'It was most likely a form of chorusing, a kind of communal singing without the words ... My guess is that this kind of social laughter came on stream, built up out of more conventional chimpanzee-like laughing, to supplement grooming as a bonding mechanism.'[21]

This suggests that laughter was a feature of ritual from the beginning, along with intoxicants, feasts, costumes, masks, body painting, drumming, chanting, dancing and sex. Many have wondered at how so many different cultures in different periods and continents discovered exactly the same kind of ritual independently, and one explanation is that, as with the near-universal discovery of alcohol, each culture found by trial and error the techniques most effective for unifying and binding.

We now know that most of these activities – drinking, feasting, music, chanting, dancing, laughter and sex – trigger the release of endorphins, neurotransmitters which generate a sense of security, wellbeing and euphoria. So any combination will enhance the effect and all together will produce a great Saturday night. And the pleasure is further intensified by company. Dunbar: 'When you experience an endorphin rush as part of a group, its effect seems to be ratcheted up massively. In particular, it makes you feel very positive towards other group members. Quite literally it creates a sense of brotherhood and communality.'[22] This would explain the combination of personal transcendence and group togetherness offered by ritual. And there is a further intensification if the group is involved in synchronised physical activity.

Dunbar and his team tested this on a rowing crew, where continuous synchrony, as near perfect as possible, is the crucial factor in speed and competitive edge. They first measured the endorphin production of crew members when rowing alone, and then when rowing together in a boat. In each case the physical exertion was the same but in synchronous rowing the activation of endorphins almost doubled. Dunbar concludes: 'There is something genuinely odd about synchrony, because it seems to ramp up the endorphin production generated by physical exercise by something close to a factor of two.'[23]

Dunbar leaves this as a mystery – but a possible explanation is that synchronising pleases the brain because this is the brain's primary function. Data inputs from the senses are processed at different speeds, with complex vision data especially slow to compute, and to produce a coherent version of reality the brain has to synchronise continuously many continuous information flows. The brain is a miracle of synchrony as the body is a miracle of rhythm, and it may well love synchronous activity because this is its thing.

Whatever the explanation, there is intense pleasure in group music-making, choral singing, and choreographed dancing. It would be interesting to research the comparative intensities of wellbeing in the various forms of physical synchrony – but it seems possible that dance, with its greater capacity for physical expression, would provide the most intense high, or at least a high as good as that of singing in choirs. Certainly group dancing has been the most common synchrony across cultures and throughout history. Though it would be typical of God the Prankster if military drill turned out to be the best fun of all.

I am not aware of any studies into the neural effects of costumes, masks and body painting but these may also provide an endorphin rush or something similar because dressing up has become a contemporary mania. I was reminded of this when I joined the queue at a wedding for what I assumed was the evening buffet of little triangular sandwiches, cocktail sausages and mini spring rolls, but turned out to be for the photobooth. This major attraction was a photographer snapping wedding guests as they donned a variety of funny hats, wigs, masks and giant specs, and waved inflated accessories such as saxophones, guitars, mikes and ice lollies. Apparently the photobooth has become yet another addition to wedding ritual, along with the rehearsal dinner, evening buffet, day-after barbecue and the ever-growing number of bridesmaids in matching off-the-shoulder Greek-maiden dresses and the same golden hue of fake tan.[24]

I quickly left the photobooth queue because I have never understood the attraction of fancy dress and have always refused to dress up. The only exception was at one of my wife's work parties, a fancy dress evening she beseeched me to attend, which I finally consented to do, but only on the condition that I could go as Leonard Cohen wearing my own black suit.

Why do so many want to dress up nowadays? My hypothesis is that dressing up manages to reconcile, if only briefly, several strong and often contradictory contemporary urges. Because fancy dress is usually for social occasions, it combines the need to stand out as an individual with the need to be accepted by, and belong to, a group. And since the costume is a personal choice but immediately recognisable as a familiar character, type or thing, it combines the desire to express a unique personal identity with the opposite desire to abandon this exhausting task for the ease of a ready-made identity as a Venetian noble, a zombie, a pirate, a chicken, or, possibly most reassuring, a banana. It also offers a form of childish play to those who are no longer children, a way to reject convention without giving offence, and above all a way to become an actor without having to act. Dressing up is an unconscious acknowledgement that life is essentially role play, a series of parts and performances rather than the discovery and expression of a true self, and that learning to play parts is a crucial skill. This is why actors, once the lowest of functionaries, have grown in prestige and status throughout the modern era and are now the new aristocracy, universally revered. We envy their ability to become, convincingly, and with apparent ease, different people. And it may be why the singer David Bowie became one of the most respected figures in popular culture and was mourned all round the world on his death in January 2016. In the seventies Bowie sensed the new need, expressed it by playing a series of roles in different costumes, and made dressing up, cross-dressing and role playing not just acceptable but the height of fashion.

And for those who find that costumes are not enough to encourage escape, masks or face paint confer the anonymity that suppresses inhibition. Even wearing sunglasses can bring a change of attitude, making this affable granddad feel coolly sinister and remote, like a Samurai-influenced hitman flown in from Detroit.

Only the masks of the early cultures, mostly now in museums, retain some sense of the occult power of their rituals. The shamans and the painted bodies are long gone, the drums long silent, and the surviving costumes look pitifully naïve, shabby and empty – but the masks can still startle and disturb. As with the rituals themselves, the masks from different cultural groups have remarkably similar features. They are all faces – but greatly exaggerated, much larger than the human face, and the expression is an extreme rictus of outrage and ferocity, the eyes madly protuberant and the oversized mouth wide open or extending a tongue. These can give even the most rigorously rational a shiver, a sense of something beyond that is huge, strong, and violently angry, with eyes that can see through all human pretence and a ravening mouth that is ready to devour.

And the masquerade, or masked ball, is an attempt by the rich and sophisticated to combine the hieratic power of the ritual mask with the transgressive carnival energy of the lower orders. Charles VI of France is credited with starting this fashion in the fifteenth century when he spiced up court life with his *Bal des Ardents* and *Bal des Sauvages*, where he and his courtiers dressed as wild men of the woods. But the definitive version of the masquerade, with the elaborate costumes, wigs and butterfly eye masks, which has passed into the popular imagination as the most potent symbol of aristocratic decadence, was developed in the sixteenth century as part of the Venetian Carnival, then taken to London high society in the eighteenth century and from there passed on to colonial America.

And since aristocratic decadence is perennially exciting in its combination of snob and sex appeal, there have been regular modern attempts to recreate the masquerade, for instance the lavish Masks and Dominoes Ball of 1951, billed as the *Fêtes des Fêtes*, the party of the century, held at the baroque Palazzo Labia in Venice by Don Carlos de Beistegui y de Yturbe, with the new mix of royalty (Princess Pignatelli), multimillionaires (the Aga Khan) and film stars (Orson Welles), and the new fashion of clothes by designers as famous as their customers (Pierre Cardin made his name by creating many of the outfits for this party). Entertainment included several orchestras, a ballet company, a ghoulish troupe called The Phantoms of Venice, created by Salvador Dali, walking on huge stilts and wearing long white robes, skull masks and tricorn hats, and, for something more robust and earthy, a team of Venetian firemen who formed a human pyramid four-men high.

In Don DeLillo's novel *Underworld* there is a marvellous description of a famous masked ball of 1966 in the Plaza Hotel in New York – the Black and White Ball organised by Truman Capote for the wealthy, famous and powerful, the men in black and the women in white. In DeLillo's imagining of this event, the seventy-one-year-old J. Edgar Hoover has a black leather mask specially designed for him by a kind of female shaman in 'heavy make-up she might have poured from a paint can and cooked', hair with 'the retouched gloss of a dead crow mounted on a stick' and 'a European accent slashed and burned by long-term residency in New York'. She has designed for Edgar 'a sleek black leather mask with handlebar extensions and a scatter of shiny sequins round the eyes', which she fits carefully over his face and adjusts before turning him to a mirror:

> The mask transformed him. For the first time in some years he did not see himself as a tenant in an old short popover body with an immense and lumpish head.
>
> 'I can call you Edgar – this is okay? I can tell you how I see you? I see you as a mature and careful man who has a sexy motorcycle thug writhing to get out. Which the spangles give a crazy twist, you know?'
>
> He felt creamy, dreamy and drugged.
>
> She made a slight adjustment in the fit and even as he cringed at her touch Edgar felt himself tingle thrillingly. She was insidious and corrupt and it was like hearing your grandmother talk dirty in your ear.
>
> 'You are a butch biker to me, you know, riding into town to take over leadership of the sadists and necrophiles.'[25]

Edgar is so excited by his mask that he wears it all through dinner and on into the night after the ball, which of course has a medieval flavour, with many women in nun's wimples and men in executioner's hoods, though Andy Warhol is defiantly postmodern in a mask made from a photograph of his own face.

Needless to say, the huddled masses yearning to be free also want their share of decadent fun, so many entrepreneurs now organise Masked Balls and many businesses hire out costumes and masks – for instance Mad World, of London, which offers over 35,000 costumes, with Eighteenth Century one of the most popular categories, and also 'the largest range of Venetian masks in the UK'. Mad World has three London outlets, with the largest down a nondescript industrial side street in Shoreditch and then down two flights of steps to a huge underground cavern filled to bursting with a staggering array of colourful costumes that not only cover the entire floor area but also the walls and ceiling (much of one wall given over to the Venetian mask collection). Even the range of categories is astounding, with costumes from every period in history to the present, arranged first by millennia, then by centuries and finally by decades, and with many other categories, including Comic Book, Military, Professional, Movies and Television, Horror, Animals (itself including a nautical sub-section, Prawns and Tuna) and Fruit and Veg for anyone who wishes to dress as a pineapple or a carrot.

The contrast with traditional dressing up is obvious. Where everyone would once have worn similar costumes for a ritual, now there is individual choice. It seems that the ironic consequence of the freedom to be one's self is a near-universal desire to be someone else. Presiding over this mad world is the ever-helpful Jill, who confirms that costume hire has indeed boomed in recent decades. Mad World began twenty years ago with a small shop in the suburbs in Crawley, then opened the much larger Shoreditch branch a few years later, adding a third shop in the heart of the West End on Charing Cross Road.

'Take a wander round,' Jill suggests, and then calls out from the desk, 'try on anything you like.'

I decline, though tempted by the disturbingly realistic Medieval Executioner (distressed brown leather jacket, shirt, breeches, boot covers and axe), and also decline to mention that I feel Jill's spirited insouciance would go well in the Pirate Wench (boots, flared mini skirt, short brocade jacket and tricorn hat).

Back at the desk she reveals that demand is strong from all age groups, all classes and both genders, and is fairly constant all year round. Halloween is indeed massive and growing ('It used to be mostly vampires but now it's more zombies', with a nod at the wall displaying an Instant Zombie Kit, Zombie Dentures and Zombie Guts), and Christmas is also busy, but throughout the year there are office parties ('going mostly for eighteenth century and the twenties, nothing too *out there*') and festivals, ever more numerous and with increasing emphasis on fancy dress. Jill's festival list has some intriguing entries, for instance National Cleavage Day, the Belle Epoque Dark Circus and the Torture Garden Valentine's Ball ('You have to fetish-up a bit for those').

But WNBR – World Naked Bike Ride? 'What *costumes* . . .?'

'Accessories,' Jill explains. 'Feather boas are especially popular.'

And in spring there are the hen and stag nights. Young men are apparently keen to look as ridiculous as possible (weary sniff from Jill) by dressing as babies, animals, or fruit (kilts with a giant penis and testicles underneath are a new trend), or going in drag (as Miss World or Droopy Granny), or in fluorescent Lycra ('very unforgiving'). Young women rarely dress up ('girls like to look pretty,' knowing laugh from Jill) but use lots of accessories, for instance L-plates and T-shirts for the bride-to-be (BRIDEZILLA This is all about me), badges, sashes and signs for the others (WARNING: HEN NIGHT IN PROGRESS) and willy whistles and willy shot glasses for everyone.

'What's the *weirdest* request you've ever had?'

'Oh,' Jill sighs, 'I'm so used to weird requests I don't know what's weird any more. Weirdness is normal for me.'

'OK. What's your own favourite?'

Immediately she brightens again. 'The Voodoo Man. It's the combination of the battered top hat and black and white face paint.' This is interesting because the Voodoo Man is a kind of shaman, from a genuinely old tradition, and mixes spirit magic with macabre humour. Jill sighs with pleasure. 'That brings out the evil in *everyone*.'

As for body decoration, face painting seems to be a feature of most children's festivities, and this century has seen an astonishing increase in the popularity of tattooing in adults. At the beginning of the century Britain had 300 tattoo parlours and a decade later there were over 1,500, including one in Selfridge's. Over 21 per cent of British adults are now 'inked' and in the 16–44 age range this rises to 29 per cent (though the USA is still ahead with 40 per cent of 20–40-year-olds). And this is not restricted to the working class. Fourteen per cent of teachers have tattoos (but only 9 per cent of service men and women).[26] Even the current Prime Minister's wife has a tattoo (a dolphin below the ankle) and the astrophysicist Matt Taylor, a classic science geek who can guide a probe to a comet billions of miles away but often has difficulty remembering where he parked his car, revealed that his body is covered in lurid tattoos.

This is despite the fact that acquiring tattoos is painful, time-consuming and expensive – a full back tattoo can take thirty hours, in six spaced all-day sessions at up to £120 per hour. And this is also despite the fact that tattoos have traditionally been associated with tribal warriors, sailors and social deviants, like bikers and criminals. What is the attraction?

Perhaps the pain suggests a warrior initiation rite, the association with deviance suggests a refusal to conform, the expense suggests disposable income, and the artwork is an expression of personal creativity. So the appeal of a tattoo is to be, at the same time, a warrior, a chieftain, a Hell's Angel and Picasso? Or, as with dressing up, the appeal is the combination of individual expression and group belonging, with the group in this case a warrior tribe or a subversive subculture?

Only a professional tattooist can provide answers and I do not have to go far – only to my corner tattoo shop, which is also a hip gallery representing artists such as Mysterious Al, D*Face and Pure E-v-i-l (who explores 'the myth of the Apocalypse and the darker side of the wreckage of Utopian dreams'). Skulls and blood are prominent in the gallery art and in the window is a work made of a partly crushed beer can with a dead rat partly stuffed down it head first.

However, the tattooist Dan Gold is a surprise, not a surly biker in a Megadeth T-shirt brandishing fistfuls of skull rings, but courteous, mild-mannered and soft-spoken, with neatly combed short hair and a houndstooth jacket, more like an Oxbridge Classics Don or even a Royal Equerry – except of course for his tattoos (though contemporary Dons and Equerrys may well now be inked). In fact, Dan is indeed something of a Don, with extensive knowledge of tattooing from its origins in the earliest cultures ('In ancient Egypt only women were tattooed'), and he explains that the current tattooing boom is merely the revival of an ancient art practised by people all over the world for thousands of years. The modern decline in interest was the aberration, not the recent revival, which he dates from 1977 when the pioneering tattooist

Dave Yurkew organised the first international tattooist convention in Houston, Texas, from which, inspired and enthused, tattooists went forth to ink the world. As with the spread of Christianity, progress was gradual at first, then suddenly speeded up, then went 'turbo', and shows no sign of slowing down.

'So what's the most popular style?'

'Fashions come and go,' Dan explains, pondering, 'but the style that is always in fashion is tribal. At first it was Celtic tribal, then the Borneo tribal style was popular, and now it's more Polynesian and Maori.'

While I am struggling to control the ecstatic shudder of the theorist who has just been offered corroborating evidence, Dan is off into a rant about the latest fashion of photorealism, an American style that specialises in fantastically detailed and convincing human portraits. Reaching for a laptop, he brings up examples, and acknowledges the technical skill, which he admits is beyond his own capability, while seriously questioning the artistic merit. It's another case of the familiar distinction between the virtuoso and the true artist.

'Like the jazz musicians who can play a thousand notes a minute?'

'Exactly.'

And Dan now reveals himself to be one of the true artists, succumbing to passion, his hands rising to sculpt in air. 'This style is all about itself rather than a marriage with a body. A tattoo should work with the three-dimensional form and the skin rather than just imposing a two-dimensional image. A 2-D image that looks good on paper won't work on skin.' And now artistic passion runs ahead of explanation. 'Nikko Hurtado ruined one of the loveliest bums in the world.' But, seeing my incomprehension, he explains. 'Nikko is one of the world's top guys, a photorealist who did a bunch of roses on Cheryl Cole's bum. But just stuck it on her bum from waist to thighs.' Dan brings up a picture on his laptop. 'It flattens out her bum instead of enhancing the curves. *See?*'

I do indeed see – and share his indignation at yet another example of Nature's loveliness ruined by human interference.

'What he *should* have done,' Dan cries, passion running away with him once again, and going seriously technical, executing dramatic air curves over the image of ruin, 'is brought lines under *here* . . . and *here* . . . and right across *here*. See what I mean?'

This time I do not entirely see but nod anyway, respecting his judgement, and continue to look. Even in its ruined state the bum is a pleasure to regard.

Finally Dan's passion subsides and he gives me a puzzled look. What is my angle? Why is a senior citizen interested in tattooing?

My own passion starts to rise as I expound my theory. The last few decades have seen the return of all the elements of the oldest human rituals and also the elements of the medieval carnival, the festivals, games and sports, subversive humour, grotesquerie and parades.

So now fancy dress is increasingly common at parties, hen and stag nights and festivals (which continue to proliferate), Halloween is ever more widely and enthusiastically celebrated, more and more adults are getting tattoos, face painting is available at every children's event and is common at adult sporting events (especially football matches), games and sport have become hugely popular (with many footballers now as heavily tattooed as Maori warriors), the youth dance scene has burgeoned, with raving and clubbing (led by the new shaman, the DJ), the purely rhythmic music spawned by this scene has spread into the mainstream, intoxicants have multiplied and are being consumed in increasing quantities, many expressions of sexuality once considered deviant have been accepted as normal (including homosexuality, lesbianism, sadomasochism and transvestism), there has been an explosive growth in clubs offering subversive, stand-up comedians (new versions of the trickster), singing in choirs has become fashionable, and the anti-capitalist protest movement has adopted many features of medieval carnival, including effigies, giant puppets, costumes, face painting, masks, group dancing and of course drumming.

'And it is fascinating to discover that tattooing took off in the seventies – because so did all the other things.'

'But why the seventies?'

The hypothesis is that these developments were the consequence of the sixties' countercultural explosion, when a new idealistic generation rejected bourgeois materialism and conformity and believed that love was all you needed to start the revolution and usher in a sexual utopia. But when the Age of Aquarius failed to dawn the flower children had to go back to work, and in the seventies they sought ways to escape in their free time. Soon they discovered, as had early cultures, the practices that helped to create group solidarity and personal transcendence, though these were now enjoyed separately rather than, as before, in unified rituals. But after the sixties there was also a demand not just for individualism but *expressive* individualism, ways to display personal creativity – individual dancing, costumes and tattoos. There was a need to express one's self as different but also a need to enjoy the support of unofficial rituals and groups. Hence the phenomenon of the deviant tribe.

'Deviant tribes,' Dan muses softly, looking out, past the dead rat, the illuminated skull and the portrait of Queen Elizabeth with blood pouring out of her right eye, in his face a growing visionary rapture: 'The world is going pagan again.'

4

Fun and the Group

Fun is a group activity and depends on group ethos, size, composition, structure and dynamics, all complex factors and dauntingly complex in combination. In even the smallest fun group of three close friends, the classic three amigos, roles and interactions are constantly changing and power is constantly shifting. Predicting behaviour is impossible, as it is in physics for any three bodies exerting forces on each other, so the three-amigos problem is the social equivalent of the scientific three-bodies problem.

Complex even in composition, a trio of friends will not form with just any three members, and certainly not with similar members, but often has a leader who is strong-willed and stern, even a little austere, then a shaman figure who is a worldly performer, a chancer, cheeky, even brazen, and a third who has no particular talent but serves the crucial functions of disciple to the leader and audience to the shaman. In the comedy film, *The Three Amigos*, Steve Martin is the leader, Chevy Chase the shaman and Martin Short the insignificant third.[1]

Of course this is too neat – the leader and shaman may be the same person, or leadership and shamanic qualities may be distributed among the three – but in general the leader decides what the group does, the shaman provides a cutting edge, for instance by talking the group into parties when they have not been invited, and the third amigo just goes along for the ride. So the tension is between the shaman, who would like to lead but lacks the authority, and the leader, who would like to charm but lacks the charisma. Both leader and shaman would like the exclusive allegiance of the third member, who may gain a measure of power by an agile shifting or division of allegiance.

In fact the third amigo may have the best of it in the long run because, in order to exercise the necessary agility, this member must fully understand the group dynamics and will often be the only one to do so – the leader and shaman will be largely unconscious of their roles. Knowledge is the true power and understanding is itself transformation, so the insignificant third may come to be the least dependent on the group and thus able to leave it for an independent existence. The three amigos group is particularly common in youth and when it breaks up in the course of time the shaman will have no difficulty in attaching to another group and finding an audience, but the leader may end up bewildered and bereft. What happened to the unity? Why did it break up? Why did my disciples forsake me?

I belonged to such a youthful three amigos and was the third amigo, patronised by the other two but useful for organising the key fun ritual of drinking in bars from 7.30 p.m. until closing time, getting in early to hold a good table that would accommodate the core three and the changing group of floaters attracted by the strength of this core, a table with protective isolation but offering a good view of the bar. When the group and the first floaters were in place and the first round of pints on the table, after being sampled with relish and serenely set back, there came a unique sense of blissful immersion, the long evening stretching ahead in an eternity of oneness. There was never any group discord in the bar, as each acknowledged the key obligation to buy one's round in turn, promptly and gladly, with no comparing of costs within or between rounds, and often tossing bags of crisps on the table with careless munificence. The worst sacrilege would have been failure to buy a round, and complaining about the injustice of the rounds system was almost as bad.

Youth groups like this usually split up when their members marry and start families, but after the sixties the growing tendency to avoid or defer marriage created a new kind of urban tribe, the group of single friends in the 20–35 age range who enjoy a decade or more of fun together. The American journalist Ethan Watters, himself a member of such a tribe, has defined it as a loosely knit, fluid, heterogenous network without membership criteria, hierarchy, gender distinctions or rules, which has formed spontaneously and may not even be aware of existing as a distinct formation.[2] And often the members have little in common beyond youth and a desire to postpone or reject traditional family life. But, as with the three amigos, these tribes are not random conglomerations but tend to have a similar composition of member types.

There is usually an organiser, who plans the fun gatherings and trips (but is not a leader and gains no respect or prestige from organising), also a comedian/extrovert, who gets the fun going, an innovator/adventurer, who suggests new experiences, an advisor/diplomat, who counsels against irresponsible behaviour and attempts to mitigate its consequences, and several 'children', who are not younger than the others but are needy, impractical and unreliable, apparently a nuisance but, like puppy dogs, serving the function of the lovably helpless who need looking after, and providing material for amusing anecdotes. For a group to be balanced, the responsible members must outnumber the children by about four to one, and for people who dislike each other to remain friends the group must have a high cluster coefficient i.e. be rich in interconnections that bind members together indirectly. These rich interconnections also bind by providing the group with its main source of fun, which is not cocaine, themed costume parties or trips to festivals, popular as all these are, but gossip. Few will admit to enjoying gossip but in fact most enjoy it, which is not surprising, since gossip, like laughter and dancing, releases endorphins, but, unlike laughter and dancing, is rarely acknowledged as a binding agent. Gossip is the secret glue that holds groups together.

All this strikes me as convincing. My student circle would probably have become an urban tribe if we had all remained single. Watters even describes a complex new ritual just like the buying of rounds in bars. Cocaine must be snorted in private, in apartments, and the owner of the apartment is expected to provide the drug, make it freely available and wave away the $100 bills that are sometimes offered. It's necessary to create an illusory atmosphere of blithe and careless magnanimity, when in reality everyone is carefully monitoring everyone else's consumption and is acutely aware of the need to be a blithe host in turn.

In fact, the ethos of these newest tribes has much in common with that of the oldest, the hunter-gatherer groups of the Palaeolithic era, which also had no fixed membership, no leaders or hierarchy and no difference in status between men and women.[3] The anthropological term for their ethos is *fierce egalitarianism*, which means that sharing was imposed as vigorously as the right to private property is imposed today. It's not that there was no selfishness or urge to dominate but that these were controlled by levelling mechanisms. 'If a would-be chief tries to dominate other group members, or to misuse a position of status, group members may ridicule, walk away, disobey, or simply ignore that individual. Other tactics are to rebuke, rebel against, remove, ostracize or expel an over-assertive individual from the group.'[4]

Anyone caught behaving selfishly would forfeit respect and be shamed and ostracised. This ferocity is important to note because there is a tendency to idealise egalitarian groups as all harmony, peace and love, and/or to regard them as easy-going, indifferent and comprehensively accepting suckers a bit soft in the head. Indeed, friendship groups often think of themselves as effortlessly benign but, as with my ritual drinkers, the conviviality is usually maintained by constant levelling. I was privileged to see that this is still happening, when sitting in a bar recently next to a group of mild-mannered, affable, laughing students as they established a drinks kitty. One angelic-looking young man counted the money on the table, counted it again, and then suddenly kicked back his chair to stand up, his face becoming a dark contusion, and roared in a deep voice, with the wrath of Yaweh, 'Who's been knocking on the whip?'

Levelling is crucial for egalitarianism but it is important to add that, as right-wing thinkers have often noted, it can be indiscriminate, more like flattening than equalising, and can suppress not just egotism and power hunger but moral and intellectual aspiration, and any form of individual development not approved by the group. My first attempts to write were savagely ridiculed by my friends as absurdly pretentious, and I learned to conceal my Penguin Classics, though I compensated by flaunting these on solitary train journeys.

But where hunter-gatherer egalitarianism was based on survival and the need to find food, that of the urban tribe is based on friendship and the need to have fun. Like many concepts and relations, friendship is often assumed to be a constant, unchanged throughout the ages and throughout individual lives – whereas it is likely to have changed continuously throughout both. It seems incontestable that it has become steadily more important, facilitated by greater affluence, freedom and mobility and easier means of communication, and simultaneously more differentiated from, and more diffused into, other relationships. Not only are you more likely to seek, value and nurture peer friends, but many previously unlikely contenders, including your dad, your boss and the author you are reading, may now desperately want to be your buddy. And the nature of friendship has also changed steadily, becoming less instrumental and more emotional, with friends chosen more for personal appeal than usefulness.[5] While, within an individual life, friends are more crucial in youth because they fulfil many necessary functions – a friend may also be an ally, mentor, teacher, protector, homoerotic attraction, or all these and more. With age these supplementary functions become less important, which is why we tend to have fewer friends as we grow older.

An advantage of friendship as a group ethos is that it is less prone to the illusion of group superiority than traditional sources of togetherness such as nationality, religion, race, gender, class or profession. Many members of urban tribes have come to the city expressly to escape from such categories. And not only do diversity and independence help to prevent groupthink, they have a positive function in improving group decision making. Studies have shown that when groups are required to find the correct solution to a problem, the diversity and independence of members are as important as intelligence and expertise.[6] And participating in decisions made by a group of diverse and independent people can improve the problem-solving ability of the individual.[7] So belonging to an urban tribe may not just improve the chances of finding the best fun but make you smarter as well, though whether or not this outweighs the effects of cocktails, coke and lack of sleep has yet to be studied.

As for fun as a goal, Watters, and many of the tribe members he has talked to, are acutely aware of the charges of immaturity and irresponsible hedonism. Watters reveals that he was never able to watch the long-running and hugely popular TV comedy series *Friends*, because the parallels with his own life were too disturbing – and he counters the charge of irresponsibility with stories of community spirit, tribe members providing each other with accommodation, loans, labour, expertise, counselling, help during illnesses, backup against threats, and support in battling addiction or depression. Of course this is biased and omits the inevitable envies, hatreds, conflicts and quarrels. It would take a new Proust to do justice to the urban tribe.

On group size, the expert is Robin Dunbar, who claims that the number in a group is usually a multiple of three and that the next common size after three itself is twelve.[8] It's odd that he misses six, which was the size of the group in *Friends*, and is also the usual size of the affinity group, the small circle based on common attributes, interests or beliefs, and so more clearly defined and focused than the friendship group, but with equally informal meetings that usually have no leaders or structure but lots of food, drink, music, humour and fun. And, unlike gatherings of friends, affinity groups are often consciously formed to promote a cause, which can range from conservative evangelical Christianity to radical anarchist protest action.[9] Whatever the cause, the small, intimate cell that has fun is a tremendously successful way of keeping its members committed to the larger group – and many religious and political movements are entirely based on such cells. Supporters of causes used to believe that asceticism was necessary for dedication but have now discovered that fun is more effective.

Moving up to twelve, psychologists have also identified this as significant for friendship, the size of the 'sympathy group', the outer circle whose deaths would cause grief. Dunbar adds that twelve is 'the typical team size in most team sports, the number of members on a jury, the number of Apostles ... the list goes on'.[10] Looking back to my drinking group, the floaters added to the core three would probably have made a dozen or so, though I would not have grieved for any of the several who were slow to buy a round. And Watters notes that the urban tribes he has studied often have a membership of 10–15, or in larger tribes an inner core of this size, with the full tribe membership ranging from around 30–60. In Dunbar's scheme this would match with the 50 or so members of an average hunting 'band' or overnight camping group.

But a viable group has an upper limit and according to Dunbar this is around 150 (now known as Dunbar's number). The theory is that, since nonhuman primates live in the largest possible social groups for defence against predators, but need major brain power to sustain the complications of face-to-face relationships with all group members, there should be a correlation between the size of a primate's neocortex and its maximum group size.[11] It turns out that this is indeed the case – the larger the neocortex, the larger the viable group – and extrapolating to the size of the human neocortex would give a maximum group size of 150. In other words, the theory suggests that the human brain can just about maintain personal relationships with 150 or so people. Supporting evidence is that hunter-gatherer communities had around 150 members, the average population of villages in tribal societies where census data are available was 153, while Neolithic villages in the Middle East are estimated to have had 120–150 inhabitants, and from information in the Domesday Book of 1086 the average population of an English village was 150. This number also turns up in modern armies where a company, the smallest independent unit, has 130–150 soldiers – and in business organisation theory 150 has been established as the maximum number of employees who can work together on a person-to-person basis.

This suggests that hierarchy tends to develop in larger groups because the close relationships necessary for levelling become more difficult to sustain as numbers rise. On the other hand, levelling enforcement is more effective as the group becomes larger. So there must be an optimal point for best combination of relationship closeness and enforcement heft. If this turned out to be twelve it would explain why sports teams and sympathy groups have a dozen or so members,[12] and why Jesus chose twelve disciples. Because he was God, he knew that one would betray him and that eleven was the best number to ensure consensus in the difficult meetings in upper rooms when he was gone. And he also understood the need for diversity. Few groups include a tax officer and fishermen.

Dunbar agrees with Watters on the importance of gossip in binding groups, and explains this as not just a luxury indulgence but necessary for the exchange of information that permits individuals to adapt their many relationships, and the group as a whole to self-regulate. However, neither Watters nor Dunbar mention the group structure necessary for friendship and the propagation of gossip – the network. The prevalence of networks in nature and society was not recognised until the current century and research has revealed many common features, often counter-intuitive. First, the efficacy of a network is determined not by the number of nodes but by the number of links between nodes. And in a growing network, when the number of interconnections reaches a critical point, the network can suddenly mutate into something new, unexpected and much more complex, a phenomenon known as emergence. From a network of molecules emerged living cells, from a network of cells emerged organisms, from a network of neurons emerged consciousness – and from friends getting together in the cities there emerged urban tribes.

However, the enrichment of connections tends not to develop uniformly but in clusters of nodes, which have many links to each other but few connections to nodes in distant clusters. Yet it's these few links that are most important, permitting rapid communication between any two nodes via a small number of links. For people, the average number of links needed to connect two individuals is the famous six degrees of separation, for websites it is nineteen and for the computers that make up the Internet housing the web, it is ten. Also, there is a tendency for some nodes to develop more links than others and become hubs. In friendship networks the hubs are the most popular people, the clusters are small circles of close friends, and the links to distant clusters are weak, acquaintanceship relations. Long before network theory, the sociologist Mark Granovetter discovered the significance of weak links when his research revealed that, for spreading gossip or news of a great new dance venue, or organising protest, or getting a job, the weak links were more important.[13] That acquaintances should be more useful than friends is not as odd as it sounds because the strong links in clusters cause propagation in circles whereas the weak link to a distant cluster opens up entire new areas – and, for receptivity, the cluster will tend to deliver what is already familiar while the weak link will introduce the new and diverse. There is an analogy with the human brain where neurons also tend to be connected in close clusters supporting established skills, habits, routines and thought processes, with few or no connections between clusters. But much creativity and imagination are based on the ability to associate distant and unrelated clusters. This is why specialisation is bad. Diversity also rules in the brain.

For anyone planning to establish a fun commune, the lesson from all this is that the maximum membership should be 150, housed in separate units of twelve or so, possibly divided into groups of six, each with a leader/organiser and shaman/comedian; and of course there would need to be daily classes (no, workshops) in ritual design, mask making, costume creation, body painting, tattooing, shamanic dance, drumming and stand-up comedy. In the evenings there would be ecstatic dance led by a shaman, once a week a comedy night with audience participation led by a trickster, and once a month a Venetian-themed Masquerade Ball. Around all these activities there should be constant socialising, especially gossiping, with at least one link from each unit to others (the clusters), and if possible between the most popular people in the units (the hubs). Also, according to Dunbar, about 40 per cent of socialising should be devoted to the inner circle, about 60 per cent to the circle of twelve, and the rest to the remaining 138. So having fun is not only complex but requires precise mathematics – and even the most detailed calculation may be futile because friendship tribes are not consciously created but emerge. No wonder so many communes fail.

Dunbar stresses that face-to-face contact is most effective, but, as Watters points out, the new urban tribes depend heavily on communication technology. The structure of friendship networks is the same as the structure of the web computer network, which is why social networks on the Internet have been so successful. And the development of the Internet has also facilitated another entirely new type of fun group – the deviant tribe, whose members long to participate in rituals but are so dispersed, and have tastes so specialised and even transgressive, that they have difficulty meeting in public. The dark side of this is that paedophiles, bigots and bullies have established online networks, but the bright side is that many others with harmless tastes, like dressing up, do not have to wait for Halloween but can display themselves in costumes all year round on websites.

Of course the terms 'fancy dress' and 'dressing up' are inadequate, even derogatory, with their suggestions of frivolity and childishness. The practice badly needed a new name to confer intellectual respectability, and it has indeed been dignified as 'cosplay', an ingenious neologism attributed to several different individuals but with a consensus that it was coined in Japan in the eighties and emerged from the new seventies ritual of dressing up as comic-book characters. Fancy dress demands to be admired and, although cosplay has its own magazines, it seems unlikely that it would have become a major worldwide phenomenon if not for websites where cosplayers show photographs of themselves in costume and exchange tips on how to paint latex monster hands, make a BL2 Deathtrap Backpack and cut out the armour for Erza Scarlet Flame Empress (use an X-ACTO knife on the EVA foam commonly found as garage mats). These websites suggest a close community whose members advise, praise, reassure and commiserate with each other. A common theme is the cruel and unjust indifference of the world to imagination and skill ('Nobody gave a rat's arse about my costume'). But once networks like these reach a certain size they 'emerge' into public conventions, and cosplay has become so popular that it now has many regular events in major cities round the world (including New York, San Diego, Tokyo, Singapore and London), where cosplayers meet to compare costumes, photograph each other, compete for prizes and shop for accessories.

The main London event takes place over three days in the vast Excel Exhibition Centre, the size of a small town, but fully booked in advance, and packed with thousands of excitable young people in a staggering variety of colourful handmade costumes and make-up. It seems as though an entire generation has made a mass escape from the Drablands of real life (in the game Legend of Zelda the Drablands are a region of Hytopia ruled by an evil witch who captures princesses and forces them to wear black), with all those not beautiful or talented enough to be models or film stars determined to claim their share of attention by dressing as faux-medieval warriors, fairy-tale princesses, space troopers, aliens, robots, zombies, cats, bears, steampunks and superheroes, Batmen,

Spidermen, Wonder and Cat Women, contemporary versions of the shamans who donned strange costumes and assumed magical powers. But the most popular single character is probably The Joker, the clown-faced villain from the Batman comics and films, a trickster attractive because he is evil just for the fun of it. Chaos and mayhem are such fun, he tells us.

However, there are none of the fantasy characters of my own benighted adolescence, no Western gunslingers or Indian maidens, no pirates or pirate wenches, and no representatives of the classical world, no Roman centurions or Cleopatras, which is disappointing because I have always had a thing for upper-arm, snake-head bracelets. It seems that fantasy has this much in common with reality – it's always on the move and always subject to fashion. And perhaps contemporary fantasy does not want to be tied to any historical period or location but to float free of all limitation in a timeless, placeless Magic World.

Invoking or coercing magic requires a magical accessory, and cosplayers like to carry something totemic – there are staffs, tridents, sceptres, parasols, assault rifles, ray guns, pikes, spears, axes, cleavers, crossbows, clubs, warhammers, and, intriguingly popular with young women, giant mallets (one bearing the message YOUR FACE HERE on the business end). Even more intriguing is a girl with a ten-foot purple spade, but an approach for information might be misunderstood as she is wearing the skimpiest and flimsiest of bikinis. Is there a superheroine known as Spade Girl? Also intriguing, but even more daunting, is a girl in stars-and-stripes hot pants and a T-shirt inscribed DADDY'S LITTLE MONSTER, gleefully brandishing a baseball bat saying GOODNIGHT![14]

But by far the most popular accessory is the sword, as important in the realm of fantasy as a laptop in the office world. 'Bring a Sword to a Gunfight', exhorts a poster above a sword stall, and these stalls are among the largest, most numerous and most crowded, with many pushing madly to get at sabres, scimitars, cutlasses, Excaliburs, samurai swords, the Folded Damascus Blue Katana and the bespoke designs of specific game heroes, the Cutting Moon, Dark Repulser, Elucidator and Oblivion Keyblade, though the young man elbowing past me is disappointed to discover that the OK is not at all OK, crying out bitterly, 'The chain is all wrong.'

It's necessary to queue for everything, and the length of the signing queues would have any realist author agog. The realistic truth is that fantasy sells. I should tour the comic-book publisher stalls pitching my idea. As with movie cops and private detectives, there has to be a superhero for every minority, so there is an obvious need for a geriatric champion. My suggestion is Silverman, who appears to be a doddery old fool playing bingo in a retirement home, but, on learning about mistreatment of senior citizens, dons his tight-fitting Silversuit to become a powerful avenger. Superheroes need a human flaw to make them credible so Silverman could suffer from memory lapses and occasionally forget where he has parked the Silvermobile.

At least the queues are useful for making contact without the embarrassment of direct accosting. While waiting in line for coffee I am bumped in the knee by a rifle butt.

'It's not real,' the owner assures me, holding up the weapon so I can see it is largely brown masking tape.

'Who are you?' I ask.

'The hunter from Bambi. And this is Bambi.' He indicates his companion, a thin girl in a beige leotard sporting a pair of beige ears, and behaving in character by tittering and stepping nervously back, as though I am an evil old wizard planning to carry her back to the Drablands.

This hunter looks intelligent so I put the question: 'Why does everyone want to dress up?'

'It's fun,' he says, giving me a suspicious once over. 'But *you're* not dressed up.'

'Actually, yes. I'm in period costume. As a Polytechnic Lecturer from the eighties. It's a character who looks normal but after marking two hundred assignments he turns into a screaming zombie.'

Bambi titters even more nervously and steps back again . . . into a girl holding a tall staff with some sort of ecclesiastical motif on the top.

'What is *that*?'

'It's for casting magic spells,' she explains apologetically. 'I'm Lux from League of Legends.'

'But on weekdays?'

'IT support.'

We are all bonding nicely but are distracted by a possibly sinister scene beside the queue, as three apes in full *Planet of the Apes* regalia, with ape heads, clubs swinging from belts and automatic weapons held high against hairy chests, stop in front of three princesses in white corsets exposing deep décolletage, and flared white skirts exposing bare thighs above white stocking tops. Is this a King Kong scenario? No, the apes just want to photograph the princesses, who are more than happy to oblige. Everyone wants to be photographed and has a special pose for the occasion.

There are no tables free so I have to share with a female zombie avidly shovelling meatballs into her face from a Styrofoam container with one hand and working a mobile phone with the thumb of the other. This girl has combined the zombie and princess themes in a Regency gown torn and stained with blood, possibly inspired by *Pride and Prejudice and Zombies*, a novel whose blurb asks, 'Can Elizabeth Bennet vanquish the spawn of Satan?' and does not answer but promises 'all-new scenes of bone-crunching zombie mayhem'.[15]

I wait for her to put down the phone and ease off on the meatballs. 'Excuse me, do you mind me asking why you're a zombie?'

She shrugs defensively. 'It's October.'

'But why a *zombie*?'

She shifts even more defensively. 'I like ripping dresses and splashing blood.'

I am curious about zombies because they are a major theme throughout the event, with artists offering zombification (your portrait as a zombie), and stalls selling zombie novels, comics, T-shirts, posters, rings, games, and box sets of the TV series *The Walking Dead*, described by the Comic Con Show Guide as 'a global phenomenon and truly must-see event TV'. The reanimation of the zombie is generally attributed to the two George A. Romero films, *Night of the Living Dead* (1968) and *Dawn of the Dead* (1978). Like fun, horror had a major resurgence in the seventies, and the connection might be that both allay fears, though in opposite ways, one by facing and one by denying. Most horror plays on fear of the evil individual but with zombie horror, it is fear of the evil horde, the contemporary fear of immigration and overcrowding, of being overrun and devoured by a multitude of ravening monsters.

It is significant that, in more recent zombie apocalypse films, the zombies are not reanimated corpses but victims of a rapidly spreading virus, often a *rage* virus, so that the survivors in their enclave fear both rage and *contagion*. And zombies are perfect for digital games because they are not only completely dehumanised, always a licence to kill, but also demonised, which makes it actually virtuous to blow away hordes.

My zombie princess has finished her meatballs so I put the basic question to her: 'Why do so many want to dress up?'

'For attention,' she confesses sadly, then brightens. 'But also the companionship. You make lots of friends online. And cosplayers are all so nice. They just want to praise each other's costumes.'

'Then how come most carry weapons and many are covered in blood?'

She ignores this. 'It's also about making the costumes. The craft. My friend ... a doctor ... spent over a hundred hours making a lace dress for today.'

It's true that the pleasure of being photographed is usually followed by the pleasure of explaining how the costume was made.

But now photographers are running from every direction to join a paparazzi melee. There must be someone famous behind the rows of upraised cameras. It turns out to be a group of six young women in high-heeled boots, tight-fitting costumes accentuating the breasts, and oversized head masks with long, fluorescent hair and the giant, wide-open eyes common in girls from comic books and Disney cartoons, no doubt to indicate sincerity and innocence. But there is something peculiar about these women. They are all wearing gloves and none exposes even an inch of flesh, whereas bare female flesh is the cosplay norm. And their movements are elaborately careful and slow. It suddenly comes to me that these are men dressed as women.

This is a combination of cosplay and cross-dressing known as female masking, which involves men donning not just women's clothes but women's bodies – heel to neck latex suits with silicon breasts and silk-lined vaginas, and latex heads with extravagant female hair. Like cosplayers and cross-dressers, maskers yearn to be seen and admired and the group of six pose endlessly for photographs.

I discover subsequently that many maskers were also happy to appear in a documentary, *The Secret Lives of the Living Dolls*[16] – for instance Robert, a seventy-year-old retired property developer who demonstrates his transformation into Sherry (as in cross-dressing, the female persona always has a name). Robert is especially proud of his own addition to the latex suit – pubic hair (cut from his own head) to improve Sherry's vagina. A traditional man, he does not approve of the contemporary fashion for shaving and waxing.

Maskers in general favour a certain type of contemporary female glamour – large breasts, protuberant lips, wide eyes, long hair and big heels – and Sherry is a traditional busty blonde who wears only the skimpiest gold lamé bikini and high heels. 'I see a very exciting female in the mirror,' Robert tells us, 'and she's all mine.' There is an element of individualistic self-reliance in cross-dressing – a man can become his own girl and take himself on a date. Posing in front of a full-length mirror, Robert now becomes Sherry who flicks back her blonde hair, lifts up her large breasts and pouting lips and cries out in uncontrollable delight, 'God, I'm *fabulous!*'

Sherry is keen to have her fabulousness more widely appreciated, to 'know what it's like to be a celebrity and get attention' (as another masker fond of appearing in public puts it) and we are privileged to accompany her to the beach, where she does indeed attract attention but, unlike the traditional busty blonde, is happy to let the many admirers squeeze her egregious wobblies. These are indeed disconcertingly convincing, as is the rest of the body – and it turns out that most of the suits, and certainly the best, are made by Femskin, a family-run business in the American bible belt, which creates individual female bodies to precise specifications at a cost of up to £10,000.

The business was established by a husband and wife but is now largely run by their sons, with Adam as the PR and marketing man, who explains that demand is growing everywhere and that they export all over the world, even to Siberia, though Germany is the biggest single market. Why are German men especially keen to be rubber dolls? Adam has no idea. Nor can he explain masking itself – and like the cosplayers asked to explain dressing up, is nonplussed by the question. 'These men aren't weirdos,' he offers at last, after long, anguished reflection, 'and they aren't gay either.' There is another long silence – but I know what he is going to say, and eventually he says it, with a sigh of relief, 'It's fun.'

This is a key word for maskers – 'I'm just able to have fun', 'Going out in public is great fun', 'Being part of the doll culture is fun.' Displaying pictures and exchanging tips on websites is also fun, but the greatest fun of all is, of course, to meet and party at the annual Rubber Doll World Rendezvous in Minneapolis.

5

Fun, Boredom, Anxiety and Authenticity

Boredom is the malign Siamese twin of fun, the dark side of the smiley face, the flatness of the bubbly personality when it is left alone, the spiritual anorexia that dogs the sensual greed, the silence that waits for the music to die, the grey ghost that haunts the gleaming temples of the contemporary world. Killing desire and expectation, depleting energy, paralysing will and casting a pall over brightness, it shocks with a preview of the worst horror, death.

Of course boredom has many precursors. Kierkegaard argued that it even preceded, and indeed was the source of, the human: 'The gods were bored; therefore they created human beings. Adam was bored because he was alone; therefore Eve was created. Since that moment boredom entered the world and grew in quantity in exact proportion to the growth of population.'[1] Then there was the 'no new thing under the sun' of Ecclesiastes, the *taedium vitae* of the classical world, the acedia of the medieval period and the melancholy of the Renaissance discussed exhaustively in Robert Burton's *The Anatomy of Melancholy*, which claimed to have discovered eighty-two different types of this affliction.

But those who have studied boredom agree that it is essentially a modern phenomenon, or at least that it has assumed a more virulent form in the modern era – a chronic, generalised, existential boredom not associated with any particular situation or circumstance, and also that it has become increasingly wide-spread and that its growth has kept pace with that of the modern world. The term 'bore' was first used in English in the eighteenth century, and in the following century boredom was recognised as a new threat peculiar to the age. The first great poet of modernity, Baudelaire, saw it as the principal vice, a kind of monster that renders its victims helplessly passive but seething with resentment and aggression.

> Among venomous insects and reptiles,
> The parasites, vermin and scavengers,
> Scorpions, vultures and jackals, who circle
> Restlessly our stale menagerie of vice,
>
> There's one even uglier and yet more vile.
> It never makes gestures, nor utters a cry,
> But it would happily pulverize planet earth
> And consign to the yawning void its dust.
>
> It's BOREDOM – impotent tears in its eyes
> As it chain smokes and dreams of the gallows.
> Reader, you know well this monster . . . *you*,
> Hypocrite reader – my double – my brother.

And boredom is all through the writings of the twentieth century, first in Pessoa's *The Book of Disquiet*, then Sartre's *Nausea*, then Beckett's plays and novels, then E. M. Cioran's philosophy, and then the science fiction of J. G. Ballard, who foresaw no relief in the twenty-first century: 'I could sum up the future in one word, and that word is boring. The future is going to be boring.'[3] According to Ballard's fiction, this future boredom will become so intense and unbearable that the mild transgression of fun will no longer provide relief and only the extreme transgression of murder will do.

Beckett's work is the most eloquent statement of boredom as the key modern problem. In *Waiting for Godot*, Vladimir says to Estragon: 'We wait. We are bored. (*He throws up his hand*). No, don't protest, we are bored to death, there's no denying it.'

And the only escape from boredom, in Beckett's bleak vision, is meaningless activity. Vladimir and Estragon are delighted to come across a pair of old boots and to pass the time trying them on. 'We always find something, eh, Didi, to give us the impression that we exist,' Estragon says, and Vladimir answers, impatiently, 'Yes yes, we're magicians.'

What was the source of this modern affliction? As always, there were many possible factors. First the Reformation and the Enlightenment delivered a deterministic double whammy, with the new science interpreting the universe as a clockwork toy wound up by God and left to run entirely predictably, and the new religion discovering a double predestination that marked everyone as saved or damned even before birth (though no one could know who was which). Acceptance of determinism, either material or spiritual, is always likely to lead to boredom. If all that happens is decided in advance then volition is powerless, and might as well be abandoned. The clockwork universe paradigm also removed from the world any sense of the divine, any presence of enchantment, and double predestination destroyed the unity and harmony of the religious community by replacing it with anxiety about who might be saved and paranoid suspicion about who might be damned.

Then the twentieth century was informed that, not only is God dead so that the universe has no one in the control tower, but the universe is not even predictably clockwork and is instead expanding randomly in every direction and may eventually die of exhaustion or blow itself up. The universe is not only meaningless but mad. Yet it is impossible to suppress the old hunger for meaning and purpose. We continue to wait for Godot in spite of knowing that he, she or it is never going to turn up. Boredom and fun are opposite responses to this lack of meaning, which may result in lethargy, a desire to do nothing because nothing is worth doing, or frantic activity, a desire to do anything to suppress the sense of futility. This could be why bipolar disorder has become so common. The individual response to lack of meaning oscillates between the extremes of depression and mania.

Another factor was the loss of the traditional carnivals, with communal feasting and dancing, and their replacement by the new eighteenth-century phenomenon of leisure, which, in another loss of unity, became separated from work and largely devoted to passive spectating. Eighteenth-century Europe saw the appearance of circuses with wild animal trainers, conjurers, jugglers and trapeze artists, and also comic opera, puppet shows, museums, zoos, professionally organised horse racing, lectures on science and exhibitions of curiosities, including deformed humans and animals.

Spectating is another phenomenon that is often taken for granted as a permanent feature of human behaviour. When we holiday by the Mediterranean and wander through the old stone seating of the ancient amphitheatres, it's easy to believe that there have always been performers and audiences – but for most societies spectating is a recent development, and in some societies it has never happened. Once a friend who went to teach English and Drama at a Nigerian university explained to me the difficulty of putting on plays there. Setting up a stage and seats was easy enough – the problem was the audience, who did not sit down in silence to experience theatrical catharsis but wandered round talking and laughing, or, if they became interested in the action on stage, climbed up to join in. At first the producers saw this as another example of the disruptive behaviour familiar to all teachers – but eventually they came to realise that there was no attempt to disrupt because the audience did not know they were an audience and in fact had no conception of 'audience'.

It was only in the more sophisticated early societies, such as those of Greece and Rome, that ritual, which began as pure participation, separated into performing and spectating. And this separation was repeated in Western Europe only in the eighteenth century. And even this spectating was nothing like the reverent silence of a contemporary theatre, classical music or opera audience, outraged by a single cough. British travellers on the Grand Tour, like James Boswell, visited the famous La Scala opera house in Milan but complained that it was impossible to hear the music because of the audience's noisy chattering, laughing, kissing, eating and drinking (not just snacks but dishes of macaroni pie and roast meat) and the slamming of doors as they went in and out of each other's boxes. It sounded and smelled like a popular restaurant on a busy night. It was only in the late nineteenth century that audiences in the West began to sit in silence, and the balance there continued to shift towards passivity, most dramatically with the arrival of television, which became the most common use of free time and often replaced 'doing' with viewing. As more people watch TV chefs, fewer actually cook. As more watch sport, fewer actually play. As more watch pornography, fewer actually have sex.[4]

There is a cautionary tale in the development of the sea squirt, a tiny creature that looks like a spongy worm but has a primitive brain that enables it to seek nutrients and avoid predators. Or, rather, the young squirt has a brain. Once it reaches adulthood the mature squirt attaches itself to a rock, boat hull or piling, takes enough nutrient from the surrounding sea, no longer needs to monitor its environment and make decisions, and *begins to eat its own brain*, since this is now redundant. It may help to recall this creature if tempted to watch golf on TV.

In *The Society of the Spectacle*, first published as long ago as 1967, Guy Debord identified passive spectating as the key contemporary development, with *Homo spectator* replacing *Homo faber*, the illusion of the spectacle replacing the old religious illusion, the unity of spectating replacing the unity of participating, and television becoming the new opium of the people. Debord overstated his case by presenting The Spectacle as an evil entity with a sinister mission, a kind of James Bond secret organisation that has succeeded in achieving world domination – the Spectacle as S.P.E.C.T.R.E – but he was certainly prescient in noticing an important trend. We are all viewers now, as Debord predicted: 'Since the spectacle's job is to cause a world that is no longer directly perceptible to be *seen* . . . it is inevitable that it should elevate the human sense of sight to the special place once occupied by touch.'[5] Debord would surely have been grimly amused to know that touch has since become the slave of sight, since what we often touch now are screens, which we carry everywhere and cherish as sacred totems, keeping us always in touch with the spectacle, as once crucifixes and rosary beads kept us in touch with the divine – but not even in his wildest dreams could Debord have imagined that these devices would offer not only several hundred television channels but access to clips from much of what has been recorded on film, plus a growing library of home movies.

Anyone who has taught young people will be familiar with the passivity of the habitual spectator, the jaded slump and loll that say in unequivocal body language to the desperate teacher, radiating enthusiasm with an energy that could power a small town, 'I expect to be entertained but not by a pitifully ingratiating old fart like you.' A few years ago I was starting the first seminar of an IT module as part of a degree course, with my enthusiasm cranked up to turbo to get things going, and finished the outline of the module programme by opening my arms and eyes wide in the joyous gesture of Christ suffering the little ones to come to him, while I cried out brightly, 'Any questions?' There was a long deathly silence – and then a query from the back, bemused and querulous: 'Is this all it is?' I was considering responding on the lines of 'What did you expect when the programme I've just been going through has been available online for months?' – but I saw that the questioner was not looking at me but staring discontentedly out of the window. His query was a rhetorical question to the world, a cry of existential anguish at its disappointing failure to entertain.

The problem with passive spectating is that it comes to place responsibility not just on the immediate performer but on all of the external world. The subjective reaction, 'I'm bored', is turned into the objective accusation, 'It's boring', a consequence of the modern emphasis on individual freedom which causes everything to be measured solely in terms of its effect on one's self, and the response of the self seems so exclusively absolute that it is projected back on to the world as a permanent feature of reality.

As our virtues are also our vices, freedom, the great gift of the modern age, is also the source of many of its problems. Jean-Paul Sartre, one of the most famous advocates of freedom in the century of freedom, the twentieth, spoke of being '*condemned* to freedom'.[6] But for most it is still too exciting a concept to be recognised as ambivalent. Freedom is the one unchallenged mantra of the times. God the Tyrant is dead and Freedom the Liberator lives. Freedom is in fact the new God. There may be many who attempt, and frequently succeed, in suppressing specific freedoms, but few would publicly dare to reject the supreme concept itself, as in the past few people would have publicly dared to reject the supreme being. It is common to have opposing forces, both political and military, who each sincerely believe they are fighting for freedom, with those in power taking action to protect freedom against those who describe themselves as freedom fighters.

But freedom, the ultimate relief, is also a new kind of burden, the ultimate blessing is also a curse, the ultimate positive is also a negative. Freedom is nothing, an absence, an emptiness. And while the possibility of infinite and endless choice is exciting, the constant need to make specific decisions and choices is exhausting. Boredom is partly a fatigue of the spirit overwhelmed by the relentless personal responsibility of freedom.

Closely associated with the development of freedom is the rise of individualism, a complex, changing concept with a complex history involving a complex mix of religious, material, social and intellectual factors. A full account would require a separate book or books[7] – but a summary version could go something like this. First there was religious individualism, the Christian insistence that salvation was a matter for the individual alone, a fundamental concept of the early Church and dramatically reinvigorated by the Reformation. Then this combined with various social and intellectual developments to produce political individualism, the idea that the individual should be liberated from social and state coercion (and, later, from all authority). After that came romantic individualism, a rejection of the urban herd in favour of solitary communing with sublime nature on rugged coastlines and mountain tops. At the end of the nineteenth, and during the first half of the twentieth century, this morphed into bohemian individualism, which recolonised the city, or a limited area of it, as a refuge from the morals, conventions and conformities of bourgeois society. All these overlapping and intermingling developments remained elitist, influencing mostly artists, intellectuals and political radicals, until, at the end of the sixties and throughout the seventies, they combined and spread through youth culture around the world to produce expressive individualism, which added to the rejection of authority and conformity the need to make a personal mark of some sort.

'Do your own thing', was the central slogan of the sixties – but who was 'you' and what was the 'thing'? The need to find one's self, then one's thing, and to do this thing and be acclaimed for it, is exhausting, a major source of the boredom of spiritual fatigue. Worse, this boredom easily mutates into anxiety, an inevitable side effect of freedom. The free life demands constant choice and is haunted by the possibility of bad choices in the past, present and future. The path of freedom leads to the prison of dread.

There is also a tendency for anxiety to develop with age, as the complexities, demands, conflicts and threats of life become more apparent and the time to find and express a true self diminishes. I have experienced anxiety increasingly myself (in fact meta anxiety – I'm anxious about being anxious). A formidable foe, anxiety is worse than boredom because it's even more nebulous and difficult to assign to any cause, even more unsettling in its effects, even harder to dispel and even more likely to become chronic. Boredom is a lack of desire to act but anxiety is a lack of ability to act. Boredom may sink into a restful lethargy but anxiety is a corrosive dread that permits no respite. And while anxiety often includes worry and doubt, it's greater and much more debilitating than these. Worry and doubt have specific objects and limited durations, but anxiety is a constant dread that something is about to go terribly wrong, or something atrocious is about to happen, though it's not clear what, when, where or how.

I think of anxiety as a general form of the experience of the guest in someone's house who is starving and shivering despite being well fed and warm. Lack of control over food and heating creates irrational sensations of hunger and cold. Similarly, the awareness of not being at home in the world produces irrational feelings of deprivation, exposure and fear, and these are likely to intensify with the growing vulnerability of age.

Youth is bored and age is anxious. Philip Larkin, a man obsessed with retaining his freedom, put it like this with brutal directness: 'Life is first boredom, then fear'.[8] The privileged are always aware at some deep level that their privileges may be taken away, either immediately by the underprivileged or by the ravages of time, ill health and death. It is no surprise that Larkin expressed fear of death with incomparable directness. 'Not to be here, / Not to be anywhere, / And soon.'[9]

There are many other sources of modern anxiety, including the fear of leading an inauthentic life. The authenticity imperative is another consequence of freedom. If everyone is completely and inescapably defined by social position then many may feel angry and resentful but no one can feel inauthentic. But with the availability of choice comes the need to choose an authentic life, first emphasised by Jean-Jacques Rousseau at the beginning of the modern age, and becoming increasingly urgent, a major concern of twentieth-century philosophy. Following Heidegger, Sartre argued that we have become inauthentic by surrendering to social roles, and illustrated this with his famous example of the waiter who is acting out the role of waiter.[10]

In the twenty-first century authenticity seems to have become an even more pressing issue. There is a growing sense that the authentic self has been lost, distracted by careerism and consumer goods, sedated by passive entertainment and distorted by social functions. So the authenticity project is to uncover and liberate the real person buried under the distractions and distortions.

This hunger for authenticity is experienced, often unconsciously, as a desire to retrieve the genuine by going back – also unconsciously, in various ways – to the play of childhood with its absorption in the moment, to the sensual joy of the body in manual work, dancing, games, and physical activity in general, to the earliest spirituality with its celebration of the cosmos itself as sacred, before institutional religion replaced this with a remote, angry God and abstract dogma, and to involvement in the group rituals of pre-history that offer the possibility of communal oneness and personal transcendence.

Everything premodern, from the Palaeolithic to the medieval, becomes attractive, but the further back in time the more authentic, which explains the recent fashion for the 'Paleo Lifestyle', celebrated in glossy Paleo magazines, websites and conferences. Paleo is the way to go, with a Paleo diet (meat, eggs, vegetables, fruit and nuts), a Paleo sleep routine (rise at dawn, retire at sunset in a totally blacked out room and if it is necessary to check emails after dark, wear amber goggles to block blue-spectrum light), Paleo beauty products (shampoo made from apple cider vinegar with a little jojoba oil for conditioner, body scrub of olive oil, and toothpaste of coconut oil, with activated charcoal for whitening), Paleo exercise (no equipment but lots of high-intensity lungeing, punching, kicking and shouting), Paleo birthing (mothers eat the placenta[11]), Paleo parenting (playing with children in muddy streams), Paleo holidays (a group called PrimalCon offer a five-day all-Paleo experience), Paleo drinks (the Paleo strawberry daiquiri made with rum, organic strawberries, honey and freshly squeezed orange juice) and Paleo snacks (the Wild Thing Organic Paleo Raw Bar with Berries and Seeds).

There is a craving for authentic products, authentic entertainment, authentic experiences, authentic places and authentic food and drink. Hence farmer's markets, sourced meat, organic vegetables, artisan bread, craft beer, biodynamic wine, home-baked cakes, hand-made chocolates and Indian/Thai/Mexican 'street' food that is prepared, purchased and consumed in restaurants with authentic untreated brick walls, bare bulbs, dangling wires, exposed girders, vents and piping, and wooden benches, another return to the premodern, before the chair replaced the bench. Often the beloved and I, hopelessly individualistic, have arrived at new restaurants to cry out in despair, 'Oh fuck, it's communal tables and benches.' But it may be worth persevering because a trip to the toilet will often reveal that the dinky little ovoid washbasins that were once the fashion have been replaced by giant cuboids with stiff, giant, brass taps attached to copper pipes (not just exposed but *flaunted*) – the ancient 'jawboxes' our parents despised and ripped out in disgust.

But even stripped pine and exposed brick are no longer sufficiently real and are being replaced by 'rammed earth', dried, moulded and compacted soil for walls, tables and countertops. This is costly, difficult to install, in need of constant maintenance and in constant danger of collapse but still well worth the expense, effort and risk. Rammed earth is especially popular in vegetarian restaurants, organic juice bars and high-end showrooms, such as those of designer Paul Smith, where the walls have been created by Adam Weismann of Clayworks: 'Anything made from clay or mud just screams out authenticity.'[12]

For authentic fun there are ancient customs, childhood games and holidays with authentic activities in authentic destinations. Anything that can be described as wild is wildly exciting, especially wild places for wild camping and wild swimming, though the less adventurous can always settle for rewilding the garden, and those who would find even this too strenuous can go wild in an armchair with a plethora of wilderness films and books.[13]

Chained to a desk and the inauthentic office work of manipulating data, the cubicle serf dreams of stripping to the waist to chop logs with an axe on a tree stump, and then relaxing in the evening by carving utensils for his woman and toys for his children. Craft and the craftsman, once dismissed as economically obsolete in the age of cheap mass production, are increasingly prized as authentic. Anything described as handcrafted is desirable, and especially if the crafting hands are one's own. So craft lessons are a new form of group fun, and craft festivals are a booming subset of the booming festival scene. The Good Life Experience teaches campfire butchery and axe throwing, The Wilderness Festival revives 'the ancient crafts of our wild forefathers', such as basket weaving, The Shambala Festival has a blacksmithing workshop, The Green Scythe Fair promotes scything as a European mind-fulness alternative to tai chi, and Spoonfest is entirely dedicated to the carving of wooden spoons, with carvers coming from as far away as Australia, Israel and the USA and a group of 200 meeting to carve spoons together.

Along with the new reverence for craft is a reverence for the workshop, a word that combines craft with group cooperation, and is used whenever possible to make abstract activity seem physical. So there are policy workshops, meditation workshops, creative writing workshops, even philosophy workshops, and the term 'tool' is used for any kind of mental activity. The fortunate participants in a philosophy workshop will usually take home 'a philosophy toolkit'.

And craft museums are proliferating as rapidly as festivals, with many towns and villages proudly displaying the authentic implements once used by the local farmers and craftsmen. In the post-industrial age anything industrial is now also authentic, and abandoned factories, foundries, steelworks and coal mines become museums. The 'dark satanic mills' that William Blake once feared are now Heritage Centres, with interactive displays, demonstrations by staff dressed as traditional millers, a gift shop selling plastic waterwheels and a café serving home-baked scones. Though some honest trades have been unjustly ignored. There ought to be an Abbatoir Experience where, after touring a converted slaughterhouse, visitors watch in fascination as a staff member in a traditional apron straddles a sheep, deftly subdues it with a hammer in one hand and cuts its throat with a knife in the other.

For authenticity in health care there is a growing belief in complementary medicine, usually based on ancient remedies, with practitioners of ancient Chinese medicine offering acupuncture and herbal treatments on many high streets – and the wellbeing industry is dominated by the ancient oriental techniques of yoga, tai chi and meditation. In agriculture there is an increasing rejection of modern technological farming, especially the use of pesticides and fertilisers, even a return to ploughing with teams of horses, and in the 'no tillage' movement even a rejection of ploughing itself. In religion the growth of fundamentalism is partly due to a desire for authenticity by returning to the simple, pure, early tradition (though the resulting fundamentalism often violates the early principles). In politics there is a growing aversion to career politicians with their platitudes designed to appeal to all and offend none, and a corresponding preference for anyone whose casual appearance and strong views appear genuine.

In the arts the new adjective 'indie' promises authentically gritty vision just as 'artisan' and 'hand-crafted' promise authenticity in products. In literature many novelists have come to regard the traditional novel, with its plot, characters and scenes, as artificial and inauthentic.[14] In popular culture there has been the growth of reality television. And contemporary philosophers are also aware of authenticity as a major issue. 'Let's call this the Age of Authenticity,' suggests the Canadian Charles Taylor, who has pondered this issue in one full book and large sections of others,[15] while several other philosophers have also written authenticity books.[16]

Even fashion, the most artificial aspect of modern culture, seeks authenticity in medieval, Paleo, pagan, gypsy and hippy chic, with floral headbands, tabards, tunics, chainmail, bell sleeves, brocade and Celtic jewellery. Last week I passed a new designer boutique called *Hunter Gatherer*, and the desire to replace the vulgarity of shopping with a Paleo experience is behind the new fad of foraging, with lifestyle articles, books, websites and smart phone apps providing guides to woodland, seashore and urban foraging. Even the exclusive world of high-end parfumerie now has artisanal fragrances and indie perfumers, while the mainstream has seized on the authentic smell of old books. 'In the Library', a fragrance in the CB Experience Series, 'is a warm blend of English Novel, Russian and Moroccan Leather Bindings, Worn Cloth and a hint of Wood Polish'; 'Library No. 35', in the True Grace Series, offers 'the scent of leather-covered books, lovingly polished furniture and ancient library shelves'; and Demeter's Paperback has 'the musty smell of aged paper'.[17] Anything old is authentic so I should launch an artisanal fragrance called *Geriatric Genitals*, with the uniquely musty scent of aged sexual organs in worn underwear.

6

Fun and Play

I am re-enacting the creation of the cosmos, defying the modern imperatives of purpose and achievement, experiencing freedom in its truest form and authenticity in its most delightful form, and banishing boredom, anxiety and the terrors of finitude and time – in other words, I am playing with my three-year-old granddaughter. Grandparents and grandchildren generally get along well because both are free from the adult tyranny of work and career. But it turns out that I am not as free as I imagined. We are building with Lego blocks and this immediately reveals a classic difference of approach. I want to build a house exactly as it appears on the Lego box whereas Mia just wants to stick blocks together and see where it takes her – the old contention of top-down versus bottom-up, the plan versus improvisation, control versus spontaneity. Mia is the dominant partner so bottom-up wins but, as a typically modern man obsessed by the necessity of goals and direction, I need to aim for something and suggest, after a while, that what she is producing looks like a pair of legs and could well be the bottom half of a robot. Why not make it into a robot? After careful consideration she agrees to this, and there is a satisfying compromise of purpose and improv, which blesses us with an interval of silent, tranquil construction.

Presently Mia remarks, without concern, and without looking up from her work, 'Granny's been on the phone a long time.'

'She certainly has. What do you think she's talking about?'

Now Mia interrupts her work to look up and ponder, then nod decisively. 'Sharks.'

'Really? What do you know about sharks?'

This time there is no hesitation. 'Never go near one except with an adult.'

We return to our absorption in work and soon the robot is almost complete. What would make a good robot head? A window? No – a clock. And, here it is, a convincingly sinister robot. We are both surprised and immensely proud. The clock head was a touch of genius.

'Ugh!' Mia grimaces.

'You don't like the head?'

'*Nooooooo*,' she snaps impatiently, 'it's his *bum*. The robot has a pooey bum.' Another connection between the old and young is excessive interest in bowel function.

'But robots don't do poos,' I explain. 'Robots aren't people.'

She considers this and appears to have accepted it, rooting around in the block box. Eventually she finds what she is looking for – a brown block which she sticks on the back of the robot. 'There's his pooey bum.'

This episode illustrates the difficulty for modern Western culture, and especially its male half, in embracing the concept of play and hence also of fun (the difference is that play can be solitary, whereas fun is social, and play is often spontaneous and unstructured, whereas fun is usually group ritual – though play is obviously a key element in the rituals of comedy, festivity, dance, holidays and sport). Dominated by instrumental rationality and the necessity of goal, plan, direction and control, the Western mindset has always tended to denigrate play as trivial and worthless. This could be a legacy of the Christian tradition and its belief in a God with a purpose and plan.

Many pre- and non-Christian world views had no such belief. In Hindu mythology the cosmos is an accidental by-product of the play of the divine absolute, Brahman, and is without plan, purpose or direction. The Sanskrit term *lila*, pronounced leela and loosely translatable as 'play', but also 'joy', describes all reality, which is ceaseless, rhythmic, dynamic mutation – a shape-shifting dance, in fact the circle dance, *Ras*, of the prankster god Krishna, who multiplies his form so that each of the young women he dances with believes him to be her sole partner. This cosmogony inverts Western values by making play the divine meaning, and purpose merely a human illusion. The pre-Socratic philosopher Heraclitus expressed the same idea in one of his aphorisms: 'The course of the world is a child at play.'[1] While the Taoist Chuang Tzu expressed it as one of his stories: 'When Prince Wen Wang was on a tour of inspection in Tsang, he saw an old man fishing. But his fishing was not real fishing, for he did not fish in order to catch fish, but to amuse himself. So Wen Wang wished to employ him in the administration of government.'[2] And the Bhagavad Gita exhorted directly: 'You must perform every action sacramentally ... and be free from all attachment to results.'[3]

However, when the Enlightenment rejected God it not only retained the idea of purpose and plan, but elevated instrumental reason into a governing principle. This faith in rational calculation has been encouraged by the success and growing prestige of technology, with the consequence that life tends to become a cost/benefit exercise ruled by optimising algorithms. The fear is that, although now religiously and politically free, we have become enslaved by the imperatives of purpose, achievement, progress and self-improvement. These imperatives can come to dominate all aspects of life, not just the financial. Every action has to be justified as serving some desirable goal. I like to think of myself as not entirely driven by financial motives but I can see that an obsessive need to produce books has come to dominate my behaviour, so that I view life as potential research material and downgrade any experience that is unlikely to provide. It is a long time since I read a book purely for pleasure.

I have been infected by this rational attitude for most of my life and so have impatiently dismissed as a waste of my precious time most forms of play, from playing with children to the organised adult play rituals. This is in spite of the fact that two of my favourite activities, writing and sex, are mostly play. Creative writing, or any writing that is not prescribed, is playful improvising in the hope of serendipitous discovery, finding one block that fits on to another and then another, and realising with a thrill that what was vaguely intended to be some sort of house has turned into a robot instead. And what play is more fun than foreplay, especially the rough play-fighting of young lovers, the tussling, wrestling, nipping, biting and smacking that release the tension of differences and antagonisms by acting them out in a way that is non-violent though violently exciting. Mature foreplay is usually more tender and has to make allowances for weak backs and arthritic knees, and this tenderness is also sublime – but, oh Lord, that *wrestling*. At least ageing lovers can still enjoy another form of erotic play, the mock insult.

Almost as soon as the Age of Reason began, play was rediscovered as a counterbalance. In the eighteenth century Rousseau drew attention to play as not just a childish indulgence but significant and valuable (as was childhood itself as a natural, blessed state of play). Before this no one had paid much attention to children, or, if they had, they regarded them only as imperfectly formed adults. But soon Wordsworth was praising childhood as the high point of life, rather than a preparation for it, the time when 'every common sight, / To me did seem / Apparelled in celestial light', and lamenting his own fall from childish grace, 'Whither is fled the visionary gleam?' – while the newly discovered children were given their own distinctive clothes, toys and books for the first time.

In 1795 Friedrich Schiller went so far as to identify play as a crucial aspect of life, indeed almost the meaning of life, and the source of self-consciousness, freedom and morality. 'Man plays only when he is in the full sense of the word a man, and he is only wholly a Man when he is playing.'[4] This theme was taken up by other thinkers, for instance Nietzsche, in the nineteenth century: 'Man's maturity is to have found again the seriousness he had as a child at play.'[5] In another work Nietzsche used 'play' in the same sense as I use 'fun', and made the connection with boredom. 'To escape boredom, man works either beyond what his usual needs require, or else he invents play, that is, work that is designed to quiet no need other than that for working in general.'[6]

In the twentieth century Johan Huizinga wrote a full manifesto on play, *Homo Ludens*,[7] which overstates the case by indeed claiming play as the meaning of life, but is eloquent in its championing of play as a necessary rejection of procedural reason and determinism. For Rousseau, play was an instinct but for Huizinga it was a conscious, deliberate choice. 'From the point of view of a world wholly determined by the operation of blind forces, play would be altogether superfluous. Play only becomes possible, thinkable and understandable when an influx of *mind* breaks down the absolute determinism of the cosmos. The very existence of play continually confirms the supra-logical nature of the human situation.'[8] Play is irrational, superfluous, disinterested, wanton, a temporary escape from the instrumentalism insisting that all activity serve a purpose. It is a way of avoiding the own goal of always pursuing one's own goals, an assertion that heaven is doing something just for the hell of it. Huizinga published *Homo Ludens* in 1938 and since then instrumentalism has become ever more prominent. It would be difficult to find a contemporary theory of human behaviour that does not view it as instrumental and/or determined in some way. Economic theory views the individual as a rational, maximising consumer, political theory as a defender of self-interest, biology as an organism optimising its environment, neo-Darwinism as a ruthless competitor for resources, and psychology as the vehicle of unconscious desires. And so much activity is indeed goal-directed – making money, building status, looking young, staying healthy and pursuing sex. Play has meaning but no function, which makes it the opposite of most activity and a useful counterbalance. Anything that encourages activity as its own reward is surely welcome.

Huizinga's book was largely ignored for several decades and play was considered of interest only as a stage in child development (and studied only by child psychologists such as Jean Piaget). But *Homo Ludens* was rediscovered in the sixties when youth rebelled against the Age of Conformity, as Rousseau had rebelled against the Age of

Reason. And in the seventies play became the subject of academic investigation, with its own research centres, conferences, journals and august institutions like The Anthropological Association for the Study of Play. Some Christian theologians, seeing which way the wind was blowing, even tried to rebrand God not as an angry old man but as a young child at play, not the man with the plan but the boy with the toy.[9]

However, as so often, definition is a problem. Play is a feature of so many activities, takes so many forms and has so many types of player, and the word itself is used so widely and loosely, that it is as difficult to define as fun. But the general consensus is that play is voluntary, apparently purposeless, usually detached from everyday life, usually pleasurable and certainly absorbing in a way that reduces awareness of the self and time, and usually offers scope for experiment and improvisation. It may be only apparently purposeless because, although it has no short-term goal, many play theorists claim that it has long-term benefits such as developing cognition, learning useful skills, and encouraging emotional growth through discovering how to communicate and bond with peers. Others argue that such claims are another example of goal fetish, an inability to believe in activity without an obvious payoff. For these theorists, play is its own reward. I have more sympathy with the latter view. Instead of turning play into yet another goal-directed activity, it might be wiser to turn goal-directed activity into play and enjoy it for its own sake. Since play is pure experience, pure process, it encourages a taste for the experiential and processual aspects of activity, even when the activity is goal-directed.

At least there is agreement that childhood play is universal, observed in all cultures whether the cultures approve of it or not, and also common among animals. Leopards playfight, monkeys jump off trees into rivers, then climb back up the trees to dive again in a different style, bonobos play a version of blind man's buff, hippos do repeated back flips in rivers, ravens slide down snow slopes, bison skate on frozen lakes, some small fish blow bubbles, dolphins and porpoises cavort with humans, goats frolic with baby rhinoceroses and polar bears dance with dogs. Some zoos encourage inter-species play among young animals in order to modify their behaviour. Dogs playing with cheetahs make the cats less wild, though much accommodating is necessary because dogs prefer to wrestle whereas cheetahs like to chase. Successful accommodation is signalled by the cheetah licking or grooming the dog.

Even reptiles have been seen playing. When Russian scientists sent geckos into space to study the effects of weightlessness, one ingenious gecko managed to remove its identifying collar, which floated in the zero gravity and was used by the group as a plaything in a variety of ways, including batting it back and forth across the tank. This raises the possibility of an exciting new range of sports, for instance weightless football, weightless basketball and weightless hockey. As in all species, some geckos were more playful than others with, as the scientists scrupulously recorded, 'Gecko No 5 accounting for up to 39.4% of play episodes.'[10]

There may even be play in the insect world. The leading myrmecologist, E. O. Wilson, has claimed that ants seem to play. But there are significant distinctions throughout the animal kingdom. The complexity of play increases with the complexity of the organism, from the solo play like running, jumping, rolling and somersaulting common in some rodents, some birds and most hoofed mammals, through the social play like chasing and play-fighting common in many ungulates and marsupials and most primates and carnivores, to the complex social play of primates, elephants, porpoises and dolphins, that involves object construction games with sticks, stones, flowers, feathers and bones, and games similar to tag, follow the leader, peekaboo and hide and seek.[11] Studies correlating play behaviour and brain size in fifteen species of mammal from dogs to dolphins found that, allowing for different body size, the larger the brain the more complex the play.[12] Subsequent, more specific, studies found a significant correlation between the extent of play and the development of the frontal cortex, the brain area responsible for executive control, monitoring, cognition and decision making, and also the cerebellum, the area responsible for attention, language processing, and awareness of musical rhythm. These results have been interpreted as evidence that play encourages crucial brain development – but it could just as easily be the development that encourages the play, and I prefer to believe that smart creatures play more.

In young children play is not just universal but constant. It's not that play is a break from more serious business, but that everything they do is play, and play *is* the serious business. Life is a series of fascinating experiments. What would it be like if I pulled this off, opened that, dropped this, threw that, kicked this, stuck that in there, put this in my mouth, rubbed that on my hands, poured this into that, stuck this to that using this marvellous stuff called glue, marked this with that using these marvellous things called pens, crayons and paint brushes, rubbed this on my hands, shoved my hand into that, and emptied the contents of this to see what sort of thrilling crash it might make.

The young child lives entirely in the present, irritated at being asked by the doting parent, 'What did you do in nursery today?' and entirely bewildered by that other doting question, 'Are you looking forward to your holiday?' Now is the time, the only time, and the only question is which experiment to try next – rock the high chair from side to side, kick the underside of the table or drop this piece of banana into that glass of milk. The immersion in the phenomenal world is total and the engagement is through all the senses, with sound, touch, taste and smell as important as sight – and this keeps them both alert and attentive while wholly absorbed in process and flow. 'And this child is the child not of Christ but of Heraclitus,'[13] Nietzsche said, referring to the Heraclitean belief that all is flux and flow. The young child is concerned only with process not product and has little awareness of goals or time limits. At lunch Mia puts a huge dollop of hummus on her toast, then spreads it out, pats it flat ... and begins to sculpt it into peaks, mesmerised, rapt, entirely forgetting that the purpose of all this is to eat, and that the toast is going cold.

Anxiety is bound up with acute awareness of time. There is always enough time for the bad thing to happen but never enough for the good thing to be achieved. The tyranny of the project is the threat of the deadline (a sinister word that originally meant the line round a prison beyond which a prisoner would be shot). Childish play escapes from the prison of time.

The fascination of children should be based less on their innocence, cuteness and adorable misconceptions, and more on their formidable range of practical skills. Adults pay gurus large sums of money to be taught these skills in courses on mindfulness, paying attention, experientialism, living in the now, going with the flow and so on – and adult success in applying them is usually only intermittent and partial. This childhood play attitude of curiosity, alertness, attention and absorption must be a factor in a phenomenon observed by child psychologists – that young children tend to be over-optimistic and to have an exaggerated sense of mastery over both their abilities and fate. (It was a mistake to allow Mia to become involved in assembling a high chair from a flat pack. 'I can do it, I can do it,' she shouted, grabbing components and scattering crucial screws everywhere.) Adult play encourages equivalent illusions. The gambler knows that the probability of winning the lottery is the same as that of being struck by lightning, but thinks, 'Yes, yes, but weren't lots of people struck by lightning last summer?' The writer knows that most writing is ultimately worthless and doomed to be forgotten but writes on in rapture, convinced of producing a timeless masterpiece.

Psychologists have also noted that pessimists have a more accurate grasp of reality and their own limited talents – but pessimists are also more prone to boredom and anxiety. Optimism may float away into fantasy and wish fulfilment but pessimism may sink into depression and lethargy. I would rather be writing this under the illusion that it is worthwhile than understand my essential worthlessness and lie in bed in the foetal position paralysed by depression. The play attitude encourages a belief in possibility and personal agency that may be unrealistic, but it is more a suspension of realism than a dismissal. The bleak truths are not rejected but merely ignored for the moment (a suspension of belief rather than of disbelief) and this is hugely enabling. To keep going it is necessary to believe that even if the endeavour fails to produce the intended house it may result in a robot instead. And even if it fails to produce either, the rapt involvement is its own reward.

But Western adults have found it difficult to value play. As Brian Sutton-Smith, one of the more thoughtful play theorists, has concluded, after reviewing the various claims that play must have some 'adaptive' purpose if animals and children expend so much energy on it, must be necessary for cognition and so on, 'The constant modern tendency to think of play as simply a function of some other more important cultural process (psychological or sociological) tends to underestimate the autonomy of such play cultures. It makes it difficult to understand that the major obvious function of play is the enjoyment of playing or being playful.'[14]

The urge to play and the urge to learn go together in the child and both tend to die together when the young adult has learned enough to survive and has adopted the adult seriousness that dismisses play as childish nonsense. Our closest relative, the bonobo, is one of the few animals to continue playing into adulthood and is rewarded by being less aggressive and enjoying more harmonious group relations, though this is an accidental reward and not the purpose of the play. Nor is learning the purpose. Play and learning are obviously linked in most species, including the human, but this does not prove that the purpose of play is learning. Regardless of connection, it would be wise to sustain both play and learning throughout adulthood.

It helps that twentieth-century physics has now accepted something close to Hindu cosmogony by rejecting determinism and accepting that the behaviour of matter is random, that reality is at base some sort of mad, dancing flux, a constantly mutating force field that exhibits order and structure only at the level of statistical aggregate. And twenty-first-century neuroscience now sees the human brain as a similar dancing flux, constantly making and breaking connections and forming interlinked networks, during sleep and in waking hours, with consciousness imposing the illusory sense of a self in control.

The anthropologist David Graeber has drawn on physics to suggest that play is a characteristic of human and animal behaviour because it is a characteristic of matter itself, that in fact 'there is a play principle at the basis of all physical reality'.[15] We now know that those wacky elementary particles refuse to obey laws and behave predictably, and insist on doing whatever they like, which is not to sit around in isolation but to form the groups we know as atoms and molecules, and neither do molecules like to sit around but prefer to link up in lines and rings to do the conga and the hokey-cokey, and generally make things more complex and lively. 'Let us imagine a principle ... call it a principle of ludic freedom. Let us imagine it to hold that the free exercise of an entity's most complex powers or capacities will, under certain circumstances at least, tend to become an end in itself. It would obviously not be the only principle active in nature. Others pull other ways. But if nothing else, it would help explain what we actually observe, such as why, despite the second law of thermodynamics, the universe seems to be getting more, rather than less, complex. Evolutionary psychologists claim they can explain ... "why sex is fun." What they can't explain is why fun is fun. This could.'[16]

So both spirituality and materialism can encourage the view that play is not a temporary withdrawal from the true order of rational progress but is itself the underlying true order; that beneath appearances all reality is a playful chaos and the modern religion of instrumental rationality is a human invention, albeit highly successful, to confer the illusion of power, control and meaning. One attraction of this play view is that it encourages a positive attitude to meaninglessness, which tends to be feared as bleak and malevolent but can also be interpreted as vibrant and joyful. The cosmos may have no one in control, no idea of why it exists, or where it is going, or how, but it seems to be having a good time in spite of this ignorance. The Great Chain of Being is more like a circle dance. So meaninglessness can become the new meaning and much that was terrifying can now be exhilarating. Vladimir and Estragon trying on old boots can be seen to be playing, and Beckett's bleak vision can be seen as playful. Note how the relevant Beckett passage ends in drollery, with Vladimir tartly commenting, 'Yes yes, we're magicians.' Sartre too reveals that his waiter, the example of a supposedly inauthentic, worthless life, is 'playing a game' and apparently enjoying this play, though Sartre does not seem to register this relish in role playing (which could be a useful strategy for all employees). If the waiter is enjoying the play where is the problem?

Play suits contemporary culture because it is freedom in its purest form, and is possibly the only true freedom, in that it escapes not just domination by others but the self-imposed tyranny of the project. Also, play counters boredom with a reason to act, in spite of the knowledge that action is pointless. In fact, the pointlessness becomes the point. And play alleviates the anxiety for achievement and status by reminding that the process is more satisfying than the goal, the anxiety about authenticity by reminding that it has all become too complex and self-conscious for *anything* to be truly authentic, the anxiety about time by dispelling awareness of time, and the anxiety about finding one's true self by the knowledge that there may be no such self to find.

Children, the world is the play of the gods. So distract the project, flummox the algorithm, shame the rules. Let us play.

And there are signs that play, rediscovered in the modern era and given a major boost in the sixties, is finally going mainstream. Sport, festivals, dancing, costuming and sex play have all been growing in popularity for decades, and there is an increasingly explicit acknowledgement of play. The digital gaming industry has taken up play theory to justify gaming, and the self-help industry has adopted play as a replacement for the over-familiar mindfulness. Art is even more enthusiastically incorporating play – and especially childish, participative play – presenting, in museums and galleries, as serious works of art, ball pits, bouncy castles, aunt sallies, funhouse mirrors, helter skelters, slides, fairground rides, mazes, crazy golf, a giant twenty-a-side table-football game and a 175-pound pile of brightly coloured sweeties wrapped in cellophane and intended to be eaten rather than admired. One of the most dramatic of such works was a life-size inflatable replica of Stonehenge, which toured the parks of the UK, encouraging adults as well as children to bounce on the site of pagan ritual, and was explained by the artist Jeremy Deller, winner of the Turner Prize and recipient of the Albert Medal of the Royal Society for the Encouragement of the Arts, as 'a way to get reacquainted with ancient Britain with your shoes off'.[17]

This play art is only one example of a return to the traditional play of childhood. Colouring books for adults are now international bestsellers, and join-the-dots books may soon be equally popular. But childish play is no longer a secret, individual pleasure. In the USA there is a boom in summer camps for adults with all the childhood activities and games. In the UK there are similar scout camps for adults, and a company called Regression Sessions that organises raves featuring bouncy castles and ball pits. Adult groups also meet to play Monopoly, Scrabble, even tag and hide and seek, and to construct with Meccano or Lego, which has become so popular that AFoL (Adult Fans of Lego), like cosplayers and female maskers, now have their own conventions (with the London event Brick extending over several days in the same vast exhibition centre as the cosplayers' weekend). Many Lego sets are specifically designed for adults[18] and many of those that have been discontinued sell for huge prices on the Internet. As an enthusiast at Brick laments, 'The Lego City Green Grocer is so collectible that now I'm priced out of the market.'[19]

The time may be right for an adult revival of hopscotch, conkers, marbles and skipping. I could have a new late career as a marbles coach, based on my skill at 'mugs', which involved shooting a marble into each of four holes (the mugs), thus making it a 'killer', entitled to hit and seize any other marble in the game. I had a tin of captured marbles of every texture, size and hue, a treasure trove of iridescent glory. Where are they now? Dispersed and lost.

Skipping is especially promising for adults, as group skipping games combine those key features of archaic ritual – choral chanting and synchronous movement to a regular beat. I am thinking in particular of the game where two girls would swing a long rope in a steady beat, while a line of four or five others ran in turns under the rope for one skip each and then around again in an endless figure of eight about the static two, all of them chanting in time to the beat. This was incredibly difficult to sustain without someone bumping into another or getting tangled in the rope, but if skilfully executed had an apparently light and effortless fluidity that was magical – the steady beat of the rope hitting the ground, the bright dresses flowing and fluttering and the high voices rising in unison in the summer dusk.

Fun and Transgression

Transgression is another broad and poorly defined term for behaviour with many motivations, often overlapping and combining, and many manifestations. It's used to describe any activity that breaks rules or violates taboos but is most appropriate where the pleasure is as much in the rule breaking as in the activity itself. Behaviour that breaks rules unconsciously, motivated only by personal drives and desires, would be better described as self-gratification.

And even conscious rule breaking may have little to do with the actual rules and much with the effects of the breaking, such as gaining attention. This is not transgression so much as rebelliousness, which usually claims to be acting on principle but is more often driven by a raging insecurity that impulsively reacts against the established order to demand recognition, and is appeased by receiving it, especially in official form. Pinning a decoration on a rebel creates a loyal officer of the Crown. As Flaubert put it, with remarkable prescience, 'Inside every revolutionary stands a policeman.'[1]

Then there is the transgression that overlaps with sensation seeking, where breaking rules and laws is enjoyed because it is dangerous, and the recklessness delivers an exhilarating sense of a new power and a new superiority over the cautious and timid. Or transgressive behaviour is used as a badge of individual or group identity and difference, as in gang culture. Or it is a source of erotic excitement, as in sexual transgression.

And transgression also provides the extra reward of experience wealth. Transgression snobbery is an important subset of experience snobbery. Everyone is fascinated by transgression, even, and perhaps especially, those who condemn it most loudly. It's possible that everyone secretly desires to transgress, and possible that this has always been so, though the modern worship of freedom and consequent dislike of constraint has certainly made transgression even more attractive. The problem is that, as the urge to transgress has grown stronger, the taboos have become fewer and weaker, and the opportunities to violate are reduced. There is a need to find new taboos to break, and even freedom from constraint can itself become a new constraint to be overthrown. This could explain the extraordinary popularity of what has come to be known as BDSM. In an age that reveres freedom, domination and submission become new taboos, and BDSM gets an erotic charge from re-enacting the roles most discredited by modern society – those of master and slave. The pursuit of freedom has had many unexpected consequences but one of the strangest must be that it has made bondage exciting.

Of course BDSM also combines sexual transgression, the danger of injury, the sensation of pain (which produces endorphins), and the satisfaction of belonging to a deviant, underground cult. But, perhaps most importantly, it has all the elements of traditional ritual – the sacred site removed from everyday life (symbolically underground, always a 'dungeon' even when on an upper floor), the costumes and accessories with magical power (BDSM enthusiasts are usually also fetishists) and the completely prescribed and stylised roles (of domination and submission). Yet within the limits there is scope for individual expression in the costumes and role play, the dramatic acting out of extremes, which, as well as violating the taboo on enslavement, offer relief from complex power relations by simplifying, exaggerating or inverting them. It is not just that weary female slaves yearn to punish the master, but that weary masters, sensing that they, too, have been warped by power, yearn to be stripped, gagged, manacled and flogged by an avenging female slave in an executioner's mask.

The appeal of transgression based solely on rule-breaking is that it confers a sense of sovereignty, of being above laws, either those of physical reality, as in the courting of danger, or those of social convention, as in BDSM, and the problem is that the forbidden is no longer forbidden once it has been enjoyed. There is always a need for a more extreme transgression to reproduce the original thrill, and a tendency to progress into cruelty, violence and, eventually, murder. Hence popular culture's obsession with the serial killer. Once the public was fascinated by crimes of passion, committed blindly in the heat of the moment, but now popular culture loves the calculating, cold-blooded murderer, usually handsome, fiendishly clever and endlessly resourceful, who kills repeatedly for pleasure and feels no remorse. There is a secret admiration for the cool sovereign who is not bound by the physical limitations of brain, body and circumstance, or the ethical limitations of morality and compassion. Such a monster must of course be caught – but by a maverick police officer who also disobeys and breaks rules.

However, as well as demonic transgression, there is also an ironic form, a fun transgression that is not above the rules but below, motivated by a profound scepticism about any claim to superior status and the right to impose on others, and more interested in laughter than danger (The Joker may be hugely popular because he combines both the demonic and ironic). This transgression does not violate just for the sake of it but breaks specific rules and taboos to isolate, expose and reveal these as possibly arbitrary or even absurd. Those who prescribe and enforce like to give the impression that the taboos are so obvious, absolute and eternal that they do not even need to be stated, much less justified. Exposure makes taboos explicit and open to question.

I discovered such fun transgression early in life. My parents were good people whose love and care gave me lifelong security, but they were also bourgeois fundamentalists, fanatical zealots of the religion of respectability, and this gave me a strong urge to expose their ridiculous prescriptions, though without bringing reprisals to disturb my comfortable situation. I have never been attracted by danger. But how to transgress in safety? It turned out to be beautifully simple – all that was needed was to repeat the prescriptions. Often mother sent me to the shops and she would always end her list with the stern injunction, 'And tell them who you are', so that I would receive the deference, and even more importantly, the discount, due to a respectable family. I never told any shopkeeper who I was but I used the phrase repeatedly at home. When any of my younger siblings were going on visits I would assume a severe expression, shout, 'And tell them who you are,' then collapse, shrieking with laughter. Of course it was necessary not to overdo this and incur the charge of 'being a smart alec', the domestic equivalent of contempt of court.

This tactic has proved successful all through my professional life. I loved my status as a university lecturer (always the bourgeois boy), and the office with desk, swivel chair and window view, and had no desire to jeopardise this, but could enjoy occasional minor transgressions.

Boss, introducing a new project at a staff meeting: 'Mike, are you busy at the moment?'

'Of course,' I snap back, 'I'm claiming ownership of my targets.'

It is safest, and often highly effective, merely to copy rather than to exaggerate or attack. The original becomes its own caricature when exposed to the light. There was a great example of this in Communist Poland, when the opposition, who would have been arrested for overt resistance, took to celebrating Communist commemorations by going on marches dressed entirely in red, waving huge red flags and chanting party slogans with demented fervour. Everyone who saw this laughed – but the Communist authorities could do nothing against an apparently pro-Communist demonstration.

This example also shows that, just like acknowledging rules and status, mocking these is more satisfactory in company and best of all in public. Peeing in the shower is enjoyable but not as much fun as ridiculing the superior in a public parade. The Polish transgression was remarkably similar to the inversion rituals that first developed in the Neolithic age and continued right up to the end of the medieval period, and involved those at the bottom of the social scale mocking those at the top by copying their dress and behaviour in rowdy parades. These rituals were a response to the hierarchies that developed after the discovery of agriculture, when the small, nomadic and egalitarian hunter-gatherer groups began to live in large, fixed settlements. These eventually coalesced into cities with a surplus of food that permitted the unproductive roles of king, priest, soldier and scribe, and the development of social and religious distinctions. Those at the top rejoiced in their superior status and those at the bottom, not wishing to run the risks of insurrection, responded by adding inversion to the ritual revelry as a way of exposing the arbitrary nature of status.

One of the earliest known examples was the Akitu festival, celebrated every spring in Babylon around 1000 BCE, when the king himself was actually slapped and humiliated. But as the powerful grew in majesty, with kings even proclaiming themselves divine, the disrespect resorted to mockery at a safe distance. In Judea the celebration of Purim included ridiculing rabbis, in the annual Roman Saturnalia slaves dressed as their masters, and the Christian Church had the Feast of Fools, between Christmas and New Year, when choirboys dressed as bishops, with a mock pontiff or Archbishop of Dolts presiding over a rowdy parody of the mass, with sausages for bread and wine, 'stinking smoke from the soles of old shoes'[2] instead of incense, and 'wanton songs'[3] in place of solemn Latin.

The most widespread of the inversion rituals was the Saturnalia, celebrated at the end of December throughout the Roman Empire in honour of the earth god Saturn, who was revered as the representative of a lost age of egalitarian harmony. So in the public holiday of Saturnalia, when no business could be transacted or war declared, slaves and masters exchanged places to preserve a memory of the egalitarian past.

Not surprisingly, the holiday was popular. Bad boy poet Catullus called it 'the best of days', canny Horace praised the 'December liberty', and though he escaped from the rowdy revelry to his Sabine farm, tells us in one of his satires that he honoured the tradition of inversion by encouraging his slave, Davus, to speak his mind for a change. 'Come on, it's December; enjoy the freedom that our fathers decreed, and say what you like.'[4] Davus takes the opportunity to tell Horace that he too is a slave to *his* masters.

Grateful Romans ushered in the holiday with a cry of '*Io Saturnalia!*', which became a catchphrase used to celebrate anything irreverently pleasing, such as a good coarse joke. And since Saturday is 'Saturn's Day' (so named by the Romans) it seems entirely appropriate to proclaim this on Friday evening. '*Io*' is pronounced 'Yo' so the phrase has a genuinely rousing ring to it. Around six on Friday I raise my glass and offer friends a jubilant toast, '*Io Saturnalia!*'[5]

An important feature of the celebrations was the choosing, usually by lot, of a Saturn substitute, a King of Saturn, who became master of revels and could issue commands, even to solemn social superiors, which had to be obeyed (the historian Tacitus gives as examples, 'Sing naked' and 'Throw him into cold water'[6]). In his youth the future emperor Nero was chosen to be such a king, which may account for much of his subsequent behaviour.

Even when Christianity spread through the Roman Empire, and eventually became its official religion, the dancing and mocking rituals continued in churches, which, until the eighteenth century, were pew-free open spaces. Eventually, after several centuries of increasing annoyance at the insolence of their flocks, the bishops banished dancing from the churches to the surrounding areas so that the original unified ritual divided into two separate forms, one religious and the other secular, with the religious rites retaining only the symbolic feast of communion bread and wine, and the secular festivity retaining only the symbolic sanctity of taking place on holy days. Now religion, which had been a general spirit infusing all of life, became a separate activity. Rarely now would worship and dancing be one again, and, as in most separations, both parties were severely impoverished. Rarely now would the ecstasy be complete.

But in Europe the secular festivity flourished as it developed into the medieval tradition of carnival, which retained full community involvement in the feasting and drinking and dancing in costumes and masks, but added games, races, competitions, parades with giants, dwarfs and trained animals (wine-drinking monkeys, pigs wearing spectacles), entertainments such as bear baiting, performances of farcical travesties, and recitation of parodies full of oaths, curses, slang, and scatological jokes. Carnival also discovered its version of the King of Saturn in the King of Fools or Lord of Misrule. In his *Anatomie of Abuses* (1585) the English Puritan Philip Stubbes denounces the 'Heathenrie, Devilrie' and 'Drunkenness' in which 'the wilde heades of the parishe conven-tynge together, chuse them a grand Capitaine (of mischeefe) whom they ennobel with the title Lorde of Misrule'. Wearing ribbons, bells and handkerchiefs 'borrowed for the most part of their prettie Mopsies' and with 'their Hobby horses and other monsters shirmishyng' this Lord and his revellers would even 'go to the churche (though the minister be at praier or preachyng) dauncying and swingyng their handkercheefes'.

I love 'swingyng the handkercheefe' as a gesture of insouciant defiance. It obviously wouldn't work with a Kleenex but I am sure my mopsie would be happy to lend me a lace handkerchief.

Until the appearance of the first Puritans, carnival was a full community celebration and it is possible that Stubbes himself suffered the fate of those who refused to contribute or participate and were 'mocked and flouted at shamefully, yea, and many times carried upon the cowlstaff, and dived head and ears in water, and other wise most horribly abused'. As well as the feasting and dancing, carnival had plenty of coercion and cruelty.

It must be significant that similar rituals of inversion emerged in so many different times and places, with direct connection unlikely (many have assumed a historical link between the King of Saturn and the Lord of Misrule but there is no direct evidence for this). As with the other ritual similarities, drumming, dancing and costuming, it seems likely that inversion developed not by influence but from the experience of a similar need to mock the superior, and similar discoveries of inversion rituals to meet this need.

The interesting question is why absolute hierarchies would tolerate being mocked (while the apparently more liberal bourgeois order did not). But it may have been just this absoluteness that made inversion possible. The hierarchy was so rigid it was flexible, so secure in its position that it could afford to be turned upside down for a short period, and even enjoy this. Another factor is that the upper levels of the hierarchy had yet to develop a bourgeois sense of fastidiousness and physical revulsion from the lower levels. It was common for kings to undress and even to take a dump in public. There may also have been an intuitive sense that order had only recently emerged from chaos, which can destroy it but is also the source of its energy, and that the form of this emergence was arbitrary and must never regard itself as divinely sanctioned but needs to be regularly reinfused with chaotic energy to save it from death by petrifaction.

As in the trickster tales, chaotic energy was invoked through laughter. The Russian philosopher Mikhail Bakhtin has argued that 'at the early stages of preclass and prepolitical social order it seems that the serious and the comic aspects of the world were equally sacred, equally "official"',[7] and that the 'carnival laughter' of the Middle Ages retained much of this inclusiveness by being cosmic in scope, with those who laughed part of the cosmic joke. 'It is, first of all, a festive laughter. Therefore it is not an individual reaction to some isolated "comic" event. Carnival laughter is the laughter of all the people. Second, it is universal in scope; it is directed at all and everyone, including the carnival's participants. The entire world is seen in its droll aspect, in its gay relativity. Third, this laughter is ambivalent: it is gay, triumphant, and at the same time mocking, deriding. It asserts and denies, it buries and revives.'[8]

Bakhtin was probably too idealistic in assuming that all carnivals were based on such sophisticated laughter, but he was certainly right to identify Rabelais as its greatest exemplar. More than any other writer, Rabelais has suffered from becoming an adjective, Rabelaisian, and being dismissed unread as a coarse-grained buffoon, when in fact he was an intellectual and scholar, and one of the most erudite men of his time. But he also understood that the thinker who argues about religion, politics and philosophy is basically an organism whose primary need is to ingest and excrete, and so, as well as learned disputation, Latin quotes, allusions, parodies, word games and puns, his work is full of eating, drinking, urinating and defecating. In *Gargantua and Pantagruel*, the young Gargantua conducts extensive research into 'arse wipes' and concludes that the most effective is a well-downed goose: 'You get a miraculous sensation in your arse-hole, both from the softness of the down and from the temperate heat of the goose herself.'[9]

Gargantua and Pantagruel is thoroughly postmodern in its lack of concern for plot, interpolated essays, frequent digressions, abrupt shifts of register, style and tone, mixture of intellectualism and grotesquerie, sophistication and vulgarity, and above all in its playfulness. (Huizinga: 'Nothing could be more playful than Rabelais – he is the play spirit incarnate.'[10]) So it's not surprising that Rabelais was championed by the arch-postmodernist Milan Kundera, who described his comedy as divine in its detachment, extent, understanding and acceptance: 'There is a fine Jewish proverb: Man thinks, God laughs. Inspired by that adage I like to imagine that Francois Rabelais heard God's laughter one day and that from this was born the idea of the first great European novel.'[11]

Rabelais certainly understood the need for inversion. When one of his characters, Epistemon, has his head chopped off and after a sojourn in hell is restored to life through having it sewn back on by Panurge, a trickster figure, he offers this report on the infernal population: 'Pope Boniface was a skimmer of pots, Pope Nicholas III was a papermaker, Pope Julius, a crier of little pies, but he had left off wearing his great, buggerly beard, Pope Alexander was a rat-catcher, Pope Sixtus was an anointer of pox sores. "What!" exclaimed Pantagruel, "Are there people with the pox down there?" "Certainly," said Epistemon, "I never saw so many. There are more than one hundred million of them. For, believe me, everyone who hasn't had the pox in this world gets it in the next." "God Almighty," cried Panurge. "Then I'm quit of it."'

Though a monk himself, an unlikely cleric eventually released from his vows by the Pope to become a physician, Rabelais was relentless in his mockery of the supreme authority of his time, the Church, and is probably unique in the history of transgression because it has never been more dangerous. He was under surveillance by the Church inquisitors, frequently denounced in public, and only by cunning and prudent disappearances escaped being burned at the stake, a punishment which then included, as an appetiser for the barbecue, having your hands cut off and your tongue pulled out. Rabelais's friend the poet-scholar Etienne Dolet suffered this fate for writing, even though only in a translation of Plato, that there is *rien du tout*, 'nothing at all', after death. So Rabelais certainly deserves the Transgressional Medal of Honour.

As well as mocking authority, Rabelais was postmodern in his refusal to accept ideology. It was not that he rejected theories and ideas, indeed he was fascinated, even intoxicated by them, but he would not acknowledge any final repository of truth. Bakhtin: 'No dogma, no authoritarianism, no narrow-minded seriousness can coexist with Rabelaisian images; these images are opposed to all that is finished and polished, to all pomposity, to every ready-made solution in the sphere of thought and world outlook.'[12]

Rabelais is frequently described as a satirist but his comedy is much richer, deeper and more generous than satire – and he was detested by leading satirists such as Pope and Voltaire, who dismissed him as 'chief among buffoons' and 'a drunken philosopher who wrote only when he was drunk'.[13] Satire seeks to expose the specific follies of specific societies, with the satirist often detached and superior, looking down from the top of a hierarchy of rational behaviour. But Rabelais's transgression was universal and timeless, even metaphysical, seeking not just to undermine a specific hierarchy but the very idea of hierarchy, any presumption of superiority and importance from the human animal. As a middle-aged Irish woman, not one of the bourgeoisie, once expressed her vision of life to me: 'The Queen shites too.'[14]

The reward for metaphysical transgression is cosmic laughter, which appears to be laughing at nothing because it is laughing at everything. This laughter can be the most intense, not just facial or shoulder-shaking but a paroxysm that seizes the entire body, squeezing tears out of its eyes like juice from a lemon. It is a peak experience, the kind of sublime possession many seek, though few mention this form of it. When I was young I used to have frequent fits of this wild, extreme laughter that began for no apparent reason and went on and on, baffling everyone present. Like other peak experiences, these fits left me exhausted but profoundly at one with the world, and like other such experiences they have become much less frequent with age. Many miss the adventures and sexual potency of youth but I wish I could laugh as I once did.

However, Rabelais's cosmic laughter and celebration of bodily functions were soon considered unacceptable, as were all the aspects of the carnival experience. High always eventually tries to dissociate from low, and after the separation of religion from social life came the separations of serious from comic, sophisticated from vulgar and mind from body. The Age of Reason was inaugurated by Descartes' famous claim, 'I think, therefore I am', which relegated the body to a disgusting and shameful support mechanism for the brain (Rabelais's body-affirming version could have been, 'I stink, therefore I am').

In religion, the Reformation introduced the crucial distinction of saved and damned, with the saved in a small minority who were in theory indistinguishable but in practice recognised by diligence, austerity and distaste for merrymaking (one of Stubbes's many aversions was to 'the horrible vice of pestiferous dancing', which, by its 'filthy groping and unclean handling' was 'an introduction to whoredom'). In science, itself a new concept, the sense of a world infused by divinity was replaced by the concept of a mechanistic universe whose workings could be understood and put to use by an instrumental reason, which would drive progress forward and make us, as Descartes bragged, 'masters and possessors of nature'.[15] In history, another new concept, time became divided into ancient, which was primitive and savage, and modern, which was sophisticated and civilised.

In festivities, the upper orders increasingly abandoned the public carnival revelry for private celebration, and Dionysian headbanging was replaced by the minuet, surely the slowest, stiffest, most formal and least rhythmic and sexual dance ever created by the human race, not so much a dance as a funereally paced joint walk of inflexible bodies keeping their distance and making no contact other than an occasional touch of hands. In comedy, the taste was now for satire, which presents the satirist as far above the deluded, vulgar world.[16] In literature, the wildness of poetry began to be replaced by the sobriety of prose, and the coarseness of the oral tradition by the sophistication of written language. In painting, the discovery of perspective introduced differentiation, separation and distance.

In homes, the single open space used by everyone and for every purpose became partitioned into rooms with specialised functions and reserved access, and the communal bench was replaced by individual chairs. In fashion, there emerged powdered wigs and elaborate clothes as visible marks of distinction. While in social life, the emerging bourgeoisie distinguished themselves from the lower orders by becoming refined. Where the mid-sixteenth-century books on etiquette had begged people to stop shitting on stairs, corridors and hallways, it was now impossible even to mention shit in polite company.

This new righteous class of the saved detested carnival and carnival laughter. Throughout Europe the traditional festivities were suppressed with equal zeal by both Catholic and Protestant authorities[17] (and, in a parallel development, European colonists and missionaries set about suppressing dancing rituals among the native peoples of the colonies). And not just the festivities themselves but the very idea of festive time came under attack from the new work ethic. The feudalism of the Middle Ages is often imagined as little better than slavery, but throughout Europe there were hundreds of holy days and those obliged to work often did so for as little as half the year and for only part of the week during that time. The idea that many could freely choose to work seventy-hour weeks with a fortnight's holiday a year would have been unthinkably grotesque.

Society became increasingly stratified, with the upper levels withdrawing as far and as frequently as possible from the low; group ritual became increasingly fragmented and specialised, with the emphasis changing from participation to spectating, usually sitting down in silence, and, increasingly, religion became a matter of abstract belief rather than practice, as the techniques of transcendence moved from the body to the head. So the dancing earth goddesses and Dionysian gods faded away and the single remaining God became angry and inscrutable, withdrawing with his entourage to a gated community in the sky. Rabelais seems to have sensed this development. Towards the end of his book there is an eerie incident where those on a ship becalmed at night hear a voice commanding them to announce, when they reach port, the news that the great god Pan is dead. And so, in the reformed churches, the dancing congregation were confined to regular rows of wooden pews and obliged to look up and listen in respectful silence as the priest mounted the pulpit, looked down and delivered a sermon.

The modern concept of fun was a response to all this and its principal champion was Nietzsche, the philosopher of fun, who sought to restore the carnival spirit, 'the glowing life of Dionysian revellers'[18] and the liberating effect of dancing and laughter. 'And let that day be lost to us on which we did not dance once! And let that wisdom be false to us that brought no laughter with it.' This quote is from his most fun book, *Thus Spoke Zarathustra*, which not only puts his ideas in the mouth of a character based on the early Persian thinker, Zoroaster, but expresses them in wild, dithy-rambic exhortations that, in the spirit of the carnival combination of serious and comic, at the same time express the aphorisms of a prophet and laugh at the very idea of prophetic utterance:

This laughter's crown, this rose-wreath crown: I myself have set this crown on my head, I myself have canonized my laughter. I have found no other strong enough for it today.

Zarathustra the dancer, Zarathustra the light, who beckons with his wings, ready for flight, beckoning to all birds, pre-pared and ready, blissfully light-hearted:

Zarathustra the prophet, Zarathustra the laughing prophet, no impatient nor uncompromising man, one who loves jump-ing and escapades; I myself have set this crown on my head!

Lift up your hearts my brothers, high! higher! And do not
forget your legs! Lift up your legs, too, you fine dancers: and
better still, stand on your heads![19]

As with Rabelais, Nietzsche's transgression was metaphysical, not
just a reaction against specific limits but against the very idea of
limit. He revelled in extravagance and excess, which even his most
enthusiastic commentators find hard to accept. R. J. Hollingdale,
who translated eleven of Nietzsche's books and wrote two books
about him, felt it necessary to apologise for Zarathustra in the
second sentence of the introduction to his translation: 'The book's
worst fault is excess.'

This distaste for imaginative excess can be explained as the
modern fear of all that not only refuses control but mocks the very
idea of control. The premodern age understood that the world was
excessive and uncontrollable and used the giant as a symbol of the
vastness, abundance, power and unpredictability of nature, often
crediting giants with creating the physical world, as in the Celtic
myth of the giant Finn McCool who made Lough Neagh by tearing up a chunk of Northern Ireland and flinging it out to sea where
it became the Isle of Man. And myths in many cultures tell of a
race of majestic giants who inhabited the earth in the Golden Age
before the Flood, and were masters of magic and occult wisdom,
believed to control weather, seasons and crops. For instance, the
Book of Genesis: 'There were giants in the earth in those days; and
also after that, when the sons of God came in unto the daughters
of men, and they bare children to them, the same became mighty
men which were of old, men of renown.'

In the frequent carnivals, processions and festivities of the premodern, giants were so popular that many Northern European towns employed a permanent 'giant'. Nor is it a coincidence that, in Rabelais's book, Gargantua and Pantagruel are both giants, with prodigious appetites and strength, though also highly intelligent, learned, compassionate and generous. But another sign of the fundamental change in the Age of Reason was its representation of the giant in the new mythology of the fairy tale. Charles Perrault's *Contes* of 1697, usually recognised as the earliest collection of such tales, saw the first appearance of the word 'ogre', now depicting the giant as a man-eating monster, angry, greedy and stupid, dangerously strong but easily outwitted and killed. And in the new literary form of the novel, *Gulliver's Travels* portrayed the giants of Brobdingnag as monstrous, disgusting and not very bright. Swift even suggested that intelligence decreases as size increases – though Rabelais might have enjoyed the episode where a saucy young giantess uses Gulliver as a nipple teaser and also, it is hinted, as a living vibrator.

As with the view of reality as play, science has come to endorse the view of reality as excess. According to the contemporary paradigm, matter is not just essentially ludic but also has an innate tendency to reject constraint and bust loose, burgeon, split, recombine, complexify and expand. The universe, once thought to be static and inert, is now believed to be expanding in every direction at an accelerating pace. For the universe, too much is never enough. And matter has created life, which yearns only to reproduce, mutate and diversify, to multiply and fill the earth. Matter and life demand excess, and the characteristic cry of *Homo sapiens* is 'More!' Life, that has finally become conscious, resents the limitations of body, society and planet and wants to be entirely free. Life itself can be understood as a metaphysical transgressor, extravagant, exuberant and unpredictable, more Finn McCool than Descartes.

Many philosophers, profoundly reluctant to stand on their heads, have also pointed out that Nietzsche is not only excessive but frequently contradicts himself. Even his tone can be contradictory, making it difficult to know how much is serious and how much play-acting – and he himself would probably not have known. Both are inseparably intertwined and this is a crucial aspect of his vision and appeal. Not only refusing to construct a consistent system, Nietzsche did not even wish to have any of his pronouncements believed and followed. He was not a philosopher-king dispensing wisdom but a philosopher-trickster interested mainly in stirring things up, subverting righteousness, challenging importance, disturbing certainty, enjoying cosmic transgression. As he wrote in a late letter in 1888, 'It is not at all necessary or even desirable to side with me; on the contrary, a dose of curiosity, as if confronted with some unfamiliar plant, and an ironic resistance would be an incomparably more *intelligent* position to adopt.'[20]

As with Rabelais, Nietzsche's excess, contradictions, play, transgression and carnival laughter help to inhibit the development of certainty, fixity, an ultimate, all-encompassing truth, and to encourage acceptance of complementarities, rival truths, contending goods, irreconcilable contradictions, opposing forces in constant tension. There is always a desire to remove tension by granting final victory to one side or the other – but this leads to lifeless petrifaction. Life is tension. And the cosmic laughter of Rabelais and Nietzsche releases the tension by understanding it as part of the joke.

However, it's important to remember that, although Nietzsche was an enthusiastic votary of Dionysus, he stressed that there must always be a struggle between the priorities of Apollo – authority, reason, discipline, order and limit – and those of Dionysus – rebelliousness, revelry, intoxication and rejection of limits. These two gods represent an inescapable 'duality', and are in 'perpetual antagonism'.[21] In general, the top of the social hierarchy is fonder of Apollo and the bottom of Dionysus. As the anthropologist I. M. Lewis remarked drily, Dionysus 'was essentially a god of the people, offering freedom and joy to all, including slaves' whereas Apollo 'moved only in the best society'.[22] Historical periods also have preferences. Apollonian values dominated the early period of modernism but more recently, and especially since the sixties, Dionysus has been the predominating spirit. And often the same antagonism rages within the individual, with the left brain representing Apollo and the right Dionysus, and with Dionysus ruling in youth and Apollo taking over in age.

I have been aware of such a personal conflict all my life, between a puritanical controller and a lunatic anarchist. Part of me has always wanted to exercise ascetic self-discipline in pursuit of achievement and status, while another part wants to laugh madly and overturn everything. Somewhere inside me Apollo and Dionysus are arm-wrestling for dominance. Often I have regretted the failure to simplify my life by letting one finally suppress the other – but when I take the side of one, I soon miss the other. And now I understand that the tension is a crucial energy source. Tension is life.

The Dionysus/Apollo duality is similar to Freud's concept of the conflict between the pleasure and reality principles, the individual desire for gratification and the social need for order. According to

Freud, the price of civilisation is the repression of instinct and the forfeiting of happiness, but Freud was an old man when he wrote *Civilisation and its Discontents*, and old men tend to privilege stability and order. I see no reason why civilisation cannot accommodate both Dionysus and Apollo, albeit in a tension that can never be resolved, and the growth of fun in the last few decades suggests that this is happening. Transgression and compliance, pleasure and reality, excess and discipline, Dionysus and Apollo – they need each other. To pursue exclusively pleasure, transgression and excess would be self-defeating. In personal terms, the road of excess does not lead to the palace of wisdom, but to the rehab clinic and the psychiatric ward. And to install Apollo as dictator would consign as many to psychiatric treatment. The trick may be to let Apollo rule some of the time, while preserving a Dionysian scepticism about the motives for his love of control, and to let Dionysus enjoy his rituals of release, while preserving an Apollonian scepticism about the motives for his recklessness.

As in carnival inversion, the function of transgressive fun is not to bring down the existing order, or even primarily to mock its hierarchy and conventions, but to encourage cosmic laughter, to reconnect with the original chaos and recover the energy, exuberance and excess of life itself. We always need a touch of craziness to vitalise the responsible behaviour that recognises and respects limits. As Zarathustra expresses it, in his inimitably excessive style: 'I say unto you: one must still have chaos in oneself to give birth to a dancing star.' Or, as Duke Ellington rephrased this for the twentieth century, we have to keep a little ragtime in our souls.

Fun and Hedonism

It's the Epicurean five-course menu, preceded by a hand-crafted champagne cocktail and accompanied by matching flights of wine.

'Epicurus will be fighting to get out of his urn!' cries an excited diner, scanning the menu with the avid gleam of a brothel customer appraising a line of girls, and lingering long over 'Cannon of marsh-reared English lamb stuffed with foraged mushrooms and truffles, with wild rowanberry jus, blistered green beans and crushed French Bar-le-Duc black potatoes from the Ardennes.'

'Probably not.'

Diner looks up in consternation. 'Excuse me?'

'The favourite evening meal of Epicurus was barley bread matched with water.'

Diner gapes, adding lamely, after a time. 'Good joke.'

'That was not a joke.'

If the best defence of fun is to describe it as play, the most effective attack is to dismiss it as hedonism. Fun always involves pleasure, and hedonism, the philosophy developed by Epicurus, believes in pleasure as the only good – so fun must be merely a new name for hedonism? Well, not exactly. Fun is complex – and so was hedonism.

For a start, Epicurus was not the kind of hedonist many imagine and, like Rabelais, has suffered from becoming an adjective. He was certainly no foodie. 'Plain dishes offer the same pleasure as a luxurious table,'[1] he said. 'He who is not satisfied with a little, is satisfied with nothing.'[2] Not that he was puritanically opposed to the blowout – but it had to be the exception to be properly appreciated: 'Those who least need extravagance enjoy it most.'[3] And his attitude to sex was similarly measured: 'I learn from your letter that carnal disturbances make you excessively inclined to sexual intercourse. Well, so long as you do not break any laws or disturb well-established conventions or annoy any of your neighbours or wear down your body or use up your funds.'[4]

Epicurus was more of an ascetic than a hedonist in the usual sense of the term – and it is this usual sense that is the source of the confusion. Hedonism is now generally understood as an excessive love of food, intoxicants and sex – but this is only its crudest form. As well as such sensual hedonism there is cerebral hedonism, which prizes the pleasures of the mind more than those of the body, and seeks ethical, aesthetic and spiritual satisfactions.

The only philosophical advocate of a purely sensual hedonism was Aristippus of Cyrene, a pupil of Socrates who rejected the teaching of the master to found the Cyreniac school of philosophy, and enjoy sex, good food and fine wines at the court of King Dionysus I of Syracuse, where he was obliged to earn his pleasures by dancing for the king dressed as a woman. Courtesans, gourmet food and fine wines have never been cheap, and no philosophers since have argued that these are the only good. So the five-course menu should have been described as Aristippean.

Epicurus understood that mere sensual gratification is often unsatisfying and can have unpleasant consequences. What he sought instead was wisdom and peace of mind. 'So when we say that pleasure is the goal we do not mean the pleasure of the profligate or the pleasures of consumption, as some believe, either from ignorance and disagreement or from deliberate misinterpretation, but rather the lack of pain in the body and disturbance in the soul. For it is not drinking bouts and continuous partying and enjoying boys and women, or consuming fish and the other dainties of an extravagant table, which produce the pleasant life, but sober calculation which searches of the reasons for every choice and avoidance and drives out the opinions which are the source of the greatest turmoil for men's souls.'[5]

This line of thought could have been usefully developed but the Christian Church hated philosophy in general and hedonism in particular, and Epicurus as a representative of both, and suppressed Epicurean ideas. It was not until the authority of religion was challenged in the eighteenth century that thinkers were again free to speculate, and the English philosopher Jeremy Bentham combined the old and the new by applying instrumental reason to Greek hedonism. The result was what he described as a 'calculus of pleasure', a cost/benefit analysis of every potential action to decide if the pleasure benefit exceeded the pain cost. This was an early example of quantophilia, the love of measurement, which easily becomes quantomania, the belief that all problems can be solved by measurement and calculation incorporated in algorithms. But, as Bentham acknowledged, it's difficult even to define pleasure, never mind measure it. In the nineteenth century John Stuart Mill also advocated a form of hedonism ('pleasure, and freedom from pain, are the only things desirable as ends'[6]) but dismissed as 'absurd' the idea that 'the estimation of pleasures should be supposed to depend on quantity alone'.[7] Instead, Mill introduced a qualitative distinction between low and high pleasures, with studying literary masterpieces and philosophy infinitely more valuable than 'sensual indulgences', which he more or less ruled out as fit only for swine. 'It is better to be a human being dissatisfied than a pig satisfied.'[8]

It is curious, given the hedonistic tendency of the modern age, that so few hedonist thinkers have followed Bentham and Mill.[9] Surely the multitude of practising hedonists would welcome theoretical support? One reason for the dearth may be simple snobbery. No one wants to be thought of as swine interested only in 'sensual indulgences'. Foodies regard themselves not as swinish but as refined connoisseurs – and the more astute modern thinkers, such as Rousseau and Nietzsche, avoided the vulgarity of hedonism by separating off the higher version and rebranding it as individualism. Hedonism differs from fun in that, while others may have to be involved, it is more interested in personal gratification than the loss of self in a group. In this sense it could even be said to be the opposite of fun. But the core belief of hedonism, that the good life is the one with most pleasure for the individual who lives it, is exactly that of individualism.

For Rousseau and Nietzsche and many since, the essential goal of the modern age was the freedom of the individual – and by the late twentieth century this was available to everyone in the Western world who could afford it. So why not take advantage of this great gain and reject the demands of family, kinship networks, group rituals and community? If financially feasible, why not live alone free of obligation and constraint?

The traditional ties have all become weaker and as living alone becomes increasingly common it is losing its stigma. The solitary who would once have been pitied as an inadequate loser is now more likely to be envied as a confident winner. And across the developed world the desire to live alone is a growing trend. According to the sociologist Eric Klinenberg, the highest rates of solo living are in the Scandinavian countries, Sweden, Norway, Finland and Denmark, 'where roughly 40 to 45 per cent of all households have just one person'.[10] Stockholm, the world capital of singletons, has an astonishing 60 per cent, and the percentage is also high in other Northern European countries, with the USA, Australia and Canada rapidly catching up. Even Japan, supposedly a traditional, family-oriented country, has 30 per cent single dwellers, and the trend is growing fastest in China, India and Brazil. Klinenberg quotes research revealing that, in the decade from 1996 to 2006, the world population of solo dwellers increased from about 153 million to 202 million, a 33 per cent rise.

The USA is not a world leader in this but has given the movement a professional lobby group, The American Association of Single People, and also energetic cheerleaders and warriors – for instance Sasha Cagen, author of *Quirkyalone: A Manifesto for Uncompromising Romantics*, who writes: 'We are the puzzle pieces who seldom fit with other puzzle pieces. Romantics, idealists, eccentrics, we inhabit singledom as our natural resting state. In a world where proms and marriage define the social order, we are, by force of our personalities and inner strength, rebels.' Nevertheless, despite their eccentricity, inner strength and rebelliousness, the Quirkyalones must organise: 'A community of like-minded souls is essential . . . When one Quirkyalone finds another, oohh la la. The earth quakes.' Cagen has initiated the organising by creating a website, Quirkyalone.net, and establishing a new ritual, International Quirkyalone Day on February 14th, as an alternative to roses and candle-lit dinners, though instead of celebrating in defiantly ecstatic solitude, as might have been expected, the Quirkies apparently have fun in dance clubs.

A prominent warrior is the psychologist Bella DePaulo, author of *Singled Out: How Singles Are Stereotyped, Stigmatised, and Ignored, and Still Live Happily Ever After*. Everyone wants to be a victim nowadays (no doubt to enjoy in principled justification the ancient pleasures of complaining and blaming) and DePaulo has coined the term 'singlism' for prejudice against singletons, though the young, intelligent and affluent professionals who live alone must be the least likely victims in the contemporary world. DePaulo also has a website where she exposes evidence of singlism and vigorously counters dubious claims for the advantages of marriage.

As to what is driving this worldwide trend, Klinenberg suggests, 'the rising status of women, the communications revolution, mass urbanisation, and the longevity revolution', and these developments have certainly hastened the spread of the trend, but the key driver is surely the emergence of individualism at the beginning of the modern era and its spread into popular culture since the sixties.

There have always been individuals seeking seclusion – prophets in the wilderness, Chinese sages on mountain tops and poet-seers in Paris garrets – but the tendency only began to gain momentum in the modern era. In the eighteenth century Rousseau discovered the self, in the sense of an individual with a unique inner life, and the Romantic era at the beginning of the nineteenth century came to regard this self as a delicate, soulful, sensitive creature in need of protection from the new horrors of industry and the new vulgarities of leisure. Intellectuals and artists felt an increasing need to escape from the multitude, first on to mountain peaks to experience sublimity and then into garrets to experience visions. In the second half of the nineteenth century the most influential modern poet, Baudelaire, the most influential modern novelist, Flaubert, and the most influential modern thinker, Nietzsche, not only lived alone but were vehement in their need for solitude and rejection of commitment. 'I have built myself a tower,' declared Flaubert, 'and let the waves of shit beat at its base.'[11] It is worth remembering, though, that these saints of solitude and self-reliance all depended heavily on their mothers. Baudelaire constantly sponged off his mother and went to live with her to escape his debtors, Flaubert needed his mother for company and when he moved from Rouen to Paris found her an apartment in the same building, and Nietzsche's mother kept him going in Turin by sending from Germany *schinkenwurst* for his evening meal and *zwiebeck* French toast for breakfast, as well as a supply of new shirts. And, in a parallel New World development, the American saint of the solitary, Thoreau, the saint of saints, had regular home-cooked meals brought to his isolated cabin in the woods by his mother.

By the mid-twentieth century individualism had percolated down into popular culture, so that the visionary in the garret was complemented by the lone private eye going down those mean streets, the lone rider entering the tyrannised Western town and the lone cop exposing the corruption of power. And by the end of the century the appeal of living alone had reached corporate lawyers and hedge-fund managers.

For the contemporary loner, purity is a penthouse apartment with floor to ceiling windows, chaste white walls unburdened by shelving, a varnished floor with as little furniture and as much empty space as possible, and everywhere gleaming surfaces uncontaminated by the sordid stains of living. It is important to have little or no evidence of clutter and baggage – but height is the crucial factor, as it was with mountaintop, garret and Flaubert's symbolic tower. Being physically above, looking down, encourages the sense of being also mentally above, looking down. This concept of a 'view' as something valuable is another modern development, a relishing of modern self-conscious detachment, a higher spectating, like watching a performance from a royal box. The pleasure is not so much in the actual sights as in the looking down on them from a privileged, secure height. Gazing down on the toilers below gives a unique feeling of freedom, superiority, invulnerability and power.

For those who have sought to live alone, rather than having solitude forced upon them, the reward can be a unique exaltation, a natural 'high' as intense as any induced by drugs. Arthur Rimbaud, the lunatic hooligan who shot his lover, Verlaine, and went on to become a gun runner and adventurer in Africa, could hardly have been more different from his contemporary, Emily Dickinson, the prim spinster who spent her entire life in a small town – but there is a similar exhilaration in the poems of Rimbaud written in a garret and in those written by Emily in her New England bedroom. Similarly, the highs of the upper rooms are similar to those of the peaks. Although separated by more than a thousand years and many thousands of miles, Po Chu-I's 'Madly Singing in the Mountains' sounds much like the exaltation of

Zarathustra after he comes down from his ten years on a mountain top to deliver lessons to the market place:

> O Solitude! Solitude, my home! How blissfully and ten-
>   derly does your voice speak to me!
> We do not question one another, we do not complain
>   to one another, we go openly together through open
>   doors.
> For with you all is open and clear; and here even the
>   hours run on lighter feet.

Nietzsche is the most instructive solitary because he was central in promoting individualism in the first place but also understood its complexities better than many of his disciples, and in his own life provided a good example of the possible consequences. His first insight was that the self is not a given but something that must be constantly constructed. 'Active, successful natures act, not according to the dictum "know thyself", but as if there hovered before them the commandment: *will* a self and thou shalt *become* a self.'[12] But he followed this with the greater insight that this self should not be willed according to some single idea. To submit to any idea is to be bullied, cowed, weakened, enslaved. There is no absolute truth beyond life, nor even any perspective point external to life, but only a self immersed in flux and constantly pulled in opposite directions by opposing forces. To attempt to suppress a force is as crippling as surrender to its opposite. These inevitable conflicts may be allowed to weaken the self – or they may become the source of its strength if the self can accept them and hold them in tension. 'Let us suppose a man,' Nietzsche says, of someone pulled by contradictory forces, but 'who deemed it impossible to resolve this contradiction by destroying the one and completely unleashing the other power; then, the only thing remaining to him would be to make such a great edifice out of himself that both powers can inhabit it, even if at opposite ends; between which are sheltered conciliatory powers, provided with the dominant strength to settle, if need be, any quarrels that break out.'[13]

What makes this so difficult to accept is the yearning for simplicity, absoluteness and finality, something to settle the conflicts once and for all. Even Nietzsche himself has been interpreted as offering a single, master idea, which is why he has been adopted as a champion both by the far left (for his libertarian anarchy) and the far right (for his aristocratic rejection of democracy).

There is no single idea. It is necessary to permit the coexistence of Apollonian order and Dionysian madness, Enlightenment rationality and romantic mysticism, authority and transgression, yin and yang, Christian love and the urge to retreat in contempt to a mountain peak. Nietzsche's quarrel with Christianity was not a rejection of Christ, whom he admired as a man, but with the Church founded in his name, which attempted to impose dogma on every aspect of life and, in particular, hated and feared the body. 'I have declared war on the anaemic Christian ideal . . . not with the intention of destroying it, but simply to put an end to its *tyranny* . . . The continuation of the Christian ideal is one of the most desirable things there is.'[14]

Nietzsche shared with Rabelais a desire to combine high and low, a rejection of the single, commanding truth, an aversion to authority, a love of parody, mockery, clowning and revelry, and an acceptance of the body ('But the awakened, the enlightened man says: I am body entirely, and nothing beside; and soul is only a word for something in the body'[15]). The crucial difference is Nietzsche's sense of intellectual superiority and contempt for the 'rabble', the 'mob', the 'common herd' (terms also dear to Baudelaire and Flaubert). He was obsessed by the idea of height as a physical reminder of superiority and remoteness.

In his last year of sanity in Turin he took a room on the upper floor of a four-storey house with a view of the Alps, where he spent the summer in another rented upper room and dreamed of building himself a hut to live in all year round. And his books teem with scornful abuse of the low ('life is a fountain of delight; but where the rabble also drinks all wells are poisoned'[16]) and rapturous praise of remote heights ('So let us live above them like strong winds, neighbours of the eagles, neighbours of the snow, neighbours of the sun: that is how strong winds live'[17]). In his last book, *Ecce Homo*, he identifies this need for cold heights as the key to his work: 'Philosophy ... is a life voluntarily spent in ice and high mountains.'

The problem is that this violates Nietzsche's own theory of balanced forces. In the struggle between love of humanity and love of the peak, the peak was definitely permitted to win (as was Dionysus in the struggle with Apollo). It also denies the pleasures of immersing, merging and belonging, the release from the 'horror of individual existence' into 'complete self-forgetfulness' and the dissolution of social hierarchy in 'mystical Oneness', which the young Nietzsche had identified as the most important feature of Dionysian revelry. 'Now the slave is a free man; now all the rigid, hostile barriers that necessity, caprice, or impudent convention have fixed between man and man are broken. Now, with the gospel of universal harmony, each one feels himself not only united, reconciled and fused with his neighbour, but as one with him.'[18] But age encourages withdrawal and the older Nietzsche, living in Nice before the final move to Turin, forgot his enthusiasm for revelry and complained about the noise of the Nice Carnival below his window.

The common objection to a solitary life is the isolation and loneliness, and Nietzsche did complain of these from time to time in his letters. But for those who have chosen to live alone, occasional loneliness is usually a small price to pay for exaltation. The real problem is the exaltation itself, which makes ordinary people seem banal and ordinary life seem insipid, and encourages a sense of superiority for this rare ability to self-intoxicate. This encourages in turn contempt for the views, tastes and activities of others and a growing certainty of the rightness of one's own beliefs, judgements and behaviour, with a parallel certainty that these deserve to be respected and indulged. The absence of any countervailing force allows self-importance and righteousness to flourish and the result is intolerance, bad temper, irritability and crankiness, an inability to accept any deviation from the expected routine and any disagreement or criticism.

When, en route from Nice to Turin, Nietzsche boarded the wrong train and ended up in Genoa, he blamed everything on the crafty, exploitative locals, and when he finally made it to Turin he began work on a book blaming all his problems on Germany and his Christian upbringing. The self-aggrandisement became ever more extreme, with chapter headings such as *Why I Am So Wise* and *Why I Write Such Clever Books*, as did the contempt for everyone else. He wrote abusive letters to his family and old friends, quarrelled with his loyal publisher, drafted a memo to European embassies advising them to set up an anti-German league, and told a friend that as Pope he would bring the Kaiser to Rome and have him publicly executed. Eventually he took to signing letters as 'Dionysus' or 'The Crucified One', described himself as 'the leading person of all millennia', declared that 'after the abdication of the old God I will reign', and asked his landlords to decorate his room like a temple so that he could receive the King and Queen of Italy, though he himself would be in shirtsleeves to show that he was a natural aristocrat. The landlords put him under surveillance and were not reassured to discover that at night he danced naked round his room and told passers-by in the street that he was the tyrant of Turin or God on earth in human form. Finally his public life came to an end with the famous tearful embrace of a horse being physically abused by its owner. (In an appropriately playful tone, Milan Kundera has speculated that Nietzsche was begging the horse to forgive Descartes for asserting that animals have no souls.[19])

Nietzsche's biographer, Lesley Chamberlain, has attributed his extreme behaviour in Turin to the 'disinhibiting' effects of syphilis contracted as a young man[20] – but there is no conclusive evidence that Nietzsche was syphilitic, and even if he was, disinhibiting can release only tendencies already there. The megalomania, anger and contempt had been aspects of his character for a long time, and are traits encouraged and exacerbated by solitude.

Many would argue that Nietzsche was only one extreme and atypical case. Of course Nietzsche was extreme – but he was an extreme version of developments I have noticed in others who have lived alone for a long time. Over many years of solitude, the feelings common to everyone, the self-centredness, the demands of memory, the desire to be always right and the knowledge of being an embodied self, tend to turn into self-obsession, righteousness, total fixation on the period of one's youth and a morbid fascination with one's own bodily functions. The result is some combination of compulsive routine, hoarding, stinginess, anxiety, hypochondria, obsession with diet and bowel function, resentment of change (especially new fashions and technology) and a doting dedication to the popular culture of one's youth. The trivial, whether problem or opportunity, victory or defeat, becomes massively important and brings the temptation of believing one's self, as did Nietzsche, to be Christ or Napoleon, depending on whether the current mood is of persecution or imperium.

For those who have lived too long alone the default emotion often becomes anger. The absence of demands from others should encourage a plateau of serenity broken by peaks of exaltation, and no doubt does so in many cases, but just as often the result is rage. Consider, for example, Philip Larkin, who lived alone to protect his freedom, refusing to commit to any of his lovers or to be involved in any social activity that did not suit him, and was also fond of remote heights, publishing a collection called *High Windows* featuring a poem with the same title and another rapturously imagining himself as a lighthouse keeper.[21] Despite his anti-social attitude, Larkin was hugely successful, critically acclaimed as well as popular, with a status and prestige many poets would sacrifice body parts to enjoy. Yet he described himself as 'boiling with rage'. If he lived only for himself, and his life was exactly as he wanted it, what was he so angry about? It could be that the growing meg-alomania of solitude demands control of a world that does not change, as the totally controlled personal world does not change, whereas the world below the high windows not only rejects control to change ceaselessly but seems determined to change in the most misguided ways, provoking fury.

This effect also works on a larger scale. In the first half of the twentieth century Irish Catholicism, despising what it saw as modern degeneracy, sought to withdraw from this corrupted world and by its example of discipline, dignity, purity and piety make the world respect, admire and profoundly wish to emulate. Instead the fallen world simply ignored the example and even intensified its concentration on base pleasures, which drove the pious pure into a frenzy of loathing and rage. Something similar may be happening with contemporary Islam.

Age of course also encourages all these megalomaniac developments, and the combination of age and living alone is often a doomsday cocktail.

However, as Rabelais and Nietzsche repeated, there are no absolute truths and no final answers. Living alone permits the fanaticism needed to produce original work but this also encourages increasing certainty and satisfaction in one's own beliefs and abilities, and increasing dismissiveness and contempt for those of everyone else. Living with a partner provides the tension of opposing forces that discourages extremism but this also makes individual achievement more difficult.

Possibly the problem is not in living alone as such, but in continuing to do so for too long or in making the isolation too complete – both allow eccentricity and madness to blossom. Even the most committed singletons realise that solo living should not be permanent. Zarathustra came down from his mountain, Thoreau left his cabin in the woods and even Miss Quirkyalone is considering the apostasy of cohabitation: 'Now I'm ready for a different experience. I've lived alone for a long time, and at this point in my life I'd grow a lot more if I were partnered.'[22] Similarly, Ethan Watters, anthropologist of the new urban tribes of singletons, and himself a singleton, eventually got married. And those who continue to make a go of living alone realise the danger of being cut off from the world. The well-adjusted singletons in Klinenberg's study are not reclusive but participate in more group activities than their married counterparts. They are more likely to go to bars and dance clubs, take part in team sports, play or sing in music groups and join political protests.

Indeed, it may be that individualism, one of the defining forces of the modern era, is finally running out of steam, as exhausted, depleted and angry individuals become aware of the demands and costs of pursuing personal autonomy. Rousseau, one of the first to promote this concept, also understood the dangers more clearly than many who followed: 'Exclusiveness is the death of pleasure. Real pleasures are those we share with people; we lose what we try to keep for ourselves alone.'[23] Individualism, which seemed to be the terminus of Western civilisation, may turn out to have been a temporary over-reaction to constraint, and we may be entering a post-individualist, or at least only partly individualist, age.

There is evidence for this from several sources. Neuroscience undermines the very basis of individualism by claiming that the individual sense of a unitary fixed self is an illusion created by the brain to provide the comfort of stability and continuity. The self is not an essence to be discovered but an ongoing process of interaction with the environment, and according to the theory of 'extended mind' is at least partly *in* the environment. Philosophy supports this by claiming that the most important environmental influence is other people. Personal identity is developed, not so much by looking inwards, as in acceptance of, or resistance to, the identities others attempt to impose.[24]

Another justification of individualism is the belief that evolution shows life to be a competition in which only the strongest and most ruthless survive and flourish – but evolutionary biology now suggests that adaptability and cooperation may be just as important, if not more so. While, from evolutionary anthropology comes the claim that the human brain evolved to be social rather than individualistic, and from child psychology the parallel claim that the infant brain is social long before it becomes individual. Social psychology supports this by emphasising the importance of empathy for wellbeing, and medical surveys reveal that social people are healthier and live longer, whereas the isolated are more likely to fall ill and die prematurely.

Revisionist history also undermines individualism by questioning its creation myth – the story that in the eighteenth century a few enlightened and courageous champions of reason broke the shackles of religious superstition and repression and set the individual free to find, express and fulfil a true self. In fact the development of individualism began much earlier and was much more gradual and complex.[25] The revolutionary liberty championed by the eighteenth century, apparently in opposition to Christianity, was made possible only by Christianity's even more revolutionary idea, a shocking novelty in the classical world, that all human beings are of equal value and subject only to the dictates of individual conscience. Secular liberalism seized on individual entitlement but forgot the corollary of individual obligation.

But as well as all these shifts in the realm of high ideas, there has also been significant change down in the popcorn-munching multiplex, where the lone hero who walked down the mean streets or rode down the main streets has largely been replaced by the buddy pair, the elite team, and the band of soldier brothers.[26] Even comic-book superheroes now prefer to fight evil in groups.

And, of course, there is the rise of fun and its emphasis on group activity, which since the seventies has developed in parallel with, and possibly in reaction to, the sense of individual entitlement. This trend towards group activity has been difficult to recognise because it is masked by the growing preference for living alone and the persisting prominence of expressive individualism – but the solo dwellers usually belong to many groups and want to do their own thing in the company of like-minded others. As Eric Klinenberg notes, 'going solo is tremendously social'.

This new social configuration is the result of eventually finding a balance between two extremes – the suffocating constraints of the formal institutions of tradition and the arid freedom of the new high-windows autonomy. The new groups are often loose and informal, short-lived and unstructured, with constantly chang-ing members but no clearly defined membership criteria, and no member lists, hierarchy, leadership or rules. In many cases the members are strangers to each other and happy to remain so. It seems as though the pleasure of belonging to a group can be more important than the actual group activity. Fun is more an excuse to form a group, more than the group is an excuse to have fun – which would explain the phenomenon of the flashmob, the group of strangers summoned by the Internet and getting together simply for the pleasure of belonging to a short-lived group.

This brings us back to Epicurus, who could well be regarded as the father of the urban group because his idea of pleasure was not solitary contemplation on a mountain top but sitting in the garden of his home in Athens with a few like-minded friends interested in discussing the meaning of life – and the ideas inspired by these sessions anticipated by thousands of years concepts in theology (the Gods are remote and unknowable and do not intervene in human affairs), physics (the universe is composed solely of atoms and emptiness), neuroscience (consciousness is due merely to the complex motion of atoms) and twenty-first-century psychology (pleasure-seeking tends to suffer from diminishing returns, a phenomenon now known as 'hedonic habituation').[27] He was modern even in making liveliness and curiosity the only membership requirements for his urban tribe, which included former slaves and women, and, again just like many in our own time, he was smeared and discredited for including in his company the dancing girls known as 'Sweet Mama', 'Baby Lion' and 'Tits'.[28]

PART III

Having Fun

9

Fun Goes Dancing

In that great scene at the end of *Zorba the Greek*, Zorba, the grizzled Dionysus played by Anthony Quinn, and his bookish, inhibited English friend (Alan Bates), invest Bates's money in a scheme to bring timber down to the sea from an inaccessible mountain forest via a series of wooden chutes. At the first trial the chutes collapse and break up in a series of spectacular, roaring crashes. For a long time the two men, waiting by the sea, look up at the devastation in appalled silence. But eventually Bates, who has been learning from the older man how to get in touch with his own inner Dionysus, turns to his mentor with an odd request: 'Zorba, teach me to dance.' At first Zorba is startled, unsure how to take this. Then a grin spreads over his grey stubble and he issues the Zorba chuckle, that unique, deep, saying-yes-to-life chuckle, cue for the unforgettable balalaika music to well up and for Zorba to lead and Bates to follow in the dance, as the tempo slowly builds and the camera slowly pulls away, back and up, to show the two dancers increasingly insignificant in the vastness of mountains, sea and cosmos yet also now profoundly at one with all of this.

It is a demonstration of the gratuitous nature of dance, its expense of energy in pure play, in this case with an added element of transgression, not appeasing but defying the gods – dance as an eloquent *fuck you* to Fate. The scene is of course an example of the feel-good, uplifting and inspirational ending beloved by Hollywood and despised by hard-headed sceptics like myself – but sometimes the crudest drama is the most effective and this scene broke through my ironic detachment to lift high my stony heart. I came out of the cinema humming the dance music, snapping my fingers and vowing to chuckle and dance away whatever catastrophes Fate had in store.

Of course it did not work out like that. I gave up dancing despite my beloved's frequent reminders that this was what had attracted her to me in the first place. I should have danced down the decades with her, defying the world by expending energy just for the fun of it, and defying the gods with human insouciance – but I rejected her entreaties with snarls of being too old, too creaky, too busy, too everything for any more of that youthful nonsense. So many lost opportunities! Men and women are meant to dance together. Women in particular love to dance. Even St Teresa of Avila danced in a chapel with her Lord, beating out time with a tambourine, undeterred by the lack of response from her partner (typical of men).

Is it too late to make amends? The beloved worries that her knees may no longer be up to it. I fear for my bad back. Also, if dad dancing is embarrassing, what will granddad dancing look like? Then there are the problems of which dance and where? London turns out to offer a staggering range of dance classes in a staggering range of venues. It seems as though every dance ever given a name can be learned and practised somewhere. There is even scope for nameless improvising in evenings of 'Ecstatic Dance' where we are exhorted to 'let the music, the community and our own inner space direct our steps, our movements, our expression, our journey'.

Line dancing would be the most appropriate to learn, in order to relive the group experience of the earliest dancers in pre-history, and line dancing has also enjoyed a resurgence in popularity – but it has been appropriated and domesticated by the faux-folksy, faux-hearty, American country tradition. Even more popular, and still with a whiff of Dionysian wildness, is salsa, a combination of the rhythms of Africa and Latin America, created in Cuba and refined in New York, and available right now in the local Community Centre.

But first it is necessary to put salsa in context.

Dancing is fundamental, universal and eternal. According to many cosmologists, the universe is doing the hokey-cokey, as galaxies rush away from each other, pause, and then rush back to reunite in an delirious crash, which starts it all off again. At the other end of the scale, atoms certainly do the conga, linking head to tail and then forming a ring. Without these congas there would be no order, no diversity, no complexity, no life. And as soon as life emerged in single cell organisms, one of these organisms, the spirochete, created the first dance – the wiggle – from which all living movement derived.

The wiggle is still effective, especially if performed by women, but eventually animals developed more complex dances. When house-hunting honey bees have checked out a new hive location, they return to the old hive and go into a jive, whose extent and orientation map the potential new site, and whose energy and enthusiasm communicate an estimate of its worth. The more vigorous and stylish the dance, the more convincing the suggestion, a form of consensus making that would certainly enliven dull meetings in the human world. Australian bowerbirds even created the first dance halls, special areas set aside for courtship, with exactly the same function as the crude building where I thrilled to Butch Moore and The Capitol Showband. Cranes developed a group dance resembling the quadrille. Scores of males and females line up facing each other, then advance, bow, withdraw, exchange partners and repeat the manoeuvre, until couples have chosen each other. Chimpanzees developed a funkier, more exuberant style that involves 'bipedal posture, rhythmic foot stamping, and hooting noises, together with emphatic arm and facial gestures'. Jane Goodall, the first close observer of chimpanzee behaviour in the wild, describes how chimpanzees react to thunderstorms. 'Sometimes when the first drops hit them they begin a display, wildly and rhythmically swaying from foot to foot, rocking saplings to and fro, stamping the ground. This spectacular performance we call a rain dance.'[1]

But the main dancing star of the animal world is Snowball, a sulphur-crested Eleonora cockatoo who became famous thanks to an Internet video of him boogying in time, with synchronised head banging and foot movement, to the music of The Backstreet Boys. The neuroscientist of music, Aniruddh Patel, investigated and had to acknowledge that 'when the tempo of a song is increased or decreased over a limited range, Snowball adjusts his movements accordingly, and stays synchronised with the music.'[2]

This seems to undermine another claim to human uniqueness – that only humans have developed the ability to synchronise movement with an external auditory source of rhythm. But in general, with the exception of Irish fathers at weddings, humans are better at keeping in time – and, as always with superior brain function, the secret is developing the right connections. The neurologist Oliver Sacks: 'The ability of human beings to keep time, to follow a beat ... physically and mentally ... depends ... on interactions between the auditory and the dorsal premotor cortex – and it is only in the human brain that a functional connection between these two cortical areas exists. Crucially, these sensory and motor activities are precisely integrated with each other.'[3] And Sacks goes on to explain that when dancing we do not merely follow a beat but learn to memorise rhythmic sequences and anticipate steps – in other words to surrender the body to the repetitive pattern.

Human dancing goes back at least to the Palaeolithic age. It is pre-speech, as fundamental as laughter and as old. There is even a theory that *Homo erectus* developed the rhythmic ability to move in time to a beat, so that dancing predated the arrival of *Homo sapiens*, around 200,000 years ago.[4]

According to the earliest graphic evidence, Palaeolithic humans were often depicted wearing animal masks, which suggests that the dancing rituals had animal origins. The first recorded masked dancer may have been the shaman in the cave paintings at Trois Frères who wears antlers, a mask and has his legs in a step position that suggests he is dancing something like the cakewalk. It's difficult to define movement from a static image but, in another cave at Tuc d'Audoubert, fifty fossilised heel prints in front of an image of copulating bison suggest a dance in imitation of the animal.

Dance is also prominent in mythology. The dance of the Hindu God Shiva is what sets the universe in motion and sustains all its rhythms, from the cosmic hokey-cokey to the conga of the atoms. Dance even has the power to awaken inert matter.

The power of dance over people is illustrated by a myth of the Onondaga Indians of North America. When a group of children were ignored by their busy parents they went to a clearing in the forest and created dances about the deer, squirrels and bears, but honouring especially the falcon, eagle and hawk. One day an old man approached them and warned them to stop or evil would come to them. For the next few days he came back to repeat his warnings but the children ignored him to dance on. Eventually the dances were so lengthy and tiring that the children asked their parents for food to eat during the dance – but the parents insisted that the children come home for meals. One day the children danced for so long without food that their heads became light with hunger and little by little they began to rise into the sky. As they rose above the forest, circling, they were seen by their parents who rushed out with great quantities of food, begging the children to come back. One child did plummet to earth but the others continued to rise into the heavens and became a constellation of dancing stars. In other words, the young constantly discover, much to the consternation of their parents, that dancing will take you as high as the stars.

The earliest agrarian communities, many millennia BCE, worshipped fertility goddesses who were importuned every spring to bring abundance to the fields. Fertility was feminine and women love to dance, so it was assumed that the goddesses danced and would reward a community dancing in their honour. This tradition persisted in the peasant communities of Eastern Europe and Russia until right into the twentieth century. Young women who died before giving birth were believed to become spirits who lived in the woods or by rivers and gathered at night to laugh, play, swing in the branches, sing and, above all, dance together. They were generally happy on their own and would not disturb the villages, but any young man foolish enough to wander in the woods at night would be seized and danced to death. These dancing goddesses were known as *rusalki* or *vily* (anglicised as 'willies', a forgotten word that persists in the phrase, 'it gave me the willies') and could be recognised by their youth, beauty, white chemises and long, loose hair, a symbol of female fertility. To distinguish themselves from these dangerous spirits, married women wore their hair braided and tucked into caps, a form of distinction that persisted into the late twentieth century in Ireland, where girls who married were expected to have their hair cut and frozen into cast-iron perms.

The *vily* had unused fertile capacity that could be called down into the earth in spring, and to do this the peasant communities danced in special festivals and rites. The dancing was especially frenzied during Rusalia, or 'Crazy' Week, sacred to the *vily*, when, in another example of carnival inversion, women ruled for a few days. During this period the madness was so general that the *vily* left their usual remote haunts to wander everywhere and would abduct anyone they came across, regardless of gender. Women who had to travel out of their villages carried garlic and wormwood to ward off these spirits.

Needless to say, the Church took an extremely dim view of young girls dancing madly and in Western Europe succeeded in stamping out the old traditions by demonising women who believed in spirits and burning them as witches, a practice that never caught on in the East, so many dancing festivities survived and succumbed only to the twentieth-century killer, TV.

The romantic ballet *Giselle* (full title *Giselle or the Willis*), is based on these pagan legends. Giselle is a beautiful peasant girl who dies of a broken heart and becomes one of the *vily*, but saves her beloved when the *vily* try to lure him to a dancing death. However, Adolphe Adam's music for *Giselle* is conventional nineteenth-century ballet music. It took twentieth-century Slavic composers to produce something more authentically old, strange and rhythmic. Stravinsky's *Rite of Spring* is a re-enactment of an archaic fertility rite, and Bartok's Romanian and Bulgarian Dances and *Out of Doors* suite are based on music used in the peasant festivities that persisted into the twentieth century. All these compositions are violently, exhilaratingly, rhythmic. *The Rite of Spring* was so strange that it caused a riot on its premiere in Paris by the *Ballets Russes* (when neurasthenic Marcel Proust, the world's unlikeliest dancer, got so fired up that he knocked the hat off a protesting financier). Bartok's Dances were composed for solo piano but use the piano as a percussion instrument and sound like some sort of weird, jagged, modern jazz.[5]

However, the goddesses were not long on top. At the beginning of the classical period, several centuries BCE, increasingly patriarchal societies demanded a male supremacy dance myth and Zeus obliged by impregnating the earth goddess Semele, who gave birth to Dionysus, Lord of the Dance, though most of the frenzied dancing was done by the female votaries of Dionysus, the Maenads (or 'Raving Ones'). These were like turbo-charged biker versions of the *vily*, wearing animal skins instead of white chemises, with live snakes for jewellery, and after dancing themselves into *ekstasis* they would roam through the forest to tear apart animals and eat them raw in a symbolic rite of god ingestion, like communion only messier. In many of the depictions on vases it is the Maenads who dance while Dionysus coolly looks on or even lolls around boozing, like a corporate executive at a lap-dancing club. Nevertheless, it is Dionysus who is largely credited as the originator of ecstatic dancing and revelry, while the dancing goddesses have been largely forgotten.

The cult of Dionysus and other similar Lords of the Dance quickly spread through Greece and around the eastern Mediterranean, while much of subsequent Greek culture involved playful choral singing and dancing (in Greek, as in many Slavic languages, the same word is used to mean 'dance' and 'play'), with dance competitions and contests and prizes for the best dancers. Plato, not much of a fun guy (he hated poetry), nevertheless advocated group singing and dancing as essential for maintaining a community spirit among citizens, and urged that these skills be taught to children from the age of six.

And, in the first centuries of Christianity, dancing in churches was encouraged in the belief that it imitated the dance of the angels round God and would help to bear souls up to Heaven. In the fourth century St Ambrose of Milan declared that 'He who dances in the spirit with a burning faith is carried aloft and is uplifted to the stars ... he who dances the spiritual dance, always moving in the ecstasy of the faith, acquires the right to dance in the ring of all Creation.'[6]

Communal dance was still an expression of religious ecstasy, but as Christian communities grew and stratified dance was increasingly associated with the lower levels of society, and when Christianity became the official religion of the Roman Empire it developed the usual upper-level distaste for, and fear of, the collective effervescence of the lower. Ecstasy was to be enjoyed only by solitary saints in the privacy of their cells. Even by the end of the fourth century bishops were beginning their denunciations of dance. St Basil the Great, Bishop of Caesarea: 'With unkempt hair, clothed in bodices and hopping about, they dance with lustful eyes and loud laughter; as if seized by a kind of frenzy they excite the lust of the youths ... With harlots' songs they pollute the air and sully the degraded earth with their feet in shameful postures.'[7] But it took nearly a thousand years to expel the dancers from church and another few centuries to suppress carnival dancing.

It's likely that these early dances varied enormously in tempo and style – but they were certainly all performed in groups.[8] According to the dance scholar Maurice Louis, couple dancing began only around 1400 and for a long time was common only among the nobility of Western Europe.[9] His theory is that, under the influence of the new courtly love, male circle dancers began to pay more attention to the ladies on their right and finally couples broke away from the circle to dance on their own. But in Eastern Europe line dancing persisted into the twentieth century, when it was finally supplanted by the glamorous couple dancing of film and television. So Fred Astaire and Ginger Rogers may have unwittingly finished off the archaic dance of the goddesses.

It was only after the Enlightenment that couple dances worked down through the classes and began to cross borders, often feared and resented as bitterly as human immigrants. Outrage at the latest 'indecent foreign dance' has been common ever since, as expressed in this fulminating article from *The Times*: 'It is quite sufficient to cast one's eyes on the voluptuous intertwining of the limbs and close compressure on the bodies in their dance to see that it is indeed far removed from the modest reserve which has hitherto been considered distinctive of English females. So long as this obscene display was confined to prostitutes and adulteresses we did not think it deserving of notice ... but now we feel it a duty to warn every parent against exposing his daughter to such a fatal contagion.'[10]

And what was this disgustingly lewd foreign dance? The waltz – imported from that filthy cesspit Vienna. It's wonderful to learn that the waltz, the dance of the bourgeoisie as the minuet was the dance of the nobility and more of a smug flounce than a dance, was once hated and feared. Yet the waltz came to dominate the nineteenth century as the minuet had dominated the eighteenth, and was challenged only by the polka, a boisterous, thigh-slapping knees-up reputedly created by a Slovakian serving girl. Once again the dance was reinvigorated from below and this has been the pattern ever since.

At the beginning of the twentieth century came the most dramatic reinvigoration of all from the New World, a return to animal roots in African-American dances such as the grizzly bear, the bunny hug, the turkey trot (similar to the twerk) and the camel walk (similar to Michael Jackson's famous moonwalk). And before bourgeois society had time to recover from this animal invasion, in 1912 there arrived in Europe from Argentina the tango, a devastatingly erotic dance developed in bordellos in the mid-nineteenth century. This was the ultimate inversion, the revenge of the zoo and the brothel. One of the crucial innovations of the tango was the slit skirt, which was not only thrillingly erotic (part exposure is always more exciting than revealing all) but freed the leg for more extravagant movement and permitted what is arguably the most devastating dance move, the high kick. Like a good joke, a good high kick must be unexpected, abrupt and swift, executed with perfect timing and no hint of hesitation or faltering, and terminated in a chest-high snap like a whip crack. What is exhilarating is the combination of liberation, rebellion and haughty disdain, the suggestion of kicking off and kicking away, but with cool self-possession and absolute control.

Dance fashions often reflect social change and a pattern in dance history is that periods of great national suffering, such as plague and war, are followed by outbreaks of manic dancing. After the Black Death in fourteenth-century Europe there was spontaneous public group dancing in many German and French towns, with hundreds literally dancing till they dropped and even, in some cases, till they died – and after the horror of the First World War came the Charleston, one of the most frenetic dances. But it was too unrelentingly frantic, with no variation in pace, no surprise. It was too naïve, too obvious, too cheerful, too chaste. The tango understood the need for sudden, dramatic freezes, which created a tension thrillingly released in explosive movement – and for solemn, impassive expressions to create mystery. Modern sophistication requires a touch of dandyism, an appearance of remoteness and hauteur, even boredom. The tango was hot because it was cool (and the Charleston was never cool because it tried too hard to be hot). The dandy must never be seen to be *trying*. Nevertheless the Jazz Age established the appearance, structure and form of sophisticated evening fun – slinky, revealing clothes, cocktails, nightclubs and dancing to the early bright.

After the Great Depression and the Second World War came another frenetic dance, the jitterbug, but in the fifties this mutated into the calmer jive, which could also be performed frenetically but was better as an expression of the new detachment and disdain of rebellious youth. Dancing was initially a group activity, then a partnership of two, and the cool version of the jive is the final stage of couple dancing, in which each individual seems to be hardly aware of a partner, much less a partnership, and too languidly hip even to be bothered to dance. The two do not even look at each other much less make eye contact as the man spins the woman violently away as though to be rid of her, and each turns in a dreamy self-absorbed circle to face once more (but not look at) each other and catch hands as though by accident.

I try not to have regrets but always feel a pang of loss at my lazy failure to learn to jive. The fashionable dance of my generation was the new sixties thing, the twist, which set the trend for solo dancing but was in all other respects undistinguished and has been justly forgotten.

The major explosion came in the seventies with the development of music specifically for dancing. The phenomenon of the discotheque, with dancing to records rather than live music, began in Paris, spread around Europe, flourished in New York, with the simplified name of disco and greatly simplified dancing music, and finally went mainstream through the 1977 movie *Saturday Night Fever*.

Everyone from that era remembers John Travolta in his white suit with the right hand arrogantly pointing to heaven, not to acknowledge God but to give him the finger and inform him that the new world is godless and belongs to strutting urban youth. The clothes and music seemed to me equally vulgar but I allowed myself to be dragged to the movie by my beloved, who, it turned out, was attracted not so much by John in his white suit as John in his black underpants. The surprise was that the movie was not a feel-good musical fantasy but a sordidly realistic story of youth, street life and sex, and a nasty surprise to the many expecting a contemporary version of *Singing in the Rain*. It is probably one of the best movies about fun – accurate in its depiction of the dreary jobs, the weekend escape into drinking and sex, and the ethos, dynamics and coarse language of the youth group, which in this case has the Travolta character, Tony Manero, as the charismatic leader of three clowns and a short hanger-on who earns his place by providing the wheels.

One classic exchange between youth and age has remained with me ever since.

Wise Old Boss: Save a little, Tony. Build a future.
Defiant Tony: Fuck the future.
Wise Old Boss: No, Tony, you can't fuck the future. The future fucks *you*.

Tony does mature and the real theme of the movie is his growing recognition of the immaturity of the group – but it's worth watching just for the dancing. In the first disco scene Tony begins with a sort of disco jive but soon abandons his partner to explode into an exhilarating solo that announces dance as a major new form of expressive individualism. Yet there is also a wonderful scene where the disco crowd unite in a disco line dance that harks back to the earliest line dancing and also anticipates the group dancing of raves. And a Puerto Rican couple perform a version of salsa, the new dance that will conquer the world. There is even a brief tango featuring a female high kick that, while not one of the greatest, is good enough to give me a shudder of awe.

By 1978 New York had over 1,500 discos, several internationally famous, though the significant development was not in the fashionable venues patronised by celebrities but in those for the outsiders – blacks, Latinos and especially gays. These clubs developed a new kind of shaman. Where the conventional DJ was an anonymous functionary who merely put hit records on a turntable, the outsider DJs became known and appreciated for specialised taste. Like the stand-up comedians who were emerging at the same time, these DJs developed a direct rapport with the crowd and responded to its mood. 'There's a feeling the crowd emanates,' explained one of the first name DJs, Terry Noel; 'it's like an unconscious grapevine. They send you a signal and then you talk back to them through the records.'[11]

The next stage for DJs was to create new effects, for instance by playing parts of two different records simultaneously, or by playing two copies of the same record so that a drum break could be repeated indefinitely by switching back and forth. The intention was to strip away melody, harmony, counterpoint and progression, everything that western music had so painstakingly developed, and leave only rhythm, the drumming. This new manic drum-break rhythm inspired a new manic break dance, often a completely individual performance with show-off solo dancers attempting to outdo each other in frenzied acrobatics that included spinning on their backs and even on their heads. But for the majority of dancers, who appeared to be dancing by themselves, the new exhilaration was the loss of individual self in becoming one with the crowd. The music journalist and chronicler of dance culture,

Sheryl Garratt: 'When the right record was played, there was no sense of *individuals* dancing any more: the club felt like one living, breathing organism.'[12] It was an unconscious return to the very beginning of dance ritual – the shaman with a drum whipping the tribe into an immersive and unifying frenzy of dance.

One difference is that in the new dance rituals the communion and unification are often between complete strangers. Here is Dela, a member of the Moontribe dance collective, on the experience of dancing all night at the collective's Full Moon Gatherings: 'Dancing for hours . . . with people who really KNOW how to let go and unite in non-verbal communication is something I've never experienced anywhere else. The experience is just that: an experience – beyond words . . . There are many people at the FMGs with whom I feel connected but with whom I've never spoken a word. This kind of non-verbal communication is hard to find.'[13]

This re-emergence of the tribe is another contemporary neo-pagan phenomenon. Where the terms 'tribe' and 'tribal' were once insults condemning behaviour and appearance as primitive, violent, stupid and backward, they are increasingly used to mean sophisticated, fun-loving, clever and radically progressive. As with Moontribe, many dance communities describe themselves as 'tribes'. An important producer of dance music is Vibe Tribe, one of the biggest dance festivals is Tribal Gathering and one of the main inspirations for mobile sound systems has been Spiral Tribe, while the tribal style of tattooing has remained the most consistently popular since the seventies, and Ethan Watters describes groups of friends as 'urban tribes'. To belong to a tribe is to be authentic and uncommercial (so some astute entrepreneur has probably opened a cool, indie coffee shop called *Kaffeine Tribe*).

The next technical development was for DJs to tape a set, edit the tape if necessary, and play it to the dancers on a reel-to-reel machine. Then came an entire set of new toys – bass and drum machines, and sampling and mixing technology. These were designed to produce cleaner, smoother music, with less distortion and, in a techno-inversion similar to the social inversion of carnival, were immediately used by the DIY DJs to make dirty, rough sounds and create new forms of distortion. The filter knobs of the Roland TB-303 bass machine were meant to be delicately turned to adjust the bass tone but a Chicago DJ called Pierre discovered that if the knobs were twisted madly, as though by an experimenting four-year-old, it made a deep squelching noise – and this became a crucial ingredient of the acid house sound. The Akai S1000 sampler was designed to time-stretch samples of music, making them longer or shorter without degrading the sound quality. But if the instructions are ignored, the time stretching, which works by chopping up the sample into minuscule pieces, can be made to introduce micro pauses and create a strobing effect – a robotic, staccato rhythm that became the foundation of drum'n'bass. One of those responsible for this innovation, the English DJ Goldie (named for his gold teeth): 'We were joy-riding the technology, like a twelve-year-old driving a Ferrari or a graffiti kid pushing the aerosol can to make the nozzle spray wide or thin.'[14]

Sampling can facilitate all kinds of insane combinations, like having the voice of a children's cartoon character sing Schubert's *Winterreise*, or using a scream from the movie *Halloween* to perform 'Peace in the Valley'. But why settle for a mere scream when entire chunks could be appropriated and pieced together? It became possible to make records without having to play instruments or indeed to create any original sounds by any means. Dance music now took to the extreme the postmodern fondness for borrowing. Everyone ripped off everyone else.[15] The novelist David Foster Wallace tells of the young female rapper Tam-Tam, who was heartbroken by a feckless lover, used her pain to create her rap masterpiece 'I'm cryin', took this round record producers but rejected offers she considered derisory – and then was heartbroken all over again to hear her rap performed on the radio by a rival called Antoinette. Once again Tam-Tam found solace in creation, with a revenge rap attack on Antoinette called, 'Ho, you're guilty'. And once again record producers liked the sound – until they discovered that the backing music for this attack on shameless plagiarism had been itself shamelessly stolen from another rap record.[16]

Dance music has also displayed an extreme version of the postmodern tendency towards fragmentation. By the end of the eighties this music was the fruit fly of culture, with the shortest generations and the fastest mutation. Soon there was hip-hop, which spawned dark hip-hop, rap, which spawned gangsta rap, house, which spawned acid house and happy house, jungle, which spawned ambient jungle, techno, which spawned nosebleed techno and playground techno, garage, which spawned speed garage and hardcore, which in turn spawned darkcore and drum'n'bass. To the uninitiated, the only common feature seems to be that the music got louder and faster, though with curious geographical variations. Speed is defined by beats per minute and the favoured bpm was greater in the Midlands than in the south of England, greater again in Scotland and Northern Ireland and off the scale in the Nordic countries. It would be interesting to plot bpm against latitude and possibly develop the results into a full-blown sociological theory – the more northerly the more mental. When I put this to professional DJ Jamie Cunningham he offered qualified agreement. 'It's not just the bpm. The music gets harder ... more aggressive. They're definitely crazier up north ... but also friendlier. Everyone wants to talk to you, hug you, drag you over to the bar and pour tequila down your neck.'

At least it's now possible to advance some suggestions for the growth in popularity of dance music (though not all of these factors apply to all dancers). First, dance is the physical expression of freedom, a freedom of the body to match the modern free spirit. Second, youth dance has been facilitated by the development of music based entirely on rhythm. Third, this dancing is a subculture that provides the transgressive pleasure of belonging to a secret society, an outlaw band, a resistance movement, an underground. Fourth, the close communion and constant feedback between the techno-shaman DJ and dancers breaks down the barrier between performer and spectator. Fifth, the practice of dancing in a group rather than as couples brings back the old joy of immersion in communal oneness. Finally, the fragmentation of dance music into a multiplicity of mutually hostile subgenres bestows on each of these the defensive solidarity of the tribe. It's a return to the ancient roots in so many ways. Hence a range of new terms such as 'techno-pagan', 'technoccult', 'occulturist', 'techno tribe' and, summarising the phenomenon, 'neo-tribalism'.[17]

As in stand-up comedy, the quality most valued seems to be authenticity. DIY music is believed to be more authentic than commercial pop, the neo-pagan mysticism is more authentic than institutional religion, the opposition to corporatism and consumerism is more authentic than the evasive clichés of left-wing

Michael Foley

politicians, and the techno tribes are more authentic than conventional groupings. Most authentic of all for the dancing tribes, the very model of dance authenticity, were the illegal raves in the UK during the late eighties and early nineties, where there were no established venues and dancers would receive last-minute instructions to gather in disused warehouses, or abandoned airfields or quarries, or often just in open fields in the countryside, taking dance back to its very beginnings, when the *vily* danced all night in the forest.

The experience sought by these dancing tribes is the 'groove', or the 'vibe', contemporary terms for Durkheim's 'collective effervescence'. As Dela the tribal dancer points out, this experience is impossible to capture in words, which has not deterred commentators such as Sally Sommer, who defines the vibe as 'an active communal force, a feeling, a rhythm that is created by the mix of dancers, the balance of loud music, the effects of darkness and light, the energy. Everything interlocks to produce a powerful sense of liberation. The vibe is an active, exhilarating feeling of "now-ness", that everything is coming together ... The vibe is constructive; it is a distinct rhythm, the groove that carries the party psychically and physically.'[18]

Dance commentators agree that the golden age of raving had an authentic vibe and that this UK golden age was brought to an end by a combination of criminal drug involvement, repressive legislation and policing, and a takeover by capitalist entrepreneurs offering the star DJs large sums to perform in new clubs specifically designed to attract ravers. To retain authenticity, Spiral Tribe (mantra: 'make some fucking noise') took a mobile sound system on the road round Western Europe, stopping wherever seemed propitious to improvise techno festivals, or 'teknivals', and in the course of time encouraging other nomadic dancing collectives, many joining up with politically active anarchist groups and/or attracting circus performers, acrobats, jugglers and fire eaters, to create travelling carnivals that energised the depressed local youth and horrified adults with their battered, heavily graffitied army trucks and school buses, sinister banners and insignia ('Poetic Terrorism', 'Remix Reality', 'Warning: CONUNDRUM'), monstrous 25-kilowatt sound systems with banks of huge speakers and bass bins pounding out continuous techno music and, not least, the combat fatigues, shaven-heads, tattoos and piercings of the tribal members themselves.

Soon nomadic dance tribes were travelling in Africa, Asia, the USA, Canada and Australia. One tribe got as far east as Ulaanbaatar in Mongolia. Another, Desert Storm, went to Bosnia while it was in the throes of civil war. 'We started playing on the move and we had thousands of people following us through the streets in two-foot snow and minus ten degrees. We played one techno record with a chorus that went, "Get going to the beat of a drum BANG!" and all the soldiers fired their AK-47s in the air "kakakakaka" and it was such a fucking buzz it was incredible . . . At one point a policeman came up to tell us to turn the volume up, but to turn off some lights as we were attracting shellfire.'[19]

All this added an outlaw rebelliousness to the Dionysian dance movement, with tribes like Renegade Virus, Havoc, Bedlam, Kamikaze, Skandalous, Blyss Abyss, DISORIENT EXPRESS, The Circus at End of the World, Tone Def Krew, Generation ov Noize, Circus Lunatek and The Mutoid Waste Company (mantra: 'mutate and survive'); groups like The Repeat Offenders,

Deviant Kickback, Conflict, Fred Nihilist, Brainsick Mob and The San Francisco League of Pissed Off Voters; DJs like Amok, Alex Malfunction, Killer Watts, Red Alert, Howie Wreckhords, Infected Mushroom, Meltdown Mickey, Ludacris, Preditah, and Catz 'N Dogz; events like Tempo Tantrum, Act Your Rage, How Weird Street Faire, Megatripolis, The Fuckparade, The Fuckfest, and the Autonomous Mutant Festival; and all this inspired and supported by written manifestoes with titles like Cyber Tribe Rising, Musikal Resistance, Guerrillas of Harmony, Carnival of Chaos and Saboteurs of the Big Daddy Mind Fuck.

These names reveal that, like 'tribe', the term 'circus' has taken on a new lease of life – and for similar reasons. Shedding its association with sad, mangy animals and bored performers squeezed into spangled costumes, in the seventies Nouveau Cirque liberated circus as disco liberated dance, and this new circus is, like dance, a skilled, hectic, intense, physical group activity, with the added romance of outsider status and the nomad life. No wonder young people are taking to it. I realised this a few years ago when I asked my niece, an English graduate, if she was going anywhere in the summer and she answered, casually, 'We're putting on a juggling workshop at the Glastonbury Festival.' And it turned out that she was in London not so much to see uncles and aunts as to visit the new Islington juggling shop, More Balls Than Most. Shortly after this, an English lecturer told of looking up in consternation from a Thomas Hardy seminar at the sight of human figures *passing by his first floor window* – and of discovering, on investigation, that this was a Circus Studies seminar going by on stilts.

The names also reveal another odd link with tradition in the tribal fondness for using 'z' instead of 's' and 'k' instead of 'c', thus establishing a connection between the members of the Kaos dance tribe and the patrons of the Kosy Korner Kafe. It is reassuring to know that we are one people after all.

At the heart of this neo-carnival of music, dancing, circus and activism is the new shaman, the DJ. In my generation, the breezy, glib, non-stop babble of DJs made them strong contenders for the most inauthentic people on earth. The sophisticated young despised DJs and wanted to be drummers or rock guitarists – but now it seems that the sophisticated young want to be DJs. When I ask Jamie Cunningham what makes a good DJ, he is perplexed. 'There are things you can do. A DJ called Cakeboy throws chocolate cakes and cupcakes into the crowd. Others crowd surf or bring people on stage. Some female DJs perform topless. I bring CDs of my music and T-shirts and throw them out.' He pauses, dissatisfied. 'But it's none of that. It's really just a personality thing. You put your personality out there . . . and some personalities work and others don't. Like with stand-up comedians. You can tell in a few seconds whether or not someone is going to make you laugh.' When I remind him that he runs a School for DJs and ought to know the secret of the art, he grimaces in the way of all those who claim to teach creativity. 'You can give them the technical stuff, how to use the equipment . . . but after that . . .' A deeper, sadder grimace. 'Some just don't have it.' It seems that the power of the shaman is a mystery – even to the shaman himself.

But it is time to stop theorising and go with the beat of the shaman's drum. The first salsa class is in a bleak community hall on a bleak, wet January evening, but the turnout is impressive and impressively mixed, with many different nationalities and social classes attending, an even balance of genders and an age range from twenty to crazy. Salsa does indeed seem to transcend all divisions. The shabby old hall is radiant with an almost religious fervour and beginners are welcomed as warmly as converts to the true faith. Salsa is surely the waltz of our era. But why this particular dance?

Most importantly, it's not a revival but a dance that has emerged from the era itself, specifically from Cuba in the seventies (again the seventies). And it's a genuine people's dance, a bottom-up development with no detectable source and no official organisation or control. No one even knows when, where or how it acquired the name salsa. Just as importantly, it is entirely rhythmic, driven by percussion-based music, with a rhythm faster than that of much popular music but slower than the manic rhythms of techno – fast enough to be thrilling but slow enough to be manageable for most dancers – and based on a simple sequence of steps (the mambo steps). It is a couple dance, with a sexual element, as in most couple dances, but not brazenly sexual like the tango. Contact is mainly hand to hand, with little hand to body, and so there is no opportunity for gropers or belly pushers and less cause for female alarm. And finally, the African-Latin-American-Caribbean connections add a crucial dash of exotic enchantment. Everything alluring comes from afar.

But the beloved and I are at the crazy end of the age range. Are we too old? George, our instructor, impatiently dismisses such negative thoughts. 'If you can walk, you can salsa.'

It seems that we will be learning 'cross-body' salsa, which turns out to be remarkably similar to the jive, is in fact a Latin American jive, a jive with Latin grace notes of ass wiggling and chest shaking. The basic couple movement is the same as in the jive – spinning the partner away and turning one's self in time. So at last I may learn to jive – and even combine fifties cool beat attitude with seventies Caribbean hot beat movement. *Caramba, daddio!*

Off we go on the basic mambo sequence of six steps to eight beats – step, step, step, pause, step, step, step, pause. Following such a simple sequence ought to be easy but I find it embarrassingly difficult. Concentrate, concentrate. Where is my neo-shamanic wildness? Even *Homo erectus* could do this, for fuck's sake. Maybe reading too much French philosophy has disconnected my auditory circuits from my dorsal premotor cortex. Or neglecting the body for too long has caused it to freeze like a polar bear turd.

Step, step, step, pause, step, step, step, pause.

Plato was right. We should be taught to dance from the age of six. We are born to learn and we are born to dance, so learning to dance should be a fundamental part of education. The right time to start is at six not the sixties. But it's never too late to learn, just increasingly difficult. And it takes even more effort to make a skill effortless.

Step, step, step, pause, step, step, step, pause.

Most of the women seem to be able to move gracefully, whereas most of the men look clumsy and awkward. The beloved takes to it as though she has been dancing in Havana bars all her life – and the rhythmic abandon does not put her in a mood to be tactful: 'You look as though you're marching in a military parade.' Then she embellishes her limber mambo steps with an insouciant tit and ass wiggle. I may not be able to move like a young man but I experience a disgraceful surge of youthful lust.

Step, step, step, pause, step, step, step, pause.

And then, just when it's starting to come together, George throws a spinner in the works by demanding that the welcome pause in the middle is replaced by a 360-degree turn *executed in one beat*.

Step, step, step, *spin*, step, step, step, pause. Instead of the body, my head spins.

The next challenge is having to synchronise with a partner. I seem to be the one exception to the cosmic urge to move in sync, and trying to spin the beloved under my raised arm knocks us both completely out of step. Then, while we are working on this, comes the most terrifying command – *Change partners* – and I find myself facing a young woman several inches taller and almost fifty years younger, whose minimal preparatory movements suggest a complete understanding of rhythm. Even her twitching is rhythmically graceful.

'You're not a beginner,' I accuse and she concedes, with an expression of suffering tolerance, that she has 'done a bit before'. This revelation and the thought of trying to spin her under my arm panics me and throws me off balance.

It's such a relief to get the beloved back, even if she is as unforgivingly sarcastic as ever. 'You should have enrolled for the Bingo instead.'

She keeps me at it, discreetly leading while giving the impression of being led (a crucial female skill) and eventually we manage a sort of spin. This is the world's slowest, clumsiest, least graceful jive – but it is definitely a jive. I have lived to jive.

10

Fun Goes Comical

As once before, thousands of years ago, when a small group met in an upper room to participate in a new ritual, so too now, except that this upper room is above a pub whose ground-level refurbishment in the latest fashion stops at a staircase that is increasingly shabby as it rises to a corridor smelling pungently of urine, with varnish worn off the floorboards and paint peeling from the walls, and leading to a draughty room with even more exhausted paint, even barer boards and a few rows of rickety, hard chairs. The arriving faithful are also scruffy, and young, most in their early twenties, and all carrying pints of beer. There are one or two reassuring bald pates but I am probably the oldest person in the room by at least forty years. Discreetly I conceal a glass of Sauvignon beneath my chair.

It reminds me of the poetry readings I attended in my own youth and of the many similarities between poetry and comedy. Because this is a club for stand-up comedy, a ritual that began in the sixties with the first comedy club in the USA and quickly spread round the Western world where it continues to flourish. This particular club is free, a venue for unknown hopefuls to have a go, and this evening a dozen or so will take turns to try to provoke laughter. But one crucial difference from the poetry reading is immediately apparent. Here an anonymous member of the audience can be singled out and ridiculed. The young MC thanks us for coming out on a wet, cold November evening, but then adopts a menacing tone, 'Have any of you got *umbrellas*?' He emphasises the noun with heavy sarcasm, sweeping the room with a challenging gaze. 'Those *fucking great* golf umbrellas ... that bang into everything?' In this audience the favoured method of rain-protection is the hood, and I am almost certainly the only one with a fucking great umbrella under my chair, in fact under three chairs. I would push it further back with a heel except that I am afraid to spill the Sauvignon. My neighbours on either side must be aware of the monstrosity below them but no one betrays me. Luckily there is no Judas in this upper room.

Another similarity between comedy and poetry is that they both seem so seductively easy – just dash off a few lines about anything that comes into your head or stand in front of a mic and talk about yourself for a few minutes. Anyone could do it – and so everyone tries (somewhere I have seen research claiming that in the UK over 20 per cent of sixteen- to twenty-four-year-olds have attempted to be stand-up comedians). But of course it's not as easy as it looks.

This evening's would-be comics have the confident manner but little else – and even the confidence often strikes a wrong note, with something already false in the exuberant bound up on to the stage to turn with a radiant grin and shout a cheery 'How y'all doin'?' Then there is no feel for timing or rhythm. They talk too fast or pause for too long, stumble over words, ramble, forget their scripts and have to consult notebooks and scraps of paper. One dressed as a vicar sets up a pulpit and begins to sing a parody of

'All Things Bright And Beautiful' to music from a mobile phone – but the mobile conks out and he has to apologise and start again. Another can't get the mic off the stand – and the next one knocks over the stand. In desperation the MC announces an *Irish* comic, Irish comics are always funny. But not this one. It's the contemporary version of stage Irish, the warm, relaxed, familiar tone of the mature, sensible best friend who understands oh so well the insanity of it all. This is too obviously ingratiating. No one laughs. So the next act takes the opposite approach and tries to be dangerous and risky by reading the vicar's notes, still on the pulpit, and accusing him, in a contemptuous tone, of following these word for word. But this attempt to get laughs from a failure to get laughs is even less funny. Not only are there no laughs but the silence returns his contempt tenfold. As the vicar retrieves his pulpit and storms out, the MC, in even greater desperation, increasingly sweaty and pallid, announces that there will be no interval because no one would return after it, a probably accurate insight that does not get a single laugh, and with terrific enthusiasm introduces the saviour of the evening, a 'professional' stand-up. But this so-called professional produces from his hip pocket a sheaf of paper and appears to be doing random bits from these notes, pausing every now and then to shuffle and read.

It is unlikely that even a good professional could rescue the gig at this stage. The many failures have discredited the very idea of stand-up by exposing it as an attempt, an *effort*, to be funny. Comedy can never seem to be trying but must simply *be* funny. Now the atmosphere is not like that of a wake – wakes are often lively – but more like a gathering of employees listening to a manager tell them that the business is about to shut down. Most agonising are the moments when the comics pause to allow laughter and are greeted by a silence as profound and terrible as the silence of God. Then they go into incredulous paralysed reverie, or do unintentional improv by muttering, 'Anyway, anyway,' 'Ah, I don't know,' 'Jesus,' 'Can this get any worse?' Or they ask the audience to explain the failure, 'Maybe too clever?' 'Too nasty?' Or they try self-flagellation, 'Scrap that, it was shite.' Or wry irony, 'That went down really well.' Or, worst of all, pitiful pleading, '*I* thought that was funny.'

What *I* once thought was that there was nothing worse than failed poetry, but failed comedy is even more embarrassing. The failure to get laughs is so immediately apparent and so brutal. The poetic equivalent would be an audience shouting in unison, 'Your poetry is shite.' So why do so many put themselves through this? The penalty for failure is hell – but the reward for success is heaven. There are few experiences more gratifying than making people laugh. I had considered trying stand-up myself, until I saw how difficult it is and how disastrous failure can be. And unlike poetry, which few read and fewer still pay for, comedy is big business. A stand-up successful enough to break out of the pub circuit and into theatres can earn money that would make even a professional footballer envious.

The roots of both comedy and poetry are in the distant past of shamans and tricksters but, unlikely though it may seem, scholars claim that modern comedy, in the sense of comedians *paid* to make an audience laugh, emerged at a specific time and place – in Venice in the mid-sixteenth century during the carnival, celebrated from St Stephen's Day to Shrove Tuesday, and the largest, longest and most lavish in Europe, with a huge range of entertainments that included banquets, balls, processions, regattas, fireworks, acrobatic displays, mock battles and sword fights, races, games and improvised plays.

But comedy emerged from the feature that was constant throughout the many weeks and many diversions – fancy dress. Anyone, rich or poor, from dignitaries to courtesans, could dress up and mask up, often to enjoy transgressive behaviour. The first reference to fancy dress and masks is a 1268 law banning the custom, popular with young masked revellers, of throwing eggs at people. This law was entirely ineffective because the custom not only persisted but became one of many ritualised ways to misbehave (and was so common that the balconies and open-air gatherings of the wealthy were protected by netting). The *mattaccini*, those in a white costume with red trimmings and a feathered hat, were permitted to throw eggs filled with rosewater (and were followed by hordes of egg sellers, also in costume, to keep them supplied with ammunition), while the *cocchieri* (coachmen) could crack whips, and the *diavoli*, in devil costumes, could whack children with water-filled bladders tied to sticks. There were opportunities to indulge simple fantasies by dressing as a wild animal, pirate or poet, and to indulge deeper, darker, more Freudian desires. The *gnaghe* were men in women's clothes, who spoke like haughty young ladies but often to utter obscenities, and the *tati* or *tate* dressed as infants and were entitled to play pranks. Those with a sadistic temperament could appear as the plague doctor, in a long black cloak, black hat, black spectacles and white mask with a huge sinister bird beak and a cane for keeping the unclean at arm's length – or as the sore-spangled victims of syphilis or plague. This is the equivalent of the contemporary taste for dressing as vampires or zombies, though it's obvious that Derry's Halloween Carnival has still a long way to go to rival Venice.

Everyone, from the Doge to beggars, could participate. It was a great time to be alive – but not if you were an animal. Games included a race between naked men to pull the head off a goose suspended from a house window, or between partly blind men to beat a pig to death, or between men with shaven skulls to headbutt to death a cat tied to a wall. Another diversion was the *cacce*, where men in fancy dress goaded dogs into a frenzy and set them loose on tethered bulls to tear their ears off. And one of the main rituals on the main day of festivities, *Giovedo Grasso* (Fat Thursday), was a bizarre celebration of a naval victory in 1162, in which a bull and twelve pigs were led into the Piazza San Marco and, in the presence of the Doge, dressed in official scarlet, and accompanied by foreign ambassadors, condemned to death by a genuine magistrate (the *Magistrato del Proprio*) and executed by beheading.

But the most influential development was a form of rowdy, ribald street theatre with masked actors improvising performances which included singing, dancing, acrobatics, juggling and coarse buffoonery of every kind but especially sexual. The performers, usually street entertainers, would literally drum up an audience by walking through the streets beating drums, and then lead the growing procession to a makeshift open-air stage and a play involving the stock characters of master, servants and lovers, and the stock plot of young love forbidden by the master but facilitated by the servants, the classic subversive combination of youth and workers against authority. This was a formalised version of the old carnival inversion, with a new sexual twist that grew out of the social situation in Venice, where the young sons of the elite families were increasingly angry at arranged marriages that often delivered the most attractive young women to wealthy old men.

These performances were so popular that in 1545 they led to the formation of the first professional theatre company of the modern age, performing shows in the style that became known later as *Commedia dell'Arte*, the tone viciously subversive and the style riotously comic, based on a new kind of mask. Where the traditional ritual mask exaggerated the eyes and mouth for spirit power, the comic mask exaggerated the nose to illustrate human absurdity. A big hooter makes everyone ludicrous, undermining self-importance by turning the nose into a proboscis, a snout, and its owner into a desperate, blindly searching animal.

The Master (the *Magnifico*) wore a mask with a hooked nose, echoed in a huge codpiece, and was always old, vain, greedy and lecherous, and spoke the Venetian dialect, while the servants (the *zanni*), wore multi-coloured patches and ambivalent black masks, spoke a rural dialect and were crafty, unscrupulous schemers bursting with anarchic energy (the adjective 'zany' derives from *zanni*). The lovers, always young and insipid, were only there to advance the plot and did not wear masks.

This *Commedia* was so popular that it quickly spread through Italy, then around Europe, though inevitably mutating in various ways and usually becoming less rowdy and ribald. The *zanni* were quickly recognised as the subversive engine and one character, Arlecchino, wearing a patchwork coat of many vivid colours and a demonic black half mask (that had no exaggerated nose), became the most important of the *zanni*, mutating into Harlequin in Western Europe and into Pierrot in France, which turned the character into its opposite, the mad, scheming, multi-coloured, worldly energy replaced by a sentimental, sickly, pale-face gazing at the moon. *Commedia* purists loathe Pierrot almost as much as they hate pizzerias named after *Commedia* characters, or sanitised, tame productions for children, or Punch and Judy shows (Punch is a debased version of the stock character Pulchinella).

The *Commedia* became a major influence on Elizabethan theatre, with *The Merchant of Venice* borrowing the theme of rich old man versus young lovers, and Ben Jonson's *Volpone*, also set in Venice, based on the master-servant relationship (in the dramatis personae Volpone, the aged Master, is described as a *Magnifico*). In the *Commedia* the characters have no inner lives or self-consciousness but in *Volpone* the crafty servant Mosca (described as a 'parasite', though he himself describes other servants as 'zanies') is given a soliloquy that captures perfectly the exhilaration of the Harlequin character at his own audacity and resourcefulness:

> I fear I shall begin to grow in love
> With my dear self, and my most prosperous parts,
> They do so spring and burgeon; I can feel
> A whimsy i' my blood: I know not how,
> Success hath made me wanton. I could skip
> Out of my skin now, like a subtle snake,
> I am so limber. Oh![1]

This is a fine expression of the comic spirit as play in Huizinga's sense of the word, an exhilarating independence that rejects all obligation and has little interest even in achieving its apparent ends, whether the schemes of the fictional character or laughter for the performer, but only in the high of enjoying the thing for its own sake. Because of its refusal to accept any ideology, religion, intellectual theory, political allegiance or social responsibility, comedy has often been described as nihilistic – but this refusal is positive rather than negative, a celebration of pure zest at the outrageous absurdity of being fully conscious of being fully alive and fully aware of the absurdity of fellow mortals – a moment of freedom in its purest form that is only momentary because freedom can never remain pure but dissipates immediately in its own expression. There is always the return to a situation with personal, social, political and ideological demands – but the brief shot of pure zest makes the return acceptable.

Shakespeare's fools are also in this tradition although, as one would expect, his treatment of the master/servant relationship is more measured and subtle, more modern. The masters are not pantomime idiots but humanly flawed, and the servants are not manic plotters and schemers but wry commentators on the follies of privilege, as when Lear asks, 'Dost thou call me fool, boy?' and his fool answers, 'All thy other titles thou hast given away; that thou wast born with.'

For several hundred years the *Commedia* flourished across Europe and didn't run out of steam until the age of steam at the end of the eighteenth century, when it lost its acrobatic and improvising energy and was perceived as too stylised and limited. (Its demise coincided with that of its source, the Venetian Carnival, which died with the fall of the Venetian Republic to Napoleon in 1797.) However, its influence continued into the twentieth century and is obvious in Beckett's work. Vladimir and Estragon, in *Waiting for Godot*, are modern *zanni*, servants, but now without masters, homes, roles, functions, or purpose, aimless tramps obliged to pass the time with zaniness. Contemporary productions of *Godot* often use comedians rather than serious actors, which would surely have pleased Beckett, who wanted Charlie Chaplin for the lead in his only film (helpfully titled *Film*), and when Chaplin was unavailable chose Buster Keaton.

The decisive break with traditional *Commedia* came in England in the early nineteenth century when an actor, Joseph Grimaldi, playing Harlequin, took the character out of the traditional plays, adapted him for individual performance and became the first professional comedian. Grimaldi reinvigorated the character by going back to the roots and concentrating on the acrobatics and buffoonery and, probably unconsciously, went even further back when he replaced the Harlequin mask with lurid face painting that exaggerated the mouth, smeared with red, and the eyes, ringed with white and topped by thick, black, arched eyebrows. Illustrations of Grimaldi in his make-up show a disturbingly demonic face remarkably similar to many ritual masks. For his costume he retained Harlequin's multi-coloured suit and baggy pants but completed his look with a Mohican wig. This is the prototype of the clown, though without the mournful expression that became a characteristic feature (a sentimental corruption similar to that of Pierrot). A more faithful version of Grimaldi's Harlequin is Batman's arch-enemy The Joker, with his clown make-up, exaggeratedly colourful outfits and love of mad scheming – a persistence of the *Commedia* in popular culture acknowledged when The Joker was given a female sidekick called Harley Quinn.

Unlike most sentimental clowns, Grimaldi seems to have been genuinely funny. One contemporary reported that he would 'put dullness to flight and make a saint laugh'.[2] The crucial feature was probably the dangerous unpredictability of his shows, which were full of lunacy and mayhem, for instance staging a detailed reconstruction of the Vauxhall Pleasure Gardens, with elegant diners enjoying a serene dinner, and then turning this into chaos with mock stealing of food, mock fights, dancing, pratfalls, disappearances through trap doors, appearances through walls or in jumps from high windows, and lots of smashed crockery, flying tables and chairs, live birds bursting out from under plates, and swarms of live bees emerging from bottles to pursue characters off stage. But as well as the farce and slapstick, Grimaldi introduced audience participation through comic songs such as 'Don't I Look Spruce On My Neddy', in which he mocked the newly fashionable jockeys on a horse made from a bench, a broomstick and a donkey skull.

He was certainly madly successful, the first celebrity comedian, performing for royalty, mixing with aristocrats (Lord Byron was an avid fan who became a friend), and famous straight actors (Edmund Kean was also a fan), and eventually selling his celebrity memoir which was edited (and possibly ghost-written) by a young Charles Dickens, an inspired choice. Grimaldi may well have influenced Dickens's many comic grotesques and the demonic vitality of Quilp in *The Old Curiosity Shop*, or at least encouraged his anarchic exuberance, distaste for authority and love of carnivalesque excess, though he could equally well have found all these qualities in Rabelais (and also the love of food and drink and convivial gatherings of every kind). The essence of the carnivalesque spirit, as exemplified by Rabelais and Dickens, is its recognition that the world is excessive, even riotous, certainly beyond the understanding and control of the masters who believe themselves to be superior and to know what is best for everyone – and the

essence of carnivalesque inversion is its recognition that the servants, unaffected by the hallucinogens of status and power, are
frequently less deluded and more aware of limitation than their
masters. Shakespeare's Touchstone expresses this neatly, 'The fool
doth think he is wise, but the wise man knows himself to be a fool.'

In *Hard Times* Dickens explicitly sets the carnivalesque,
represented by Sleary's Circus, against the rational utilitarian,
represented by the 'eminently practical' Gradgrind's evangelical
belief in 'Plain Fact' and mathematical calculation, which he
attempts to instil into his 'model' children. But his daughter Louisa
becomes broken in spirit and depressed, and his rebellious son Tom
becomes a gambler and thief. When a major theft is discovered,
Tom takes refuge with Sleary's Circus, performing with the Clown
as 'comic blackamoor' servants of the giant in a Jack the Giantkiller
burlesque. Other performers include the 'Emperor of Japan, on a
steady old white horse stencilled with black spots . . . twirling five
wash-hand basins at once, as it is the favourite recreation of that
monarch to do', 'Miss Josephine Sleary, in her celebrated graceful
Equestrian Tyrolean Flower Act', and a child rider known as 'the
Little Wonder of Scholastic Equitation'.

Gradgrind tracks his son to the circus and after a performance
confronts his model boy in a 'comic livery' of clothes several sizes
too big and 'of coarse material, moth-eaten and full of holes, with
seams in his black face, where fear and heat had started through the
greasy composition daubed all over it'. In a neat touch of symbolic
inversion, Gradgrind, appalled and forlorn, sinks down 'on the
Clown's performing chair in the middle of the ring'.

The circus clown was one aspect of Grimaldi's legacy, but
more important for comedy was his rejection of genre and theatre

characters to create his own individual comic persona, in which, again like so many who followed, the manic figure on stage had a depressive double in real life. Crippled by the physical demands of his act, Grimaldi retired early and died young, at forty-nine, but his creation, the individual comic performer, flamboyantly dressed and heavily made up, with an act mixing slapstick and comic songs, became the mainstay of the new English music halls in the second half of the nineteenth century, and then of their American counterpart, vaudeville.

Most of the famous American comedians of the first half of the twentieth century emerged from vaudeville, for instance Buster Keaton, Charlie Chaplin, the Marx Brothers, Mae West, W. C. Fields, Bob Hope, Jack Benny and Milton Berle, but in the course of the century comedy evolved, from physical to verbal, from slapstick to drollery, from the bolstering of superiority by laughing at others to the acceptance of inferiority by laughing at one's self. In this more subtle comedy of incongruity, the laughter is caused by having an expectation rather than a person knocked down. Not just any overturning is funny – it has to be lightning fast, almost instantaneous, and to have an appropriateness, a clever rightness, in the manner of the overturning. We laugh at what is simultaneously wrong and right – and this is why comedy is the deepest expression of the human predicament, the existential incongruity of being both wrong and right in the world (Nietzsche described laughter as 'the one true metaphysical consolation'[3]). What could be more wrong than an animal that has become aware of itself and feels as though it is an immortal soul while knowing it is really just a rapidly deteriorating body, that has a brain with 100 billion densely networked neurons but is connected to a donkey cock, and with, as Robin Williams once put it, sufficient blood flow to power each of these but rarely both at the same time? On the other hand, what could be more right than an animal with the consciousness to celebrate the miracle of being alive? At once absurd and sublime, the only human response is to laugh.

Around the middle of the twentieth century, the younger generation of comedians, including Benny, Hope and Berle, abandoned the costumes, slapstick, comic songs and sketch routines to develop a new style of talking directly to audiences in their everyday clothes as what appeared to be their real selves. These comics were known as the 'monologuists' and at some point after the mid-century their style was copied by the next generation and became known as 'stand-up', a term that first appeared in dictionaries in the early sixties.

There is a claim that stand-up evolved independently in England as the music hall comics increasingly used 'patter' around and during their slapstick and songs – but the consensus view recognises it as an indigenous American phenomenon, like jazz, with which it has many similarities – anti-authoritarian, bohemian, cultish, nocturnal, blooming darkly in smoky, often underground, clubs. The most influential of the early stand-ups, Lenny Bruce, was a fervent jazz fan, performed frequently in jazz clubs, enjoyed improvisation and hated repetition ('As soon as it becomes repetitive to me, I can't cook with it any more, man'[4]) and regarded it as his major triumph if he could make the ultra-cool jazz men laugh.

Everything about stand-up is quintessentially American – the rejection of traditional artifice, the breaking of taboos, the autobiographical emphasis on individualism and authenticity, the casual, direct, intimate style, the spontaneity, improvisation and free-flowing formlessness, and above all the fundamental belief that ordinary life can, without undue exaggeration, be made interesting enough for a poem and funny enough for a comic routine. It is the democratisation, the Whitmanisation, of comedy. Walt Whitman got the ball rolling in poetry with 'Song of Myself' and a century later comedy followed with 'Joke of Myself'.

The most obvious similarity between comedy and poetry is their total dependence on timing and rhythm – but there is also the dependence on personality, tone, the *voice*. The great American poets are immediately recognisable from even a few lines chosen at random because all the lines are in the voice, which reveals the personality. It's fascinating to discover that stand-up comedians use exactly the same term as poets to describe the search for an individual style – 'finding the voice'. It is not 'creating' or 'developing' but 'finding', because the process is gradual, blind and entirely intuitive, a lengthy trial and error that, with persistence and a measure of luck, eventually stumbles on something that works. One of the greatest stand-ups, Richard Pryor, has claimed that finding the voice can take fifteen years.

Of course this personality expressed by the voice is really a persona, a role, a selective, concentrated and heightened version of the real personality, itself based on a series of roles, and the life roles that produced the persona role are in turn influenced by the persona. It is all fascinatingly complicated.

As is the vexing issue of timing and rhythm. Everyone agrees that these are crucial but no one can define exactly what the terms mean. There is certainly no doubting the fatal consequences of a failure in either. The novelist Zadie Smith follows her stand-up brother and was perturbed to find that a routine which brought the house down on one occasion, and was repeated exactly in a similar venue to a similar audience, died, as Max Wall once put it, 'like a louse in a Russian beard'.[5] In the course of a melancholic post-mortem she and her brother came to the conclusion that the difference between success and failure was a variation in timing so minute as to be barely perceptible. I discovered this myself when giving a talk to two literary festival audiences of similar make-up and size, in venues only a few miles apart. The first time I died a lonely, anonymous death and was buried swiftly, without cere-mony, in an unmarked grave. But the second time, a few months later, when I was about a third of the way through, I suddenly became aware that people were actually laughing – and I assumed that I had forgotten to zip up after the nervous pre-talk pee. But no, they really were laughing at the jokes. The script was exactly the same so the difference had to be in the delivery. But where?

Part of the problem is the attempt to extract timing and rhythm and treat them as abstract qualities separate from the performer and performance, when in fact they are inextricably bound up with the persona, which is in turn inextricably bound up with the person, who is in turn inextricably bound up with a life history and the pressures of current circumstances. In a successful performance everything depends upon everything else, and the parts and the whole have been developed together, unconsciously, intuitively, in the course of many performances, so that not even the performer understands what is going on.

But whatever the mix of skills, and whatever the relation of persona to person, the crucial thing is that the performance, though obviously an act, must not seem like an act but be credible, authentic, making the performer sound like a genuine person (not necessarily admirable or likeable). By the mid-twentieth century the demand for authenticity had worked its way through to popular culture, when many popular singers took to writing their own songs and a new generation of stand-up comedians began writing their own material. This was the final break with the idea of the comedian as an actor performing a script, and must have caused a major rise in unemployment in the USA. Bob Hope used eighty-eight different writers throughout his career, with, in any one period, up to thirteen working full-time in his team.

Authentic performers of any kind expose the sham social self and inspire the failing inner self. There is no example more direct, more immediate or more reviving. Authentic performance is mouth-to-mouth resuscitation for the soul.

And comic authenticity is especially useful because it prevents the self-centredness of individualism from turning into self-importance or, even worse, self-righteousness: it reminds us forcefully that we are all inadequate, ignorant, conflicted, uncertain, neurotic, anxious, fearful and absurd. It is no accident that the characteristic shared by the best stand-up comics – Lenny Bruce, Richard Pryor, Bill Hicks, Joan Rivers, Billy Connolly – is an immediate and overwhelming impression of authenticity, of a real individual talking with candour. Richard Pryor, a strong contender for best of the best, advised comics to be 'truthful, always truthful. And funny will come.' There can be no doubting Pryor's own honesty. After setting himself on fire in the course of free-basing cocaine he made a comic routine out of it ('Thank you God for not burning my dick'). After suffering a heart attack he re-enacted it on stage, imagining his heart addressing him: 'Don't breathe,' it tells him, and then adds a taunt, 'Thinkin' 'bout dyin' now, aintcha?' To which he replies in a panicky, pleading, high-pitched voice, 'Yeah, I'm thinkin' 'bout dyin', I'm thinkin' 'bout dyin'.' The heart pauses for a moment, and then says in a sinisterly calm tone, 'You didn't think about it when you was eatin' all that *pork*.' After the heavily emphasised *pork* Pryor squeezes his fist to illustrate the revenge of the heart and drops to the floor to writhe in a silent scream.[6]

Pryor's performances have a manic energy that seems to be driven by some sort of desperation. Even watching a performance on film it is possible to feel the steam rising off him. It is this sense of an inner turmoil verging on breakdown that gives much of the best comedy its edge. Not only does this comedy acknowledge tension, the comedian actually *embodies* it, and connects at a visceral level with our own repressed terrors, which intensifies enormously the release in laughter. Freud argued that comedy is release of sexual repression but it's surely more general than that – a release from the fear of the many forms of inadequacy that haunt us, sexual, social, personal, physical (Pryor illustrates physical inadequacy by giving his body parts independent and dissenting voices, as in a routine about his boxing career when he has his arms say, 'I ain't got nothin' to do with it,' and his legs, 'Why the fuck should *I* fall?').

Comedy is based on insecurity, the feeling of being under threat, which explains why it is expressed in the apparently opposite forms of aggression and submission. This ambivalence goes all the way back to pre-human primate behaviour. Laughter is thought to have developed from the barking sounds used by primates in aggressive response to a threat, and the smile from the silent bared-teeth display used to express appeasing submission to a threat.

So comedians, notoriously insecure, respond with aggression or ingratiation, and attempt to unsettle, disturb, jolt and be feared, or to settle, soothe, reassure and be loved (the English comedian Alan Davies has divided his professional colleagues into self-harmers and golfers[7]).

When I was growing up, most professional comedians fell into the golfer category and I rejected them with contempt in favour of the street comedians who told dirty jokes and sneered at authority and pretension. For me, there are few things more inspiring than accurate mockery of the self-important and few things more dispiriting than the laughter of sycophants, which used to resound at the tables of kings and is ringing out again at this moment round the tables of conference rooms.

Lenny Bruce changed everything. His battles with authority began early when he joined the US Navy, became bored with it after the Second World War and got out by claiming to be a transvestite. The story, which may be apocryphal but is certainly a good one, is that, when asked by a naval psychiatrist if he really did enjoy wearing women's clothes, he replied, 'Sometimes' and when asked 'When was that?', like a true comic timed a pause and adopted a straight face for the answer, 'When they fit.' But even Bruce took a while to find the voice. His early material was the usual inoffensive humour that wanted to be liked, and it was only in the course of a long apprenticeship playing burlesque clubs that he developed the style which made him famous and introduced to comedy, sex, religion, racism and the full range of swear words.

The comedy of incongruity has continued to evolve and diversify into many sub-genres such as surreal fantasy, observational humour, political satire, found comedy, and imaginative insult (the speciality of Joan Rivers), and the personal styles of the comics are just as diverse. As well as the manic energy driven by turmoil, which can never find enough words, there is the opposite style of detached, deadpan drollery inspired by a sort of stupefied wonder, which appears to have difficulty in finding any words at all. Theorising about comedy is always dubious, contentious and incomplete, because it is in the very nature of comedy to reject tidy categorisation and exegesis. It is that which refuses to be contained or explained. It is also the form of communication most subject to personal taste. What makes a Mount Etna of one face will turn another into Mount Rushmore. So my dubious theorising is based on entirely subjective reactions.

Nevertheless, it seems safe to make the broad distinction between ingratiaters and transgressors, the big cheesy grins wanting to reassure in order to be loved, and the taboo breakers wanting to shock in order to be admired – Richard Pryor making jokes about the white fear of black people, Bill Hicks about wanting a cigarette moistened in Claudia Schiffer's vagina, Joan Rivers about the suicide of her husband (during her notorious 'Merry Widow Tour'), Frank Skinner about heterosexual sodomy and the stoning to death of Islamic women, and Billy Connolly about a hostage beheaded by Islamic fighters.

The constant factor is the need for an audience. Stand-up comedy is a group ritual, a tense interplay that is risky both for members of the audience, who may be singled out for ridicule, and the comedian, who may not get laughs and die, or be heckled and obliged to turn the tables by outwitting the heckler (failing in this is also death).

Anyone willing to risk stand-up must have a desperate hunger for attention, an insatiable neediness (depression and addiction are common among comics) – but to succeed must be able to conceal this completely. Successful stand-up requires insecurity for its inspiration but assurance for its delivery (Dudley Moore once said of his comedy partner Peter Cook that he had 'professional confidence combined with personal un-confidence'[8]). Any hint of fear will bring instant death. But the best comics also have a touch of craziness, a touch of the shaman. And there is an unbroken lineage – shaman, trickster, Lord of Saturn, Lord of Misrule, jester, Harlequin, clown and stand-up comedian. A shaman who persuaded the spirit world to grant him immortal life would have enjoyed continuous employment for several hundred thousand years and might be doing better than ever today, especially if he could swing a slot on a TV panel show, a few character roles in movies, a Perrier Award at the Edinburgh Festival, and a nationwide tour of town halls with a filmed show released as a DVD. And he would probably be considering a change of gender to capitalise on a new trend. One of the most welcome developments in comedy has been the appearance of many young female stand-ups.

But the financial rewards for comedy success are now so great and the venues so huge that the shaman is likely to turn into a rock star, a dot on a distant stage visible only on screens. This destroys any possibility of intimacy with the audience. Stand-up works best in a small venue (it could be that Dunbar's number applies here as well, with 150 as the upper limit for an intimate connection) and usually only young comics starting out play to such small audiences.[9]

It is instructive to observe two such comics in turn, both in their late twenties, both becoming established, both hailed as promising newcomers after success at the Edinburgh Festival, both described as not the usual stand-up, both performing sets of the same duration in the same venue (a 180-seat theatre) – the two similar in many ways, except for the crucial difference that to me one is funny and the other is not.

The first comic, John Kearns, is already on stage as the audience shuffle in, pacing nervously back and forth, making O-mouths and taking deep breaths, constantly pushing his spectacles back up his nose, like an unexceptional little man bracing himself for some terrible ordeal. I begin to feel anxious myself. Surely to God the venue could have given the poor guy somewhere to prepare in private – but of course this is part of the act, a postmodern effect, like the Pompidou Centre showing its pipes on the outside, or a po-mo novelist commenting on the action of a novel. Except that this is not just another exhausted cliché. By making the audience nervous he is establishing in advance his theme – anxiety, the modern affliction.

Now he has paused to gulp down a pint of water while staring in perplexity at the arrivals. And well might he be puzzled. The comedy audience is as difficult to define as the phenomenon itself. They are almost all young – or rather youngish, around thirty, no teenagers, but strangely nondescript, with none of the tacky glamour of the theatre-goers, or the clichéd shock effects of the music fans, the tattoos, piercings and fluorescent hair, or the brazen sexuality of the clubbers. Who are these people and why are they here?

Kearns begins with a quote from one of his reviews: 'If you've never been to a comedy gig this is probably not the place to start.' He allows the ambiguity of this to hang in the air. Is it criticism or praise? Then he dons a cheap joke-shop wig and protruding teeth and tells us that we are watching 'a man grappling with a joke that has gone a bit too far'. This sets the tone of ambivalence, uncertainty and fear. There are constant hesitations, long pauses, much brooding and frowning. Everything is inconclusive. Instead of building to punchlines, the anecdotes peter out in bewildered silence. He has the house lights dimmed to read from Mary Shelley's *Frankenstein*, does some comic business with a torch, begins to read a passage, pauses in perplexity and then throws the book away. The audience participation is equally half-hearted. He takes a man from the front row, places him on a stool, puts a white wig on his head, gives him a pint glass and fills it very slowly and carefully from a brandy bottle, then appears to forget about him. Eventually he sends him back to his seat and with terrific grimacing concentration carefully pours all the liquid back into the bottle using a plastic funnel, carefully tapping off the last drops and putting the bottle aside, muttering, 'This cost fifteen quid.'

Again and again he reminds us that he is doing this for a living, that he is actually *at work*, a notion he seems to find difficult to understand. He tells us that he is now self-employed and so has to keep receipts in his pockets – but in constantly checking them pulls out and loses banknotes. He now has nothing to do during the day and sits about in a dressing gown with its pockets full of crumpled tissues and pistachio nut shells. He's like that guy in the movie *The Diving Bell and the Butterfly*, who can move only one eyelid – except that *he* can move everything. But he is reassured by the eloquent authority of the intellectuals and politicians on the serious late-evening, topical TV shows like *Newsnight* and *Question Time*. Not that he would ever wish to debate with such titans – how, when he can never even understand them – but he would like to be a baby asleep in his cot and just have them look in to see that he is all right.

One especially effective trick is to keep looking at his wrist for the time – when in fact he is not wearing a watch.

After another long agonising silence, when he seems to have forgotten the audience entirely, he says to himself, 'You get driven to this' – and after a few moments adds, with a brief ironic gleam, 'It's not level one.' At other times he acknowledges the audience, '*You* bring your fifty per cent and *I* bring my fifty per cent.' Towards the end he tells us that when we go home and are asked by our loved ones what we saw and what made us laugh, we will have to admit, in confusion, 'Nothing.' He is right – it is more satisfying to laugh at something that does not seem to be funny, rather than at obvious jokes. This becomes a kind of deep, existential laughter, an inexplicable response to an inexplicable world. At the end of his act, as he fastidiously packs into a wooden case his wig, teeth and funnel, which he wipes dry with the white wig, Kearns asks in wonderment, 'Why the fuck are we here?'

This performance is a good example of the paradox that comedy is a confident version of diffidence. Without the dark undercurrent of insecurity, assurance can seem merely slick professionalism, empty entertainment.

The second comic puts on a terrifically energetic show with lots of running around, frequent, rapid costume changes and much darting back and forth to do, in different voices, all the characters in sketches that end in punchlines heavily underlined by loud sound effects. The audience participation is just as whole-hearted. He has us scrunching paper balls to throw at him, brings up four young women to rub his back with sun cream, and at the end of the set has the entire three front rows disco dancing on stage.

None of this made me laugh – and the difference between the two sets was summed up by their conclusions. Where Kearns asked, 'Why the fuck are we here?' the second guy begged us to follow him on Twitter and Instagram and stood at the door handing out business cards, which finally made his earlier satirising of business careerism a joke.

The two styles revealed another truth – that trying hard can be self-defeating (or, rather, *seeming* to try hard). The most effective artists in any medium are those who appear to be making no effort at all and give the impression that anyone could do it. Examples outside comedy include Picasso's childish paintings and the poems of William Carlos Williams, which look like a few simple, banal sentences randomly chopped into short lines. Couldn't anyone do that? The answer is, go ahead and try. That apparent effortlessness was the result of years of effort. You have to try really hard in order not to appear to be trying at all.

The energetic comic got laughs but it seemed to me that they were willed and dutiful, a good-natured reward for so much hard work. Whereas, with Kearns, the laughter was involuntary, surprised, even a little reluctant and guilty, because there did not seem to be anything funny in what he said and did. What was his secret? For one thing, the anxiety and fear of failure set up a tension that was aching for release. For another, his persona was a contemporary version of the character at the heart of modern comedy, the bemused everyman baffled and marginalised by complexity. In the course of his set he claimed to have worked in a series of dead-end, service-sector jobs, the perfect everyman career, and he caught the contemporary everyman mix of passivity, ignorance, boredom and respectful bewilderment at the glib assurance of public figures. Kearns may well have worked in service-sector jobs but is much cleverer than his persona. There was a even a touch of Beckett in his strangely resonant banalities, painful silences, inconclusive trailings off and pointless business executed with fanatical precision and care.

But after all the analysing of successful comics something mysterious remains, as it does with successful poets, a rare gift that eludes definition. Sometimes, and this is even more rare, the comic and poetic gifts come together, as they did in the poetry of John Berryman, who had many of the characteristics of the stand-up comedian, in particular a raging insecurity that made him an alcoholic and a womaniser, needy, intense, obsessive and driven, desperate to find his own voice, which he did only towards the end of his life in *The Dream Songs*:

> Life, friends, is boring. We must not say so.
> After all, the sky flashes, the great sea yearns,
> we ourselves flash and yearn,
> and moreover my mother told me as a boy
> (repeatedly) 'Ever to confess you're bored
> means you have no
> Inner Resources.'[10]

11

Fun Goes Sexual

Many varieties of fun were rediscovered in the seventies and if I had known that the decade would be so significant I would have paid more attention. To live it again I would even wear flares and a polyester shirt. In particular, this was when sex went mainstream and public. The maxim of the sixties, 'All you need is love', became in the seventies 'All you need is sex', which was even less true and even more exciting. After disco music, the identifying sound of the decade was the joyous slam of closet doors being flung open. The gay and lesbian sex scene exploded, and for heteros there were swingers' clubs, soft-porn films like *Emmanuelle*, sex manuals like *The Joy of Sex*, and sex toys like *The Non-Doctor Vibrator* in an astounding new retail outlet – the sex shop. Even stuffy academics got the hots when Michel Foucault published *The History of Sexuality* and opened up a virgin area of study to penetrate. Over the following decades scholars revealed how different cultures had circumscribed in various ways the diverse sex of pre-history, when polygamy, polyandry, group activity and homosexuality were all common.

In particular there has been mounting evidence, from several different disciplines, to suggest that heterosexual monogamy is not

Nature's Way. Zoologists have claimed that, of the more than 30 million species on the planet, the only definite sexual monogamists are the Kirk's dik-dik (an African antelope), the convict cichlid (a Central American fish), the shingle-backed skink (an Australian reptile), the scrub jay in Florida, the albatross in the Southern Ocean and the jackdaw in Europe.[1] There are probably others but a few examples per continent are scarcely enough to establish faithfulness as natural (and the theory is that the faithful creatures have not chosen monogamy but, for various reasons, had it forced upon them by circumstances).[2] Primatologists have revealed that chimpanzees and bonobos, the two primates closest to humans in terms of DNA, both live in groups and practise frequent multimale-multi-female mating, though the bonobos complement this with regular girl-on-girl and boy-on-boy action, especially vulva rubbing and penis fencing. And their hetero foreplay includes massage, oral sex, hugging and kissing, often with deep tongue penetration. These sophisticated lovers do not go ape but *go for French*. Factor in the ability to laugh, dance, play Blind Man's Buff, and beat out a funky rhythm on drums, and it is obvious that the bonobo discovered fun long before *Homo sapiens*.[3]

And anthropologists believe that the egalitarianism of the hunter-gatherer groups also extended to sex, a theory supported by evidence from surviving premodern groups.[4] What changed all this was the development of agriculture. In parallel with the replacement of social equality by hierarchy, sexual equality was replaced by patriarchy. There was a drastic reduction in the status of women, who became the property of men rather than their partners, and a corresponding rise in male possessiveness and jealousy, two developments that were to warp sexual relations for thousands of years.

This combination of social hierarchy and male domination was the central feature of life in Greece and Rome, where male citizens were entitled to enjoy at will wives, concubines, prostitutes, boys, and foreigners and slaves of both sexes. The first interesting thing is that there was little distinction between sex with either gender. The terms heterosexuality, homosexuality and bisexuality, indeed the term sexuality itself, were all inventions of the nineteenth century, products of the modern tendency to classify, categorise and specialise. There were no classical equivalents for these because they would have had no meaning. Sexual behaviour did not define personal identity, another modern concept, but was merely the satisfaction of appetite, like eating, with a taste for boys no more significant than preferring lamb to beef. And, as with food, the issue was not so much what was on the menu as the dangers of overindulgence in dining.

The second interesting thing is that the crucial factor in sex was not gender or status but physical position – who was active and who passive – with the male citizen required to be on top in every sense. What shocked Romans most about Nero was not that he slept with his mother, dressed in animal skins to rape men and women tied to stakes, or staged a public wedding to a boy called Sporus dressed as a bride, but that he publicly acknowledged being penetrated by a freedman called Doryphorus and not only staged another wedding to Doryphorus with himself as the bride, but left no doubt of its outcome by imitating the cries of a virgin being raped. The crucial act for the man was penetration, with no concern for the pleasure of the penetrated. In Greece cunnilingus was considered especially demeaning and a public figure could be seriously discredited by an accusation of going down on a woman.

For a male citizen, to be passive was to behave like a female and forfeit dominant status. However, the problem with domination is that it always suspects the dominated of secret deviance, and since constraint and surveillance can rarely be total, suspicion grows and can easily develop into paranoid fear. This encourages an even more extreme domination, which only increases the suspicion and fear. If the dominance is cultural rather than merely personal, the result is a general suspicion of the dominated and, in the case of male sexual domination of women, a general belief that women are cunning, deceitful and sexually voracious.

The vast majority of classical writings were by men, so it's impossible to know what women believed, thought, felt or did with each other in private, though many scholars suspect that the women-only festivals included girl-on-girl fun. However, there is plenty of evidence of male paranoia, especially from poets. Catullus and Propertius constantly suspected women of duplicity, and Catullus raged at the imagined multiple infidelities of his girlfriend, Lesbia:

> I send Lesbia this valediction,
>   succinctly discourteous:
> live with your three hundred lovers,
> open your legs to them all (simultaneously)
> lovelessly dragging the guts out of each of them
>   each time you do it,
> blind to the love that I had for you
> once, and that you, tart, wantonly crushed
> as the passing plough-blade slashes the flower
>   at the field's edge.[5]

So the idea that only hetero monogamy is natural has as little support from the evidence of the classical period as it does from the study of hunter-gatherers or the observation of animal behaviour, and was largely the product of the Judaeo-Christian tradition. The Jewish religion restricted sex to the marital bed for the purpose of procreation and proclaimed this the 'natural' human way. In fact, procreational sex is more animal than human, while recreational sex is more human than animal. But at least the Jewish husband and wife were allowed to enjoy each other. Christianity made even this restricted sex a sin, and to add to the fun, intensified the view of women as treacherous and deceitful with the doctrine that Eve's transgression infected the entire human race with an original sin that can never be effaced. Celibacy was the new ideal and the Virgin Mary the new role model for women who were henceforth either Madonnas or whores, a simple form of classification that has persisted in the Christian world. In *Saturday Night Fever* John Travolta tells a female dancing partner, 'You can be a nice girl or a cunt but not both.'

At the beginning of the second millennium CE when Hindu temples were being decorated with sculptures of women washing their hair, putting on make-up, playing games, dancing and participating in penetrative and oral group sex, Christian artists were filling the churches with portraits of a sorrowful Virgin looking down from her immaculate detachment on a contaminated world.

Of course, most ordinary people ignored the Church teaching on sex. It was even common for priests to live openly with concubines and have children by them, and clerical marriage was not officially prohibited until 1123. The modern notion of European sex in the twelfth and thirteenth centuries is of courtly love, with

troubadours singing songs of eternal devotion to chaste high-born
ladies, but the village equivalent of the troubadours in the castles
were the jongleurs in the taverns, comic entertainers whose equivalent of the romantic ballads were the folk tales known as *fabliaux*.
These were wildly exaggerated yarns of sensual, and usually sexual,
abundance and excess, with the voracity of women a constant
theme. In one *fabliau* St Martin appears to a hungry peasant and
his wife and offers four wishes. The peasant is about to request
food when his sexually frustrated wife wishes that her husband has
cocks all over his body, 'and let not one be soft or limp, but stiffer
than an iron bar'.[6] St Martin obliges and cocks sprout all over the
husband, who then wishes for cunts to appear all over his wife,
which the saint also arranges, thoughtfully adding variety with
'hairless cunts, cunts piled and plushy'.[7] However, the couple have
such difficulty in manipulating multiple sex organs that they wish
all of them away, leaving no genitals at all, so that the final wish is
for the restoration of the faulty original pair.

Another common theme was the autonomy of the genitals,
portrayed as independent and insatiable creatures taking over their
hosts, with the genitals of older women, and especially widows,
uncontrollably demanding. Another *fabliau* tells of a widow who
has just lost her husband and is immediately overcome by desire,
as 'a sweet sensation pricks her heart and lifts up her spirit, and
arouses in the bearded counsellor under her skirts an appetite for
meat, neither peacock nor crane, but that dangling sausage for
which so many are eager'.[8] These tales influenced both Chaucer
and Rabelais, who tells us that in women, 'nature hath posited in
a privy, secret and intestine place ... a sort of member, by some
not impertinently treated as an animal', which causes 'certain

humours, so saltish, brackish, clammy, sharp, nipping, tearing, prickling, and most eagerly tickling, that ... their whole body is shaken and ebrangled, their senses totally ravished and transported, the operations of their judgement and understanding utterly confounded'. Book Three of *Gargantua and Pantagruel* is largely concerned with Panurge's desire to be married but fear of being cuckolded. He consults a series of sages, sibyls, soothsayers, poets and philosophers, and even an astrologer, but is not reassured to discover that while this learned man was discussing 'celestial and transcendent matters' with the king, 'the court lacqueys were screwing his wife to their hearts' content on the stairs between the doors'. Nor does the astrologer himself assuage his fears: 'In a basin of water I'll show you your future wife being rogered by two rustics.' Panurge, however, does not care to witness this dramatic feat of divination: 'When you poke your nose up my arse,' he tells the clairvoyant, 'don't forget to take off your spectacles.'[9]

However, the theme of the voracious widow was most fully developed by Chaucer in *The Wife of Bath's Tale*. The monologue of this five-times-married wife ('that's to say in church, not counting other loves') is a rare literary example of an older woman expressing enjoyment of sex in startlingly uninhibited language ('You'll have cunt enough and plenty, every night').[10] There is nothing like it in literature until Molly Bloom's monologue in *Ulysses*. But it is not just a woman talking dirty, enjoyable though this is. It is also a remarkably sophisticated analysis of the tribulations and rewards of marriage, with the wife describing wedlock as a perpetual power struggle but arguing that the relationship *depends* on this struggle. A marriage succeeds through a tension between partners and fails if one gains final dominance. But the Law and the Church grant the husband brute power so the wife has to resort to devious tactics. The Wife cheerfully admits to behaving unreasonably in order to resist domination and maintain the power balance ('God has granted women / Three things by nature: lies, and tears, and spinning'). One of her tactics is the pre-emptive strike ('I'd scold them even when I was at fault / For otherwise I'd often have been dished').

Her message is that the wife will submit only if the husband does not force her to submit, and grant allegiance only if he permits her to be free. Marriage is complex and demanding but satisfying for this very reason, and despite the struggles and sorrows she is keen to get back into it. 'Blessed be God that I have married five! Here's to the sixth whenever he turns up.' Not that she intends to mope during the wait. 'Age, alas, that cankers everything' may have destroyed her youthful beauty, 'But all the same I mean to have my fun.'

Chaucer is remarkably similar in tone to Rabelais. No more a cheerful naïf than Rabelais was a coarse buffoon, Chaucer had the same keen observation and sharp wit, the same qualities of generosity and tolerance, and the same corresponding lack of anger, superiority and reforming zeal. Take life as you find it, both seem to advise, and make what you can of what you find. So both also indiscriminately mixed high and low and happily acknowledged bodily functions and sex.[11]

This generous, comic spirit of the jongleurs, Chaucer and Rabelais was crushed by the Church as it gained increasing control of social and personal life by means of the surveillance of the Inquisition and its sanctions of torture and burning at the stake.[12]

The fear of sex intensified into hysteria with the belief in succubi and incubi, nocturnal demons who could have sex with men and women as they slept. A cunning succubus would make a sleeping man ejaculate, then cunningly turn into an incubus to deposit the semen in a sleeping woman, quite a rewarding job despite the unsocial hours. And the fear of women developed into witch hunts, which condemned to the stake a multitude of women for a multitude of reasons, including possession of a prominent clitoris ('the devil's teat'). Scholars estimate that in the 300 years of witch mania in Europe somewhere between 40,000 and 100,000 people were executed, with the vast majority women and the vast majority of these from the lower social classes. Assertive or openly sexual women were especially singled out, as were widows, so that if the Wife of Bath had been born a little later she would probably have gone to the stake instead of surviving five husbands and going in search of a sixth.

After the Reformation, witch hunting intensified and all popular public entertainment – carnival, ribald comic performances, dancing and sexual licence – was discouraged or suppressed. Now Dionysus completed his transformation – from the revered Greek god of revelry to the semi-human Roman satyr, eventually a joke figure, and then in the medieval period becoming the horned and hoofed manifestation of the arch-fiend Satan. In Catholic countries nightmarish sightings of the cloven hoof have been as frequent as visions of the Virgin Mary. Even in the swinging sixties there were reports of handsome strangers turning up in Irish dance halls and attempting to seduce the local colleens, but these canny girls always spotted, in the nick of time, the distinctive hoof.

There was still plenty of open fun for aristocrats and those at court, who could resist clerical pressure, and no doubt also for many others if they had the sense to keep it quiet. Comedy and dancing soon returned, but overt acknowledgement of sexual pleasure remained forbidden and became the central taboo of the emerging bourgeoisie keen to distinguish themselves from the common herd. Where the medieval response to transgression had been burning at the stake, the new bourgeois, shuddering at the thought of such frightful barbarity, developed the novel response of pretending that the transgression did not exist. By the nineteenth century Western attitudes to female sexuality had undergone an astounding reversal, from the extreme of many believing that female libido was universal, rampant and insatiable, to the opposite extreme of many believing that there was virtually no such thing. In 1875 Lord Acton declared that 'The majority of women, happily for them and for society, are not very much troubled with sexual feelings of any kind.'[13] This was not just the view of Victorian England. In his influential *Psychopathia Sexualis* of 1886 the German sexologist Richard von Krafft-Ebing wrote that if a woman 'is normally developed mentally and well-bred, her sexual desire is small. If this were not so, the whole world would become a brothel and marriage and a family impossible.'[14]

As a consequence, many women were diagnosed with the new affliction of 'hysteria', which, as the historian Rachel Maines has pointed out, was a condition with symptoms remarkably similar to those of sexual frustration, i.e. 'anxiety, sleeplessness, irritability, nervousness, erotic fantasy, sensations of heaviness in the abdomen, lower pelvic edema, and vaginal lubrication'.[15] The treatment was 'vulvular massage', which produced a 'nervous paroxysm' and gave the sufferer temporary relief. Apparently male physicians disliked massaging with their fingers and invented the vibrator to do the job (which explains something that always puzzled me – why that first seventies vibrator was known as The Non-Doctor). In the USA this new medical instrument was made available for home use in 1902 and by 1917 American homes had more vibrators than toasters. It's a crying shame that no one seems to have considered cunnilingus, which would surely have been the most effective form of treatment, though defending this might have required an even more nimble tongue. And in the twenties women were denied even the consolation of the vibrator when it became a star of the first porn movies. Stripped of its medical disguise, it quickly disappeared from homes, not to re-emerge, buzzing with renewed energy, until the seventies.

The denial of female libido was common right up to the mid-twentieth century and still persists in the sociobiological theory that women have sex just for procreation or to keep their men happy. What changed everything was the sexual explosion of the sixties, which surprised most people at the time, though in retrospect it is possible to see it as inevitable. Even in the nineteenth century men found a way of writing about sex by inventing the new title of 'sexologist' and claiming the dispassionate interest of science.[16] Then, in the twentieth century, literary writers like Joyce and Lawrence flouted the taboos and the censorship laws, and eventually the UK publication of *Lady Chatterley's Lover* coincided neatly with the birth of rock music that took over the promotion of sexual freedom, a conjunction noted by Philip Larkin in *Annus Mirabilis*:

Sexual intercourse began
In nineteen sixty-three
(Which was rather late for me) –
Between the end of the *Chatterley* ban
And the Beatles' first LP.[17]

One problem with the sixties was the combination of wildly extravagant aspiration with a total ignorance of ways to implement change. It was all just sure to happen in a revolution that would bring a sexual utopia and release everyone from drudgery into an idyll of peace and love. But while the political half of the dream faded in the seventies, the sexual half flourished, and the most astounding of all the new sexual developments were two books which revealed that women not only fantasised about sex but actively sought it and were prepared to acknowledge this in writing. Erica Jong's novel *Fear of Flying* was an autobiographical account of a married American woman who not only fantasised about anonymous quickies with strangers on trains, and was not only seeking such encounters round Europe, but defined her sexual holy grail as 'the zipless fuck'. This ideal experience was zipless '*not* because European men have button-flies rather than zipper-flies, and not because the participants are so devastatingly attractive, but because the incident has all the swift compression of a dream and is seemingly free of all remorse and guilt; … because there is no rationalising; because there is no talk at *all*. The zipless fuck is absolutely pure.'[18] And in case anyone believed Jong to be a unique aberration, Nancy Friday's non-fiction *My Secret Garden: Women's Sexual Fantasies* revealed that women fantasised not just about anonymous sex with strangers but sex with dogs, donkeys and even a black octopus with many adroit tentacles. Friday claimed that women's fantasies were wilder and stranger because of long repression, but the encouraging feature of her survey was the revelation that many of the female fantasies were the familiar male favourites – sex with strangers, authority figures, other races, and group sex, bondage, spanking and so on.

These two books appeared in the same year, making this a second *Annus Mirabilis*:

> Female Sexuality was freed
> In nineteen seventy-three
> (Which was just in time for me)
> With Erica's zipless fuck crusade
> And Nancy's Secret Fantasies.

John Updike compared Jong to Chaucer ('the Wife of Bath, were she young and gorgeous, neurotic and Jewish, urban and contemporary, might have written like this'[19]) and could also have mentioned Rabelais because the dirty talk is not confined to sex. The narrator complains about a former lover leaving shit stripes on her sheets and digresses into a detailed analysis of the different ways European toilets dispose of shit, concluding that German toilets are the worst because there is no water before flushing and the shit falls first on a porcelain platform causing the 'strongest shit smell of any toilets anywhere'.

Shit-stained sex from a woman naturally provoked uproar, as did Updike's revelation in *Couples* that group sex was no longer confined to hippy communes but had spread to the supposedly conservative middle classes in the suburbs and satellite towns.

Where Jong was entirely a sixties child of Dionysus, obsessed with pleasure seeking, Updike was more complex because he not only combined Apollo and Dionysus but extreme versions of both. He supported the Vietnam War and was a practising Christian, a member of the First Congregational Church, serving on church committees and as an usher during services, and bringing his children to Sunday school. Yet, as his biography reveals, and most readers suspected, the adultery and group sex in his novels were based on his own experience.

The other crucial difference between the two writers was that Jong's narrator was an expressive individualist, seeking to find her true self through sex and to express this self by writing about the experience. She was not much interested in her partners, never mind community, whereas Updike valued the group experience as much as if not more than the sex. It's odd that Updike, who made the apparently backward step of moving from New York to Ipswich, a small New England dormitory town for commuters to Boston, now looks more ahead of his time than Jong travelling the cities of Europe in search of the zipless fuck. Updike's life in Ipswich was the complete group fun package now sought by so many, with he and his wife involved in music, singing, dancing, games, sports, dressing up and, of course, sex. As he described this experience in an essay:

> There was a surge of belonging – we joined committees and societies, belonged to a recorder group and a poker group, played volleyball and touch football in season, read plays aloud, and went Greek dancing and gave dinner parties and attended clambakes and concerts and costume balls, all within

a rather narrow society, so that everything resonated ... As a group, we had lovely times being young adults in Ipswich, while raising our children more or less absent-mindedly ... .[20]

In the same piece Updike confirms Ethan Watters's insight on urban tribes by identifying gossip as the group's binding agent: 'under the tireless supervision of gossip all misfortunes were compared, and confessed, and revealed as relative. Egoistic dread faded within the shared life.' And he compares the sense of belonging to that of the earliest communities. 'An illusion of eternal comfort reposes in clubbiness – an assurance that members of tribes and villages have extended to one another for millennia.'

The Ipswich group even conformed to Dunbar's theory, with a membership of around twelve couples and a core of around six, and within this Updike played the standard group role of clown. As one of the group members explained to Updike's biographer, 'If he's not being paid enough attention, he'll fall off the couch.'[21] The autobiographical *Couples* reveals that the suburban tribe of young couples with their pitchers of martinis is the precursor of the urban tribes of young singletons with their lines of coke, but with the crucial difference of marriage and adultery, which make sexual tension the explosive energising feature and add extra spice to the gossip. In the *Couples* group most covet the spouses of others and adulteries are legion. The situation teeters on the verge of overt swapping, and Updike is insightful on why this never quite happens. When two couples are involved in adultery with each other and the husbands suggest dropping the tiresome pretence of secrecy, one of the wives is outraged and breaks off all relations. She was happy with the two 'secret' affairs, and indeed initiated her own, but regards making the adultery open as 'corrupt'.

Other real-life couples took the inevitable next step. In the early seventies group sex evolved rapidly from informal swapping parties in private homes to highly organised activity in specialised clubs, often with luxurious and extensive premises (even ranch-style resorts of many acres), [22] rigorous member screening (couples where the woman seemed coerced were rejected), codes of conduct (no drug use, all contact strictly consensual, no always meaning no) and affiliation to overseeing, regulatory associations. One of the visionary entrepreneurs was Robert McGinley, a former aerospace engineer, who attracted middle-class professionals with a country club setup that included interviews for membership and access to a luxurious clubhouse with a bar, dining room, dance floor, swimming pool, hot tubs, and most reassuring of all, a fireplace, which McGinley would stand before to host warm-up discussions.

McGinley's Club WideWorld, founded in California in 1969, was an immediate success – but even more important than a congenial ambience was congenial language, and his greatest stroke of genius was to replace, in 1972, the hated terms 'swinging' and 'swingers' with the much more attractive 'lifestyle' and 'playcouples'. Another astute move was to understand the new need for costuming and meet this with theme nights and Erotic Masquerade Balls. But the most important factor was that, as well as imposing a code of conduct, the clubs allowed degrees of involvement. Sexual activity could range from voyeurism to soft swinging (nudity with limited contact), side-by-side (no-exchange sex beside other couples), open swinging (partners exchange but remain in the same room), closed swinging (partner exchange in separate rooms) and interpersonal swinging (threesomes). The only activity mostly lacking was the one most imagined by non-swingers – the orgy. The sex was selective, usually involving small groups of three or four, and was carefully negotiated. In fact, even in the premodern festivals of sexual licence, selective coupling was more common than an indiscriminate everybody-with-everybody. And while ancient Rome is as famous for orgies as for gladiators, historians have pointed out that there is surprisingly little evidence of wild mass Roman sex, though this has not diminished the popularity of toga parties in lifestyle clubs.

The McGinley model was immediately and widely copied, first round the USA and then round the world and, after a dip in the eighties due to AIDS, has continued to grow in popularity, especially since wide availability of the Internet. There are no figures available for swinging but what convinced me of its continuing expansion was a news article with the astounding headline, 'Swingers Groups in Ireland Are Growing at a Massive Rate'.[23] If even the Irish are increasingly into it then everyone else must be too.

Yet despite the growing popularity of swinging, there remains a stigma. Most of the forms of sexuality once considered deviant – homosexuality, lesbianism, transvestism, sado-masochism – are now widely regarded as normal, and many of those who practise these forms wish to be free of secrecy and to have their sexuality publicly accepted. But few swingers are prepared to come out of the closet, however crowded this particular closet has become, and however independent, intelligent and articulate its many occupants.

It's typical of the hypocrisy surrounding sex that adultery, with its need for deception and lies and frequent humiliation of the deceived spouse, seems still to be more socially acceptable than swinging, which attempts to satisfy the same urges but in an open, honest way. The social response to adultery is often a knowing sigh or a knowing joke, whereas swinging often inspires revulsion (as in the reaction of the wife in *Couples* who had no problem with deceiving her husband but regarded open exchange as corrupt). This antipathy must be based on deep, primal fears – possibly of the group as a potentially violent raping gang, or of family life and the social order breaking down if monogamy is not upheld, publicly at least, or of female sexuality becoming rampant if not controlled. Or it could be that adultery does not challenge the belief in romantic love whereas the joint willingness of couples to share seems to banish romance. There may also be an element of snobbery in the distaste for swingers, who are mostly older people with bodies that do not conform to the sexual ideal. Many find it disgusting that such people should openly enjoy sex in public.

It may be that, whereas free love communes break down because they have no structure, rules or ritual, swinging in clubs is more successful because it is a group ritual enacted at ritualised times in a ritualised setting and firmly regulated by rules and conventions (which makes it similar to the sexual licence permitted by early communities in festivals). It takes place between initiates in a special place that is not only separate from the community but often unknown to it, and as in many rituals (for instance initiation ceremonies), it first separates and then brings people back together in an enhanced sense of belonging. It also matches the three stages of the quest myth – leaving the familiar environment, venturing forth into a dangerous unknown to encounter strange, alarming creatures, and then returning to the familiar environment enriched.

For swingers, the three stages are preparation, participation and reunion. In the preparation stage spouses are especially attentive and discuss anxieties about bestowing each other on partners who may be more experienced, more attractive, and more generously endowed; in the participation stage each ensures that all transactions (usually exchange with another couple) are sanctioned by the spouse; and in the reunion stage there is a reaffirming of affection and exchange of esoteric knowledge (her fanny farts, his cock is bent). Often the problem is not sex with another but a display of affection. Hugging may be more of a threat than fucking, and post-sex tenderness is especially challenging, as when a husband raged at his wife, 'Why did you suck his dick *after* he came?'[24]

Observers of swinging have also noticed common patterns of behaviour. As with other forms of fun, many value the group experience as much as the actual activity. And while women tend to be initially reluctant, and have to be persuaded by their men, they often become as enthusiastic, if not more so, and often conduct the negotiations. They are more rigid in their expressed opinions but more fluid in their sexual behaviour. Lesbian activity is common whereas homosexual contact is rare, even taboo. The anthropologist Katherine Frank noted a range of female self-definitions as 'bisexual, bisensual, bicurious, bicomfortable, biplayful, or even bi-when-drinking-tequila'.[25] This fits with what Nancy Friday found in her surveys – lesbianism was common in the fantasies of heterosexual women but there was no male equivalent in the fantasises of heterosexual men. And a surprising number of women fantasised about having an audience for sex, while as many men fantasised about being the audience. It seems that women like to be watched and men like to watch.

Another common phenomenon is hot-wife syndrome, where husbands enjoy seeing their wives have sex with other men. And while swinging can go disastrously wrong for couples, it can also enhance the relationship. The ambivalence and anxiety, and the revelation of the spouse as attractive to others, create an over-powering urge to reconnect and a need for the couple to stop the car on the way home to jump on each other. Swinging, with its occasional dash of transgression, renews the habitual, whereas a constant pursuit of transgression becomes the habitual and suffers the deadening effect of habituation.

These behaviours may have a physical basis. When the biolo-gists Robin Baker and Mark Bellis investigated bodily responses to multiple mating (several men having sex with the same woman over a short period), they produced surprising conclusions for both genders (though these are as fiercely disputed as all other theories of sexual behaviour).[26] It had always been assumed that the average 200 million sperm cells in male ejaculate were all identical and identically motivated, as undifferentiated as the hordes of baddies in a blockbuster action movie – but according to Baker and Bellis less than 1 per cent of the cells are programmed to fertilise an egg, with the rest dedicated to blocking or killing the cells of rival lovers. Even more surprising, when a man is aware, or suspects, that his female partner has recently had a rival lover, he unconsciously drives deeper and ejaculates three times as much, 600 million cells, so the ejaculation is three times more delirious than usual, which would explain the benefit of watching a hot wife. However, producing all the extra cells requires extra energy so that the lover who shoots like a lion is left weak as a kitten. Many biologists also believe that even the physical presence of rivals stimulates extra sperm production. However, sperm competition is difficult to investigate as it would involve taking sperm samples at a swing club or establishing a swing club in a lab, but certainly bucktooth parrotfish shoot more sperm when mating in groups. It seems that male jealousy can be expressed either as rage or ecstasy, a desire to murder the sexual rival or merely to murder his sperm, and the second option is safer and much more fun. The obvious lesson: shoot a load not a man.

The female equivalent of Sperm Competition (SC) is Cryptic Female Choice (CFC), a wonderful phrase for a range of techniques to facilitate the passage of sperm from some males but to expel, hinder or kill that of others. Animals have developed an impressive variety of techniques for differentiating or expelling, with even the most apparently limited showing great sophistication. Female chickens and turkeys actually store sperm from different copulations in separate containers and decide later which to use, while female house mice can adapt their ova, making them easier to fertilise in monogamous situations and more resistant in a polyandrous environment.[27] In humans, CFC is even more difficult to study than SC because it happens internally, has complex physiology and chemistry and would be invasive to investigate, but it seems that the human sperm journey is not just a sprint through a passive conduit but more like hurdling a series of obstacles while under attack by chemical weapons – and it is thought that the occurrence and timing of the female orgasm is crucial. When the woman has an orgasm along with, or just after, the man, both physiological and chemical responses help his sperm on its way. So men seeking children should understand that it may not be enough to shoot a load and fall asleep. There may even be some fantastically complex CFC process, whereby the body sends a message to the chemical warfare division in the uterus: 'Can you *believe this*? The bastard is *snoring*. Blitz his come.'

The theory is that both SC and CFC evolved in an arms race to deal with female polyandry, one woman mating with several men, a common practice to increase the possibility of procreation, with SC a way of defeating male rivals and CFC a way of selecting from multiple inputs. Anthropology supports this with evidence that polyandry was indeed common in early communities, with some, for instance the Matis of north-west Brazil and the Lusi of Papua New Guinea, actually believing that conception is cumulative, requiring the semen of many men, and that a woman who has had a mix of variously talented contributors has the best chance of producing a multi-talented child. And studies of contemporary women who practise polyandry show that they are more likely to double mate in the period when conception is most likely.

These patterns are also evident in dogging, the British contribution to group sex, a combination of exhibitionism and voyeurism where couples have sex in car parks or woodland and encourage others to watch and sometimes join in. Doggers are even more secretive than swingers but a documentary on the subject, featuring interviews with doggers and film of their activity, reveals that, while this is a different form of group sex performed by a different class of people (all those interviewed were working class) in a different environment and on a different continent from the American swingers, the behaviours are similar in many ways.[28] Although the numerous voyeurs were all men there was no homosexual activity, whereas a husband brought his wife and her female friend into the woods and encouraged them to 'play'. Other husbands enjoyed watching their wives have sex with the voyeurs ('I like to think that my wife is desirable'), while the wives appreciated the attention ('I like them to like what they're looking at'). And it made couples more attractive and exciting to each other ('It's like foreplay. I enjoy it but the best thing is coming home').

Dogging, the fish and chips of sexual cuisine, is also evidence of the increasing diversification of group sex. And while the large group is still often regarded as deviant, though increasingly popular, the threesome is becoming more acceptable, with websites and apps for arranging compatible trios, either couples plus a 'guest star' or three singletons, giving new meaning to the old conundrum known as 'the three-body problem', but promising, if the mechanics can be satisfactorily arranged, what William Blake described as 'Threefold each in the other clos'd, – O what a pleasant trembling fear'.[29] These websites and apps have no restrictions on gender or sexual orientation, and MMF is common as well as FFM, which suggests that the taboo on homosexual contact between heterosexual men may finally be weakening. There is further evidence for this in surveys revealing that, in marked contrast to older generations, a majority in the 18–24 age group (74 per cent in one survey)[30] believe that sexuality is fluid rather than fixed and almost half (49 per cent) do not classify themselves as entirely straight or gay but by the increasingly popular new term 'polyamorous'. In yet another return to the factory settings, sexual fluidity is making a comeback after several millennia of banishment.

Fun in general is also becoming more fluid, with the different varieties tending to merge. Many clubs now offer facilities and special events to cater for the growing interest in BDSM, cross-dressing and transvestism, and try to attract younger customers with DJs, techno music and a more hip environment. For instance, post-communist Berlin has reclaimed its brand as the capital of decadence, and replaced country-house opulence with the post-apocalypse chic of dark clubs in decommissioned Soviet power stations and disused Nazi bunkers and air-raid shelters. Other clubs retain the luxury but vary the fun. A new London venue advertises not its sexual facilities, which are taken for granted, but four street-food outlets and two 9-hole crazy golf courses.

But the clubs face increasing competition from one-off events, where organisers avoid the overheads of buying and maintaining property, and the familiarity of a single location. The gay scene has Internet-organised 'chill-out parties', where gay men meet in private apartments and houses for group sex, and often take drugs to keep going but not coming for days on end. The heterosexual equivalent seems to require more elaborate staging (but less stamina), with single nights in hired mansions, villas and chateaux, for events that often have fancy-dress themes (Mythological, Roman and Venetian are common favourites), and can include organised role play.

Seeking enlightenment on this interesting conjunction of group sex and costuming, I talk to an adult fancy-dress impresario in an outer London suburb that would seem the very picture of sedate, semi-detached conservatism, had not John Updike shown that these apparently conventional places seethe with transgressive desire. Peter Birch (his stage name) fits right in and could pass for a solicitor or a GP (which means that from now on I will see such professionals in a different light). As with Updike, Peter's group sex began when he and his wife partied with other couples, but it soon went beyond Updike into 'playing'. From there they progressed to the fetish scene, which, in the eighties was beginning to boom, with many new BDSM clubs opening.

'Why do so many want to role play nowadays?'

'It's certainly a lot more popular.' He pauses to ponder. 'People want to be taken to the hidden academy, where the everyday roles and rules no longer apply, and you can discover a different self.'

'But what I've never understood is why so many want to be *submissive*. In a competitive age where everyone seems to want to *dominate*.'

'That's precisely the *reason*. Many subs are highly successful people but they want to escape the pressure and the public façade, the act ... and above all to surrender responsibility.'

'And the doms?'

'Male doms tend to be skilled manual ... mechanics, electricians, engineers ... often independent, owning their own businesses. Lots of them called Dave, for some reason. Sir Guy Masterly was actually the garage owner Dave.' A laugh and a pause to remember Dave playing Sir Guy. 'Difficult to generalise though. Everyone has different and complex motivations ... that they probably couldn't even explain themselves. And most doms and subs will switch ... I'd say about ninety per cent will switch.' This seems to suggest that the roleplaying, the acting, is more important than the role. 'But not in the USA, oddly enough. There's little acceptance of switching ... everyone's expected to stick to a role. Here it's very flexible and playful but over there it's formal and serious. Totally ritualised. The gay leather scene is full of arbitrary rules ... for instance you must never touch the peak of anyone's cap.' So the land of the free is the land of constraint and those who most wish to give the impression of breaking rules also most wish to set binding new rules. As so often, the escape replicates what it is trying to flee. 'There was this Mistress in Club Submission ... gorgeous woman, acted the role to perfection ... black leather catsuit, ferocious, all the men wanted her to be their dom ... but she told me that what *she* really wanted was to be spanked.'

In the interests of discretion we are talking in a pub garden, and alone in it, but I cannot escape a sense of hidden eavesdroppers. Someone has been working for a suspiciously long time near the window of the bar kitchen. On the other side, the shrubbery seems to be alive with prurient interest. But Peter is uninhibited, only beginning to get into his stride. He has been drinking cider for thirst and is now ready for a glass of wine, grimacing at the prospect of Chilean Merlot, but giving it the full sniffing, swirling and pouting treatment.

'People love this sort of thing. Even the great clarets taste Chilean now. Even a classic Bordeaux like Pontet-Canet Pauillac fourth growth.'

After a sigh at the vulgarity of popular taste, he resumes. 'But the BDSM club scene got very predictable. I had a stall in Torture Garden and I remember sitting behind it looking at the whole thing and feeling really jaded.'

'What were you selling?'

'Bridles and harnesses.' There is a pause for reminiscence. 'Good-quality leather products. Many still in use.' He laughs. 'So this man commissioned me to make him a saddle. Which I did and was rather proud of ... stirrups and everything. But it turned out that he wanted a saddle he could wear *standing up* ... more like a chair. Refused to pay and left me with this thing. Took it home and had fun with it at parties . . . in time trials. Then it came to me, the idea for the Pony Club. Doms driving carriages pulled by subs in harness and bridle. We'd meet once a month somewhere, always different. For fun, free, but invitation only. And only couples, some gay and lesbian, no single males.'

As often happens, I have so many questions I hardly know where to start. 'Where could you do this?'

'Forestry Commission roads away from beauty spots. Always deserted at weekends.'

'Why go to such trouble?'

'I'm an organiser!' Peter cries. 'I love putting events together, finding a location, selecting the people, getting them all to mesh. So satisfying just to stand back and see it work.' Having always hated organising as a tedious chore, I suddenly see it as creative, like piecing together a novel – setting, characters, interaction.

'But carriages are not cheap. Who paid for it all?'

'*Eurotrash*,' Peter explains happily. 'The TV show. They filmed a few of the meets and were great. Funny thing – the people despised as scum of the earth . . . *Eurotrash* and the *Sun* . . . treated us really well, proper contracts and good money, whereas the people supposedly with high standards, like the BBC, treated us like dirt. They seem to believe that people who have sexual fun are a threat, potential rapists and/or paedophiles, ready to jump on anyone.' Peter looks away, brooding on injustice, and takes a consoling sip of Merlot.

Imagining what it would be like to spend Saturday in a bridle and harness dragging a cart of whip-wielding doms over a dirt track, I forget to act the connoisseur and take a beer drinker's swig of my Sauvignon blanc.

It's starting to get dark in the garden. I feel that the eavesdroppers are inching closer, and possibly shiver.

'Are you cold?'

'No no no no,' I protest, though freezing.

Peter returns to happy memories. 'One of my favourite things was erotic clowning.' I take this to be figurative language for fooling around – but it is literal. 'Clowns already have a licence, even an obligation, to misbehave, and the clown-face make-up is as good as a mask for anonymity. I made it more bizarre and grotesque by having genitals painted scarlet … works especially well with cock and balls … and nipples circled with bright red. Then there's the erotic pleasure of splosh, the custard pie in the face and the strawberry dessert down the pants. And you can play on the sinister aspect of clowns, the coulrophobia, fear of clowns. I found it worked best with a hierarchy, an evil cackling leader who plays pranks on a buffoon, with a third sort of intermediate who can side with either.'[31]

This sets off a firestorm of connections in my head. The clown threesome recreates in erotic terms the three-friends dynamic. The Three Amigos Go Out To Play. Then there is the link to The Joker, then back to Grimaldi, and back again to *Commedia Dell'Arte* and even before that to the carnivalesque. Also a link back to autonomous genitals and the Rabelaisian grotesque. And a link to BDSM but with the prankster/buffoon relation more imaginative than dom/sub. Not to mention combining comedy, play, absurdity, transgression, and tapping into the new interest in circus. Why not extend erotic clowning into a full-scale erotic circus? The pony trap could be incorporated and a trapeze act could make use of BDSM suspension play.

Before I can suggest this, Peter's mobile goes off – his wife is threatening to eat the pasta bake if he doesn't come home. And it's getting darker and colder. There is the usual host of questions but probably time only for one more.

'What's your most memorable fun experience?'

'Oh . . . there's so many.' About to rise, he sits again. Like all the funists I have talked to, he is remarkably generous with his time. 'What stands out? One Christmas this club asked me to be Santa. It paid well so I took it on as a job, a chore. But it turned out that practically every woman there wanted to have her bare bottom spanked by Santa. Nothing to do with me, it was Santa. There was a queue all night . . . and several came back for more.'

In some weird way I understand this. A sort of authority/father figure, but reassuringly benign. The safe, fun way to be punished. Philip Larkin, a spanking fan with a large collection of spanking porn, might have been less angry if he had taken Christmas jobs in BDSM clubs, though it's difficult to imagine him as Santa.

Peter has forgotten his pasta bake. 'It was a cheap Santa suit and eventually the elbows and knees came through. And my hand was sore, throbbing with pain, and eventually swollen.' He raises his right hand and regards it in wonder. 'But my God it was certainly worth it.'

12

Fun Goes on Holiday

The woman was loitering with intent in the photocopy room, wearing a little smirk of anticipation that I immediately recognised. This was September. I knew what was coming.

'Been anywhere nice?' she asked at once.

My mutter and shrug were sufficient because all she wanted was to recount her own experience. I had to say it. 'And you?'

'Peru!' she cried in triumph. 'My God, to stand on those *floating islands*. And the mountain trekking! You know, we climbed this isolated peak in the Andes, absolutely beautiful . . . and guess what we found at the very top?'

'Spectacular views?'

'An Internet café!' she screamed in delight. And now, to confirm her superior experience, she had to know mine. 'But what did *you* do?'

The curse of snobbery is that, even when recognised as abhorrent and pitiful, it provokes an overwhelming desire to out-snob the snob. I would have loved to say, 'Camel trekking in Nagorno-Karabakh.' And to have added airily, as though it was the sort of thing everyone ought to know, 'Lovely little unspoiled republic surrounded by Azerbaijan.' And to have finished with the casual,

smiling clincher, 'Totally off the grid.' Instead I mumbled misera-
bly, 'I was at a family wedding in Ireland.'

'Lovely!' she cried, in utter insincerity of meaning, though with
utterly sincere joy of tone at her crushing victory.

This was a highly successful application of holiday snobbery,
possibly the most important subset of fun snobbery, a flaunting of
experience wealth, the new form of conspicuous consumption that
is not yet conspicuous in the sense of being recognised as bragging.
It was also an example of holiday addiction. As with the fantasy
activities of digital gaming and transgressive sex, the holiday escape
from dreary routine may be ultimately unsatisfying but the return
makes the everyday seem even drearier, and the desire for escape
even stronger, bringing a spiral into addiction. The difference is
that, as with the snobbery, holiday addiction is not generally recognised as such, though specialists in pathology have given it the
wonderful name of dromomania.

This addicted colleague needed her regular fix. The year before
she had been to Vietnam ('The amazing puppet theatres of Hanoi!')
and the year before that to China ('The amazing terracotta army!').

'You'll soon be running out of places to go,' I suggested, with a
touch of sarcasm that went unnoticed.

'I *will*,' she agreed in happy sorrow.

'Don't worry,' I consoled her, 'space tourism will soon be available . . . and the cosmos will then be your oyster.'

This time the sarcasm was unmistakable and she scowled in
displeasure. A small but significant moment of payback.

In many ways the holiday is the most extreme form of fun – the
most widely practised, the most expensive and time-consuming,
the most thoroughly ritualised, the most religious but also the

most hedonistic, the most keenly anticipated but also the most disappointing, the most effective for fun snobbery, the most likely to become an addiction, and the most difficult to admit to hating. Revealing an aversion to holidays would be social suicide.

The heart of the holiday problem is that the impulse is religious but the experience is secular. You pay for the sacred but get the profane. The religious impulse is based on the belief in a sacred elsewhere, which seems to be a fundamental human trait. The early religious rituals, which belonged to a sacred time outside everyday routine, were enhanced by being enacted in a sacred place, literally outside. The temple became the first elsewhere. And rites considered to be essential, such as initiation into adulthood, had to be enacted even further outside, so initiates were usually taken to a place unknown to them, far from the community. Further afield again was the elsewhere of spirits, fabulous creatures, monsters, goddesses and gods – and in the universal myth of the quest, the quest hero must venture forth into this dangerous realm, travelling over mountains and across oceans and deserts, in search of the mystical object – the Golden Fleece, the Holy Grail – that confers esoteric knowledge, magical powers, sometimes even immortality, and brings release and rebirth. Where shall wisdom be found? Not at home, but on the purifying mountain peak, in the hidden valley, the enchanted forest, the mysterious island, the legendary land beyond the sea.

Elsewhere is mysterious, enchanted, alluring, and we are irresistibly drawn to it. The problem is that as soon as we arrive it is no longer elsewhere. Millions have been discovering this for thousands of years and yet the mystical belief in elsewhere has continued to intensify and in this secular and sceptical age is overwhelmingly strong. The holiday involving a journey and a sojourn away from home is a recent calendrical ritual (at least compared to the archaic dancing rituals) and its mass availability is more recent still, yet it is considered more fundamental and necessary than any other, not a luxury but an entitlement, even a right. 'I *need* a holiday,' is the groan that goes up from millions of workplaces round the world – and the holiday longed for, needed, *demanded*, is not an opportunity to sit in the garden and think. To be deprived of the annual holiday abroad (or, more likely, holidays) is a form of sensory deprivation like being locked up in solitary confinement in the dark. 'I haven't had a holiday in *nearly two years*!'

As in the early rituals, the desire is for transcendence and transformation, and this has been given added urgency by the modern hunger for authenticity and re-enchantment. The easiest form of transcendence is travel, the easiest form of re-enchantment is an exciting new place, the easiest form of transformation is to shed the constraints of routine, and the easiest way to acquire authenticity is to buy native souvenirs.

The concept of the holiday was born in the nineteenth century, grew in popularity with the affluent throughout the twentieth century, and became a universal Western ritual in the seventies. Since then the tourist industry has grown steadily every year and by the turn of the century was the major economic activity of the planet, accounting for an estimated 9 per cent of global GDP. As soon as people have money they want to go elsewhere. In the fifties and sixties it was the affluent Americans. In the seventies and eighties, when Japan had its economic boom, Japanese tourists were everywhere. In the nineties and beyond it was the Russians who had done well in the free-market smash and grab after the fall of communism. Now China is booming and it's the turn of the Chinese to travel, though this is such a novel experience for most that the Chinese government has issued a sixty-four-page *Handbook for Civilised Tourists* with useful advice such as 'Don't steal the lifejacket from the airplane' and 'Don't dry your smalls over hotel lampshades'.[1]

The holiday is a modern version of the ancient group ritual of pilgrimage to the temple to beg the god or goddess for magical rewards. The pilgrimage lodges spiritual capital in the Bank of God and the holiday lodges experience capital in the Bank of Fun.

Recently archaeologists in the Turkish province of Anatolia discovered the Göbekli Tepe, a buried temple 11,000 years old (6,000 years older than Stonehenge), and since there is no evidence of settlements anywhere in the vicinity, the hypothesis is that pilgrims journeyed to the temple from as much as 100 miles away. This is speculation – but there are records of pilgrimages over 4,500 years ago in Egypt, where hundreds of thousands of pilgrims would journey in groups to Bubastis on the Nile Delta, site of the temple of Bastet, the cat-headed female fertility goddess of joy, love, song, dance and the moon – the Goddess of Fun (who should surely be adopted as the Goddess of the Rave).

Believers around the world have been travelling to sacred places ever since. As soon as Christianity became established in the third century CE there were pilgrimages to the Holy Land, and then to Rome, where the apostle Peter was reputedly buried. In the ninth century Santiago de Compostela in Spain set up in competition and quickly became the most popular through clever marketing, claiming to have the bones of the apostle James, though he had been beheaded in Jerusalem, and justifying this with the story that the ghost of James had not only inspired the Spanish army to its victory over the Moors but had killed 70,000 of the invaders with his own hand. This was soon standard marketing practice for new shrine start-ups.[2] But Compostela consolidated its dominance with another shrewd marketing innovation – one of the first travel guides, the *Liber Sancti Jacobi*, which had details of the route to Compostela, giving the Bordeaux region five stars for its excellent cuisine and wines, but taking an extremely dim view of the Basque Country: 'They eat with their hands, slobbering over the food like any dog or pig ... They have dark, evil, ugly faces. They are debauched, perverse, treacherous and disloyal, corrupt and sensual drunkards ... They will kill you for a penny. Men and women alike warm themselves by the fire, revealing those parts which are better hidden. They fornicate unceasingly, and not only with humans.'[3]

The traditional pilgrimages are increasingly popular, with the numbers visiting Mecca rising annually into the millions, and for the Hindu Kumbh Mela, where pilgrims come every few years to bathe in the sacred Ganges, the latest numbers were estimated at a staggering 100 million, with approximately 80 million attending on one day in February, thought to be the largest ever gathering of people on a single day. For Christians, a mere 2,491 completed the pilgrimage to Santiago in 1985, but by 2010 the number had risen more than tenfold to over 27,000.

The new factor is the number of pilgrims who are non-believers – another example of the craving for religious ritual without the religion. The Compostela pilgrimage is once again the market leader. I have been at dinner parties where lifelong atheists have solemnly pledged, after several bottles of wine, to undertake the journey on foot from Paris to Santiago. 'Drunken fantasy,' I snarled on one such occasion, which turned out to be accurate but was a tad insensitive and not helpful in understanding the phenomenon. This was some time ago, in my snarling years. What I should have said, softly and wonderingly, was, '*Why?*'

The beauty of the pilgrimage is that it pretends to be about the destination but is really about the journey. The pilgrim is always on the way, enjoying the travelling, and the faith and the grail can be largely excuses, or entirely ignored by the secular pilgrim. So the attraction of the Santiago pilgrimage may just be its length, with the requirement to travel on foot from Paris making it not only long but authentically arduous. Those who complete the full journey on foot are given a certificate known as *La Autentica*. A Certificate of Authenticity – what could be more desirable in our inauthentic age! What would look better on the wall next to the primitive art?

Pilgrimage also provides another great combination – the illusion of pursuing elevated purpose while actually enjoying base pleasures. The Egyptians journeying to honour Cat Woman, the Goddess of Fun, were surely obliged to have fun en route – and the medieval Christian pilgrims certainly had fun. Many groups included musicians to keep them entertained while travelling, and the inns where they stayed provided hearty food, lots of wine, prostitutes and more musicians, singers, dancers, jugglers, magicians and novelty acts. Avignon, a major stopover on the route to Rome, had a one-armed woman who could sew, spin, juggle a ball and play dice with her toes. Souvenir shops were also common – and once again Compostela showed the way. The emblem of St James was the cockleshell and, to show that they had completed the journey, pilgrims were originally obliged to go to the sea to find their own shells but by the twelfth century vendors were selling these in the cathedral square, the vendors had also tired of going to the sea and sold shells made of lead.

In *The Canterbury Tales*, written in 1386, Chaucer captured the fun-loving nature of medieval pilgrimage with his account of a group journeying from the Tabard Inn in Southwark to the shrine of St Thomas à Becket in Canterbury (but never arriving). There were twenty-nine pilgrims and Chaucer himself decided to go along, making a group of thirty (a satisfying multiple of three in accordance with Dunbar's theory). Among those individually described by Chaucer were a knight whose son sang and played the flute 'the livelong day', a singing nun, a merry monk who 'didn't give so much as a plucked hen' for pious maxims, a singing and fiddle-playing friar, a wine-and-food-loving country gentleman, a scurrilous, bagpipes-playing miller, a vendor of pardons who sang loudly, 'Come to me, love, come hither', and of course the laughing and joking big-hipped wife from near Bath, a pilgrimage veteran who had been to Rome and Compostela and 'thrice to Jerusalem'. It is significant that there is no solemnity in any of the religious but only in a wealthy merchant and money-changer, 'who gave out his opinions pompously' and 'kept talking of the profits that he'd made'. The landlord of the Tabard recognises immediately the orientation of the pilgrims:

> All year I've seen no jollier company
> At one time in this inn, than I have now.
> I'd make some fun for you, if I knew how.[4]

But soon enough he comes up with a fun idea – that on the way to Canterbury the pilgrims compete to tell the most entertaining story, and these become *The Canterbury Tales*.

None of Chaucer's pilgrims mentions the supposedly religious reason for their journey, least of all the eight religious. The fervently pious pilgrim was a phenomenon of the nineteenth and twentieth centuries, while the medieval pilgrims wanted fun, which was often sexual. In sites across Northern Europe, including Britain, archaeologists have discovered thousands of cheap, mass-produced, lead-tin badges worn by pilgrims from the thirteenth to the mid-sixteenth century, the medieval equivalent of the holiday T-shirt. Many of these are brazenly sexual and feature walking and flying phalluses, vulvas on horseback or stilts, or carrying pilgrim staffs and rosaries, phalluses and vulvas about to conjoin, and female pilgrims merrily roasting phalluses.[5] It's those wacky autonomous genitals again – in the medieval age they just refused to stay in place and behave. The Wife of Bath could well have sported one of these badges, and my feeling is that she would have opted for the vulva on stilts.

However, by the end of Chaucer's life objections to pilgrimage fun were beginning to be raised, and subsequently the Reformation, and Calvinism in particular, denounced pilgrimage directly. According to Calvin, pilgrimage 'aided no man's salvation'.[6]

But like the festivals and carnivals, the fun pilgrimage was not to be denied. It would make a surprise return in the twenty-first century, and in the meantime went secular as the holiday, a pilgrimage to an elsewhere still sacred though now for different reasons, as art replaced religion and the imagination replaced the soul. For two centuries, from the mid-seventeenth to the mid-nineteenth, English, Germans, Scandinavians and a few Americans embarked on a Grand Tour to worship at the places in Europe made sacred by genius. The full Tour required at least a year and usually several, so that only the sons of the wealthy could afford it, and to keep these young men on the straight and narrow they were usually accompanied by a tutor and, with numbers depending on wealth, an entourage of coachmen, grooms, footmen, valets and a painter to record scenes and copy masterpieces (the third Earl of Burlington brought two painters, one for architecture and sculpture and the other for landscapes). Tour guidebooks also recommended supplementing the basic travelling necessities with 'a portable tea caddy, an inflatable bath with bellows, a pocket inkstand, a complete medicine chest, at least a dozen changes of linen' and a wardrobe that included 'a summer suit of camlet with gold thread buttons, a winter suit of worked flower velvet with velvet buttons, red-and-white pumps with diamond buttons, white silk stockings, at least four pairs of fine Swiss ruffles, several Spanish lace handkerchiefs, and a snuffbox and toothpick case'.[7]

Italian art replaced religion as the ostensible reason for the pilgrimage, but the fun remained the same – heavy feasting, drinking, singing, dancing and whoring, with the Paris brothels en route offering the widest range, though it was advisable to reserve in advance, if requiring a precise combination of age, physical measurements, attributes, colouring and specialist services. Those too exhausted to go to brothels could fall back on chambermaids, and the phrasebook for gentlemen offered useful sentences in five languages:

Sweetheart, is my bed made?
Pull off my stockings and warm my bed for I am much
    out of order.
Draw the curtains and pin them together.
Where is the chamberpot? Where is the privy?
Put out the candle and come nearer to me.[8]

In Venice the Grand Tourists from the hypocritical North mar-
velled at the phenomenon of the *cicisbei*, the openly accepted lovers
of noble ladies, whose husbands performed a similar role for other
wives. Venice was swinging over two centuries before the USA,
especially during the carnival weeks with their many opportunities
for dressing up, dancing in the streets and masked balls. Disguise
encouraged sexual adventure, though Lord Byron got in trouble
when his Italian mistress Margarita Cogni became suspicious of
his mysterious companion and ripped the mask off to discover her
sister. Time to move on, though for Byron a swift getaway was
not easy since his entourage included a valet, sparring partner,
tour guide and personal physician, and he travelled in an enlarged
copy of Napoleon's coach, which had sleeping, dining and library
areas, not to mention a travelling zoo with a monkey, peacocks,
birds and a dog.

It was on to the Renaissance glories of Florence and Rome,
though classical Rome was a disappointment, with artisans' huts
and animal pens in the Forum, and a Catholic Stations of the
Cross erected in the Coliseum, which was also full of beggars and
animal dung. The art, too, was frequently disappointing, though
only the likes of sceptical Yankee Mark Twain would admit it: 'The
Last Supper is painted on a dilapidated wall of what was a little

chapel attached to the main church in ancient times, I suppose. It is battered and scarred in every direction, and stained and discoloured by time, and Napoleon's horses kicked the legs off most of the disciples when they (the horses, not the disciples) were stabled there more than half a century ago.'[9]

But the intrinsic quality of the tourist attraction is not important. The attraction is only a symbol, an image, of the sacred or the authentic (and, like the bones of St James, need not even exist). What matters is the ritual of the pilgrimage to the holy site and the joining with many other pilgrims in silent veneration. It is the homage that makes the shrine and not the other way round. In his novel *White Noise*, Don DeLillo enjoyed exposing this embarrassing truth in the episode of 'the most photographed barn in America'.[10] The barn in question is utterly undistinguished but accidentally appears in many photographs, which leads others to photograph it in turn. Soon, like a celebrity famous for being famous, the barn is being visited by crowds taking photographs from a specially constructed elevated viewing area. Two men drive twenty-two miles to see this, park with forty other cars (and a tour bus) in the new lot and spend a long time observing the photographers. Finally one speaks: 'No one sees the barn.' He has just recognised the unique double feat of sightseeing – it makes the sights invisible and the seers blind.

DeLillo was astute in identifying the photograph as the contemporary form of homage. The act of taking a photograph enrols the photographer in a virtual congregation of all the believers who have previously taken pictures of the holy place, and these pictures need never be looked at again, as the shrine itself need never be observed in the first place. Taking the photograph is sufficient homage.

Sight is the most detached sense and therefore the sense most prized in the detached modern age. Hence the invention in the nineteenth century of scenery, the scenic and especially the 'view', which adds the pleasures of detachment and superiority, a development perfectly captured in another new word, 'picturesque'. But the modern age not only wished to be detached but to dominate, control and own nature, which gave the tourist a need to turn it into images to take home. So the aristocrats on the Grand Tour brought along painters, and in 1840 Fox Talbot invented photography, which had long been technically possible, after lamenting the lack of a visual record of his Italian holiday by Lake Como.

Later, the need for individual expression and experience wealth gave the tourist a need to appear in the foreground of the picture, both as proof of having been there and claim to personal ownership. This was a further downgrading and appropriation of the scene as it became merely a backdrop, not even observed but *donned* briefly, like a funny cloak and hat in a wedding photo booth. In due course technology facilitated this, first with the delayed action photograph and then with the selfie stick.

The addition of cameras to smart phones and tablet computers surprised me as a redundant luxury add-on, but now I see it as an inevitable consequence of the need for detached control. The camera controls the immediate environment by capturing it in photographs and video, and the Internet connection oversees the hinterland of social life and the distant penumbra of world events. The combination is an all-areas surveillance device. There is a tendency to associate surveillance only with sinister corporations and paternalistic governments but now everyone is spying. The new hand-held device is the true remote control, providing high-windows detachment everywhere on the ground, like the magic ring of myth that confers on the hand supernatural powers. The mythical aid is usually a ring or sword because these are in or on the right hand, which exercises power – and the smart phone became irresistible when it could fit comfortably in the hand. No wonder people are distraught when they lose this magical remote control. As a lover of high-windows, my own tourist weakness is for 'views'. En route to a recent holiday in Cefalù, Sicily, the beloved and I spent much of the flight wondering if the rented apartment would have a balcony with a view over the main square and cathedral, as on previous holidays we had fretted over the possibility of a sea view or a view over the bustling market (is there a market anywhere in the world that does not bustle?). Wouldn't it be delightful to see an *authentic* Sicilian wedding, as in *The Godfather*? And, goddamn it, we forgot to borrow *The Godfather* box set from our daughter.

The beloved argued that the apartment-building website had talked glowingly of balconies with just such a unique view and I conceded this but pointed out that it did not say these were a feature of *every* apartment. As it turned out, there was no balcony never mind view, and in any case the main square did not have authentic weddings but crowds of tourists queuing for takeaway pizza and triple-scoop ice creams, though it would still have been pleasant to look down on all this, especially with an Aperol spritz in one hand. As James Howell recommended in his *Instructions for Forraine Travel* back in 1642, the tourist's 'chamber' should 'be streetward to take in the common cry and language and to see how the town is served and the world wags about him'.[11] But never mind. We were mature enough to cope with such setbacks. Why worry about a balcony view when the next day we would have the spectacular view from the rock that soared up behind the town?

The first surprise was that it was necessary to pay four Euros for the privilege of climbing a steep, rough track full of sharp stones that cut my expensive Terra Plana 'active shape memory' barefoot walking shoes to shreds, while exposed to the fierce Sicilian sun and the equally fierce insect defenders of the rock, who left us covered in malignant bites. The second surprise was that most other tourists were determined to do the same, despite many difficulties. There were overweight people who would have had trouble walking on carpets, senior citizens on sticks, women carrying babies and an energetic but mad young couple in flip-flops. 'Hard work,' groaned those toiling up, and 'Well worth it,' joyously cried those coming back down; 'Well worth it for the *view*', though in fact all that could be viewed was the shabby back end of town that tourists avoided.

By the mid-nineteenth century the new steamships and rail-ways encouraged the new middle classes to embark on the Grand Tour and deprive the aristos of their exclusive advantage. The last straw was when Thomas Cook, who had had a road-to-Damascus vision of package travel in 1841 on his way from Harborough to Leicester for a temperance meeting, arranged first a package for attending temperance meetings, and later a package Grand Tour by steamship and rail that took a month instead of a year. The rise of the bourgeoisie at home intensified the new desire for escape to authenticity and the invasion of bourgeois tourists finished Italy as an exotic destination. The lost authenticity is always further back in time and further away in space, and usually both – and when Europe became too familiar, authenticity was sought in the Orient.

Byron, an early adventure tourist, travelled to Turkey via Albania, camping out in the mountains with bands of soldiers, all formerly brigands, drinking *raki* and dancing round the fire where a whole goat was roasting – and later swimming the Hellespont against the current, as Leander had done for love of Hero. Flaubert, a fan of Rabelais and Byron, loather of the bourgeoisie, lover of antiquity, and an early sex tourist, journeyed to Egypt in search of the authentically real and authentically erotic. 'Oh how willingly I would give up all the women in the world to possess the mummy of Cleopatra!'[12]

But Thomas Cook was hot on their heels, launching, in 1869, an Egyptian package which began with a stay in Shepheard's Hotel in Cairo, described by Cook as that 'strange combination of ancient Orientalism with Parisian innovations', and then conveyed the tourist by boat along the Nile to the Pyramids, where a swarm of pedlars now solicited with souvenirs that included the hands and feet of mummies, and, thanks to a group fee negotiated by Cook with the Sheikh of Giza, the sightseer could be hauled up a Pyramid by three Arabs singing 'God Save the Queen',[13] one on each side and one at the back.

The trick was to keep ahead of Thomas Cook and the package hordes. Tourism is like fashion in that a few innovators discover something new, which is immediately copied by the multitude, destroying its distinction and obliging the innovators to find a new new thing. For the twentieth century the new thing was once again discovered by artists, principally the American painter Gerald Murphy in the early twenties. If pale skin was the mark of distinction and the sun was to be avoided at all costs, then one way to recover authenticity would be to seek out the sun and become as brown as a peasant or a sailor and, to complete the authentic make-over, wear the cheap light clothes of peasant and sailor. So when the fashionable rich moved from the Riviera to Normandy in the summer, Murphy and his wife not only moved in the opposite direction but lay on the beach in the summer sun. Soon they had a villa on Cap d'Antibes and established an entirely new fashion by having glamorous guests like Rudolf Valentino, Picasso, Scott and Zelda Fitzgerald and the Hemingways.

Now the beach holiday, with trips to the sand in light clothes for tanning instead of arduous sightseeing in formal clothes, became the template for the rest of the century. Hedonism had always been a feature of tourism but where the food, drink, sex and luxury accommodation had been understood as secondary, a reward for the travelling and virtuous sightseeing, they were now the primary, and often sole, purpose of the holiday. This remained fashionable as long as it was exclusive but in the sixties the concept of the charter flight made air travel cheap and in the seventies the masses arrived on the beach in Hawaiian shirts.

Everything that goes up must come down, everything that lives must die, and everything that comes into fashion must soon go out. It was difficult for golden skin to remain a mark of distinction when there was Vertical Turbo Tanning available on the local high street. The attractions of passive hedonism also began to wear off and the package holiday became too restrictive for the expressive individual.

Now active experience is becoming more popular, even with the old. Decaying seaside resorts are enjoying an unexpected revival because the rigour of the coastal walk is replacing the rigor mortis of the beach. And if the walk is along a cliff top so much the better. The views ... *oh*!

But the truly authentic adventure involves a dangerous activity in a remote location. The trick seems to be to invent a new sport that combines as many insane skills as possible and then to make it available as far away as possible, in a place not just 'unspoiled' but 'hidden', 'secret', 'undiscovered', 'off the grid'. So kiteboarding involves controlling a lunging and plunging kite while trying to stay upright on a surf board, volcano sledding is going down an active volcano dodging lava bombs, and canyoning varies the fun with a combination of abseiling, rock climbing and white-water canoeing. Book now for kiteboarding in Wadi Lahami, volcano sledding on Mount Yasur in the South Pacific island of Tanna, or canyoning in the Azores, lyrically described by the *Guardian* as 'a place of wild rugged landscapes whipped by the ever-changing elements, where sailors swap tales of derring-do'.[14]

And of course there is the experience that combines adventure, risk, danger, transgression, spontaneity, physicality and authenticity – holiday sex, as easy to buy as the hand-made necklace and straw hat (and often from the same vendor). Like swinging, sex tourism is still a love that dare not speak its name, rejected as disgustingly depraved by the conservative and disgustingly exploitative by the liberal.

However, the inescapable problem with tourism is that, however strenuous the attempt to go native, even to the extent of sex with natives, the tourist remains irredeemably inauthentic. In fact the modern quest for authenticity is futile because the authenticity project, in the sense of a true self engaging with a real world, is itself inauthentic. There is no true self, now that life has become role-playing, and no real world now that nature has become scenery. The solution is not only to accept inauthenticity (the postmodern approach) but to go further and actually *relish* the inauthentic, the tacky and trashy, the copies and fakes, the simulated and the staged (the post-postmodern approach).

I had this revelation in Sicily when a group of Japanese tourists stopped to photograph a local selling vegetables from a rickety stall built on to a motor bike, and then a group of smirking Germans also stopped and began to photograph the Japanese. I wished I had a camera to add another level and photograph the Germans photographing the Japanese photographing the Sicilian. This was my breakthrough into the meta-tourism of studying tourists, which I have extended into a more general ironic tourism that opens up entire new areas of intellectual and aesthetic pleasure, such as exulting in holiday-brochure prose, elevator music and hotel-bedroom art. And, instead of being embarrassed by my new leisurewear, I don it with pride and glee as a form of cosplay, like dressing up as a superhero or a pineapple.

Activity/adventure holidays are the newest development but the other three types – pilgrimage, sightseeing and the beach – remain hugely popular. A smart tour operator should combine all of these in the Fourfold Transformation Experience, which mixes days of foot pilgrimage, days of cultural-site guided tours, days of extreme sports, and days sipping cocktails on sunloungers. The FTE will also meet the need for individual expression by allowing a 'tailor-made' or 'bespoke' pick 'n' mix. Accommodation will of course be authentic, with stays in mountain caves, mud houses, log cabins, shepherd's huts, igloos or yurts, and the only alternatives to walking will be rickshaws in town and ox carts in the fields.

It may be that cruises are increasingly popular because they combine many features of the Fourfold Experience, as well as meeting other contemporary needs. After the financial crash of

2008 worldwide spending on holidays in general plummeted – but spending on cruises continued to rise.

One obvious factor is, of course, price. Cruising is at the same stage as the package holiday in the seventies – retaining vestiges of exclusive glamour but cheap enough for anyone in regular employment to afford. And with a growing diversity of ships and services, cruising has shaken off its senior-citizen image of Bingo, Ballroom Dancing and aged crooners singing 'My Way'.

At the top end of the market there is still the traditional luxury cruise that appeals to seniors – luxury is the hedonism of age as partying is the hedonism of youth – but now often offering a more sophisticated, state-of-the-art luxury. Regent Lines, for instance, has launched the *Seven Seas Explorer*, which they claim is 'the most luxurious ship ever built', 'with a level of sumptuousness that has never been seen before' – and their slogan, which it would take a European semiotician to explain, is TRUE LUXURY IS INTANGIBLE – displayed above a photograph of an attractive thirty-something couple reclining on cushions holding flutes of Champagne. 'Every inch of the ship exudes luxury and excellence,' the brochure continues, and you will be 'treated to the ultimate indulgence of having a personal butler tend to your every whim'. But as well as luxurious indulgence there is top-of-the-range culture from the mysterious but obviously classy Smithsonian Collection by Smithsonian Journeys, 'an engaging enrichment programme lead by a wide range of experts' – though this is somewhat undermined by the suggestion that you 'relax in your private sitting area with a best-selling novel from the Library' or 'draw the curtains closed to watch the latest blockbuster on your interactive flat-screen television'.

In his classic account of a Caribbean luxury cruise on a liner called the *Zenith*, which he refers to throughout as the *Nadir*, David Foster Wallace tries to enjoy himself by releasing his inner infant and succumbing to indulgence, only to experience what psychologists describe as 'hedonic habituation' – the inner infant immediately becomes accustomed to the level of luxury, begins to notice things to complain about, and demands more and better, is in fact revealed to be 'insatiable'. So the luxury cruise slogan ought to read TRUE LUXURY IS UNATTAINABLE. In the end Foster Wallace suffers from something much worse than dissatisfaction: 'There is something about a mass-market Luxury Cruise that's unbearably sad. Like most unbearably sad things, it seems incredibly elusive and complex in its causes and simple in its effect: on board the *Nadir* – especially at night, when all the ship's structured fun and reassurances and gaiety noise ceased – I felt despair.'[15]

For the less traditional and more hip, Celebrity Cruises has liners such as *Celebrity Silhouette*, *Celebrity Century* and *Celebrity Reflection*, which still provide luxury but also offer transgression lite in the 'authentic, edgy, innovative' Sizzling Sin City Comedy, a blend of 'renowned stand-up comedians' and 'seductive dancers performing modern burlesque acts'. And at the booming youth end of the market there is Carnival, a name to inspire fear and loathing in anyone over fifty, which now has twenty-three liners with names like *Carnival Inspiration*, *Carnival Dream*, *Carnival Glory*, *Carnival Magic* and *Carnival Triumph*, and boasts that 'there's always a reason to party on a Carnival Cruise'. Getting down to detail, the brochure adds, 'You won't be surprised that we take our pool and deck parties very seriously, and pull out all the stops to keep things kickin'.'

There is now even an indie cruise ship, the SS *Coachella*, a sea-faring offshoot of the Californian indie rock festival of the same name, with rock groups, DJs, parties, dancing, a DIY Arts 'n' Crafts workshop ('with opportunities to make fashion accessories or a zine'), a Snowball Bar Crawl ('where everyone has a blast'), and DJ Tutorials ('where each participant will receive their very own SS *Coachella* poster with their own name prominently featured in the line-up'). This may sound like the ultimate in excitement but new rival Groove Cruise promises to 'blow *Coachella* out of the water' with a ninety-six-hour non-stop set list rave that 'will keep you moving right past those notions that you need that thing people onshore call sleep'. As well as raving there are 'theme days and cos-tumery to put a seal on the group debauchery', and the company of no one but twenty-one-plus party people ('this isn't anyone's first rodeo') 'surrounding you all the way to the very last, very blurry, sunrise set back into port during that 95th hour of insanity and on into a piece of lifetime memoria you'll never forget'.

So there is high seas hedonism to suit all ages – go lazy or go crazy. But the cruise ships themselves are also part of the attraction. The mega liners are now the size of major corporate buildings and have many of the same features – towering structures offering secure enclosure always within reassuring sight of other people, but avoiding any sense of confinement with spacious atriums, concourses and esplanades, and everywhere gleaming surfaces that reject even the possibility of blemish or stain. The attraction is per-sonal freedom within company, and protection from the external threat of the polluted and dangerous city and the internal threat of personal deterioration and decay. Though, unlike office buildings, cruise ships have the added advantage of being as dazzlingly white as film-star teeth, which defy in a radiant smile the degradations of age.[16]

And the cruise ship brings together more desirable urban facilities than the corporate building – the gated accommodation, the shopping mall, the entertainment complex, the bars and restaurants, the night club, the casino, the basketball court, the roller-skating rink, the swimming pool, the health spa and the gym – and adds to these with even more experiential facilities like assault courses, rock climbing, surfing and on Royal Caribbean's *Anthem of the Seas* (sister ship to *Rhapsody of the Seas*), a mini golf course, a sky-diving simulator and a circus school that offers to 'unleash your inner trapeze artist'. So, meeting the contemporary demand for cake that can be both eaten and retained, the fortunate passenger is simultaneously at home and at sea, simultaneously protected and enjoying adventure.

As with office buildings, size matters – and *Anthem* is proud to be the largest white whale to date, 40 per cent bigger than its biggest predecessor, and if stood on its stern 50 per cent taller than London's Canary Wharf tower, with accommodation for 6,296 on sixteen passenger decks and a crew of 2,165 from 71 different countries. As well as providing all the usual indulgences, it meets the contemporary need for transgression with a comedy club, the need for ecological concern with a central park featuring 12,000 specimens of trees and plants, and the need for cultural dignity with 7,000 specially commissioned works of art. Many of the cabins face on to the inner park so that these passengers need never see the ocean – and with a vessel the size of a resort town why bother sailing forth at all? Royal Caribbean did consider the possibility of keeping the *Anthem* berthed, and commissioned market research to investigate the potential reaction of customers. All those surveyed vehemently rejected the idea of stasis, revealing that the deepest reason for the popularity of the cruise is also the simplest and most obvious – the fact that the cruise ship is always on the move. (The RC execs took this on board, both symbolically and literally, and met the desire for movement not just by horizontal sailing from port to port but by a moving bar that vertically glides between three decks.)

For, although the cruise is still one of the most hedonistic forms of one of the most hedonistic rituals, the holiday, its basic appeal remains essentially religious – the sanction and renewal promise of the pilgrimage and the mystical lure of the quest. Like the pilgrimage, the cruise ship is always on the way and brings along its own fun. Never tarrying long in port and always glad to be setting sail, the immaculate white prow cleaves the blue in its endless shining voyage to the sacred elsewhere.

13

Fun Goes to the Game

Games and sport are as old as dance and, like dance, have for long periods been denigrated and even suppressed, but in the seventies they regained a popularity that has continued to grow and diversify into a multitude of new forms. It sometimes seems that every fantasy, from playing rock guitar solos to saving the planet from alien attack, can become a digital game, and every physical activity, from bog snorkelling to wrestling with alligators, can be turned into a sport.

This is yet another return to the beginning. As with dance, there is evidence of prehistoric sport in cave art showing wrestlers using a variety of holds, and there is evidence of prehistoric gaming in archaeological finds of boards, counters and dice. On good days our early ancestors may have enjoyed open-air wrestling and on bad days retreated into the cave for a tournament of Ludo. Games and sports were also common in all the early civilisations, in Mesopotamia, Egypt, India, China, and later in Greece and Rome, and included track and field events, fighting contests, gymnastics and ball games. Evidence from ancient Egypt shows astounding variety – many board and ball games, marbles, ninepins, athletics, hunting, stick fighting, archery, competitive running and swimming, bull fighting, tug of war, hoop and throwing games.[1]

The Greeks were more particular, not keen on ball games but enjoying boxing, wrestling, rowing, swimming, bowling, archery, javelin and discus throwing, while the Romans were not keen on athletics, which they considered too effete, and preferred fighting events – boxing, wrestling and the notorious gladiatorial contests that began in 264 BCE and continued for centuries with many innovations, such as swords against nets, men against wild animals, and, following an ingenious suggestion of the emperor Diocletian, women in a fight to the death against dwarfs.

All these games and sports were religious rituals, honouring the gods or attempting to defy the gods and fate, but, as with the festivals and dancing, if they were universally played, at the expense of much precious time and energy, and often with the risk of injury, they must have met many secular needs, which indeed they did and continue to do. Games and sports are rituals which create and therefore acknowledge tension between opposing forces, the fundamental injustice of life, the urge for mind and body to move beyond familiar activities and exceed limitations, the need to operate within arbitrary but binding rules, the possibility of personal transcendence by immersion in a group or absorption in a skill, and the possibility of demonstrating personal and group superiority without having to kill. Though the wheeze of playing games to reduce violence sometimes has the opposite effect. When the Greeks, who first articulated this use of games as a substitute for war, staged the first modern Olympic Games in 1893, they became so excited by their sporting success that they declared war on Turkey – and were immediately stuffed by the Turks. Further evidence, if any were needed, that God is a Merry Prankster.

Different games and sports have predominated in different cultures at different times but, given the current global prominence of football as the most popular form of sporting fun, and the fact that this has happened only in the last few decades, it's interesting to trace its early history. I have always shared the lazy assumption that football was an English invention of the late nineteenth century, but it turns out to have precursors as far back as the first millennia BCE. It's impossible to establish who was first – but in China a game called *cuju*, meaning kickball, may have been played as early as two millennia BCE and was certainly formalised in the Han dynasty (206 BCE–221 CE). This was played by two teams on a marked pitch with a goal at each end and a ball of stitched leather filled with feathers or fur propelled mostly by kicking, though handling was also allowed, as was robust tackling, and the game survived until the early Ming dynasty (1368–1644 CE).

Roughly contemporaneous with this was a Meso-American ball game, also remarkably like football, which may have been played as far back as the Olmec Era (1200–400 BCE) and was certainly played by the Mayans (1000 BCE–1500 CE), who called it *pok-ta-pok*, and the Aztecs (1200–1500 CE) who knew it as *tlachtli*. The game was played with ferocious intensity and losers were likely to have their heads chopped off or their hearts cut out, a punishment many contemporary fans would like to inflict on their own underachieving players. There is evidence that versions of this game were played for hundreds if not thousands of years, as far north as Arizona, as far west as the Pacific coast of Mexico, as far east as Puerto Rico and as far south as Honduras, though there is speculation that it was also played in South America, and it would surely be fitting if football originated in South America rather than England.

The warrior culture that ruled Europe from the fall of Rome to the early medieval period had no time for sports that did not teach fighting skills – but ancient Celtic ball games were preserved on the western fringes of the continent. Games resembling football were played in Ireland, Wales, Cornwall, Brittany and Normandy and may have inspired the medieval English version of football, a violent free-for-all played with a pig's bladder, and with few rules or restrictions on number of players (often all the inhabitants of one village played all the inhabitants of a neighbouring village), role of players (everyone chased the ball), length of game (it could last all day) or on the distinction between players and spectators (players could drop out to watch and spectators could join in for a kick, either at the ball or a hated neighbour). These rowdy events often ended in mass brawls, and royal edicts banning football were issued regularly until the seventeenth century, though with little effect. The new Puritanism of the Churches was more successful, denouncing sports as sinful worship of the body. And the new bourgeoisie, increasingly fearful of crowds and rowdiness, were only too happy to encourage suppression. By the mid-nineteenth century folk football in England had almost died out but found an unlikely saviour in the upper classes when it was taken on by public schools as character building. The products of these schools then took it round the world, with football brought to Brazil in 1894 by a young man called Charles Miller, son of an English father and Brazilian mother, who was sent to school in England, played football for his school (and even occasionally for a professional club, Southampton) and returned to São Paulo with two leather balls.

Why did football become the global sport of the late twentieth century? The fact that similar games were prominent on three different continents in earlier periods, often at the heart of cultures and played for centuries, suggests that it is something in the game itself rather than the cultures. Kicking a ball must be more satisfying than hitting it with a stick, bat, racquet or club, and is certainly more satisfying than throwing or palming. The games based on these, basketball and volleyball, were invented in the late nineteenth century and had no early precursors, so far as I can tell. Handball does have a long history, but has never been as popular as football.

Kicking is the most effective form of human defence or attack, deeply instinctive, and is therefore a fierce primeval joy, enhanced by the sensation of launching a projectile, which may be further enhanced by an accelerating run-up to deliver the kick. It occurs to me that children can probably kick a ball before they can throw, certainly before they can use any form of bat – and even at sixty-seven I can't see anything on a pavement without a mad desire to run and kick it, preferably between the posts of a gateway, and preferably right into a corner. *Goal!*

At the beginning of the twentieth century other sports, such as rugby, hockey and tennis, also prospered, if not with the global appeal of football, and were formalised and organised, with rules and regulations, governing bodies and sometimes professional players. This happened first in England, also the first country to industrialise, and then most quickly in the countries with most economic growth –France, Germany, Sweden and the USA. The growth of sport in the modern era matches economic growth, which leads to two opposing explanations – that sport was a reaction against industrialisation or a product of it, a defiant use of the autonomy and freedom of play, or a submission to the bread-and-circuses diversion encouraged by the society of the spectacle to keep its citizens sedated and docile. Both explanations have been passionately argued, with the right favouring the defiance theory and the left denouncing sport as a capitalist conspiracy. It's possible that both explanations are true. Sport can be as complex and ambivalent as carnival.

By the mid-twentieth century the growth and spread of sport seemed to have reached a limit. Sport had never been favoured by the Church and was largely dismissed by intellectuals as philistine (though bull fighting was an exception because of its sexy association with death). Football was the diversion of the philistine working classes, tennis and golf of the philistine bourgeoisie, and hunting and sailing of the philistine rich, these divisions maintained by snobbish exclusivity and the expense of the equipment and facilities, from pig's bladder on back street, to tennis racquets and golf clubs on members-only courts and courses, and on up to the exorbitant costs of hunting and yachts. And the sixties' espousal of fun specifically excluded sport as regressive and aggressive, not conducive to love. Contact sports like football, rugby and boxing were for violent, atavistic cavemen, tennis and golf the ridiculous recreation of the respectable suburbs, and hunting and fishing typical of the predatory cruelty of the upper class. For the flower children, to wish to become a professional sports person was as inexplicable and disgusting as wanting to become a professional soldier.

All this changed dramatically in the seventies. Sport became more popular with the middle classes and even intellectually fashionable. Politicians began to attend sporting events, historians and sociologists began to analyse it and literary writers to describe it.[2]

Even philosophy took an interest with the appearance of the *Journal of the Philosophy of Sport* in 1973. Sport might seem the opposite of philosophy but many prominent thinkers have played physical as well as mental games. Plato was a prize-winning wrestler in his youth, Socrates admired physical ability and participated in the Isthmian Games, Aristotle wanted to be a pentathlete because 'they are equipped by nature at one and the same time for brawn and for speed',[3] Jean-Paul Sartre was a trained boxer (and defined boxing as a 'binary praxis of antagonistic reciprocity'[4]), A. J. Ayer was a county cricketer, and Jacques Derrida a goalkeeper ('Beyond the touchline there is nothing'[5]), as was Albert Camus, who played in goal for the Algerian university team, *Racing Universitaire Algérois* (and wrote in the university's sports magazine, 'What I know most surely about morality and the duties of men . . . I learned from football'). Goalkeeper is surely the perfect position for a philosopher, both in the team and detached from it, wearing a different jersey and following different rules, not involved in the play for much of the game but every now and then required to block an attack. *Camus saves!*

Hollywood, never slow to capitalise on a trend, went from making hardly any sports movies to churning them out as it once did Westerns. In fact the sports movie became the new Western, transferring to sport the eternal tale of the victory of the apparently no-hope underdog. Even the Churches, realising that distaste for sport was now a PR disaster, relented and climbed on the bandwagon. The Cathedral of St John the Divine in New York actually commissioned a stained-glass window with sports scenes, and in 1976 the Christian country singer Bobby Bare had a major hit with 'Drop Kick Me, Jesus, Through the Goalposts of Life'.

So why did sport begin to extend its appeal in the seventies? As with any social change, there were numerous factors involved. Many intellectuals would probably interpret the phenomenon as evidence of the society of the spectacle reasserting its sedation after the frolics of the sixties. But another reason may be that sport benefited from the seventies' hunger for group fun that brought a new interest in comedy, dancing, holidays and sex. Sport involves physical synchrony, like dancing and sex, offers escape from routine, like holidays, and is a means of personal expression, like comedy.

Football was slower to become fashionable, blighted by the hooliganism of the seventies and eighties and the disasters caused by overcrowding, and seemed to be in terminal decline, with steadily falling attendances at old, deteriorating stadiums – only to rise from the dead once again and soar past all other sports to world domination. The World Cup Final is now watched by over half the population of the planet, several billion people, a simultaneous mass participation unprecedented and unparalleled. One explanation could be that football is not just a team game but the team game that developed the most dynamic and intricate synchrony, an interconnected and interdependent constant flow that maintains tension balance, with protracted and often frustrated foreplay enhancing the rare orgasm of the goal.

In a football game all the outfield players are ceaselessly on the move, with attackers probing together for openings and defenders repositioning to block, and then turn defence into attack with a speed that takes by surprise, like Napoleon's baggage-free army always arriving before expected. Professional players have detailed roles and tactics dictated by a coach but must also be able to improvise while running with the ball and facing heavy tackles, and to anticipate and synchronise, hitting the ball precisely into space knowing intuitively that a teammate will arrive there at exactly the same time as the ball, while the teammate runs into the space knowing intuitively that the ball will appear in front of him. It's like a jazz group improvising on a tune, each following a general score but responding to and inspiring the others – except that there is a rival group attempting to impose a different tune. There is also something of the marvel of organic life spontaneously creating order, complexity and synchrony, though a better analogy might be with the human body's immune system, an immensely sophisticated network that must constantly adapt to defend itself against cunning new forms of attack.

As in comedy and dance, it is timing, speed and precision that make the excellence dazzling – the one-touch technical skills of passing the ball into the crucial space with a single deft flick or meeting the ball in midair to volley into a corner of the net, the execution of such fluency and confidence that it seems natural, as though anyone could do it. Excellence must always seem effortless.

Football's popularity and its prized qualities have grown together in a positive feedback loop. The tactics are ever more complex, the players ever faster and ever more technically adept, and ever better at anticipating the play. It was said of the French player Thierry Henry that his greatness was not so much in his speed or technique, outstanding though both of these were, but in his ability to see several moves ahead like a chess player. So the great sin for defenders is watching the ball instead of anticipating the movement of attackers – and the great sin for attackers is grandstanding, showing off individual flair instead of working for the team. In the early history of modern football, from the late nineteenth century through most of the twentieth, individual dribbling was the skill prized as the most effective (and most entertaining) way to get past defenders, and, while this is still important, just as much prized and often more is the ability to make an incisive pass to a teammate between or above the heads of defenders. It's a sign of the times that teamwork has become more important than individual skill.

Of course most matches are messy, clumsy affairs and even the best have only brief flashes of vision and grace. Sport is intuitive, like creative work, and the moments of miraculous synchrony must be as rapturous for the players as the equally rare moments when the creative artist suddenly sees the parts come together to form a unique new whole. As a priggish intellectual snob, I gave up the childish vulgarity of playing football, but the few student park games I did join gave the unique satisfaction of a random group of individuals, without agreed tactics or even positions, discovering intuitively how to play together as a team.

Another factor in the appeal of football is that the spectators can also enjoy the endorphins of synchrony. Entirely unlike the theatre audience, rigidly forward-looking, passive and silent, the stadium crowd is noisily aware of itself as a unity, an active presence, a major contributing force. And this crowd is complex, containing not just the two sets of fans but within these many overlapping groups, loose alliances of friends who occasionally attend, and a core of obsessives who go to every home match, which group itself often breaks down into sub-groups of the relatively restrained and the completely mad. Then there are the extremists who make long pilgrimages to away games at the other end of the country or in distant countries, braving expensive, lengthy and uncomfortable travel, the hostility of the locals and the brutal corralling of baton-wielding police. This sense of being a tiny, embattled group surrounded by numerically superior and more powerful enemies creates the most intense group cohesion, the band-of-brothers solidarity of soldiers under fire.

There is also the solidarity of the underdog. Most teams never win trophies or achieve any kind of eminence and many run the risk of disastrous relegation to a lower league, and I have often wondered why anyone would support such habitual lack of success. But this is the attitude of a winner-takes-all culture. Lack of success may actually be the *reason* for the support. The suffering underdogs in life are consoled by uniting in sorrow and grief for the similar problems of the underdog club – the disparities in wealth (big clubs becoming even bigger by buying up the best players), the injustices of authority (referees favouring the big teams), the temptations of greed (little clubs cashing in on their best players), the cruel caprices of fate (the last-minute freak goal caused by a deflection), the fallibility of supposedly superior judgement (the atrocious decisions of managers), and the selfish ambition and vainglory of individuals (players showboating on the pitch or wanting to move to bigger clubs). There seems to be a redemptive catharsis in experiencing all this as part of a crowd, in a solidarity of disappointment and loss. To suffer in company reduces pain, as to celebrate in company increases pleasure.

My father would never have dreamt of submitting me to the vulgarity of a football match so I knew nothing of the local team or its players – but the bitter regret of its supporters made a lifelong impression. A sentence repeated by several tough middle-aged men undone by grief is burned into my consciousness, as though with the gnomic power of a mythological axiom of the tribe: *City should never have dropped Jumbo Crossan*.

The football crowd participates with furious passion, responding to the rhythms of the game, urging its team on when the players seem to be on the defensive and losing heart, encouraging attacks with a rising roar that bears the attackers forward like boats on a great ocean surge, and rewarding moments of daring and skill with fervent *Olés*. Team managers depend on this response and complain if the crowd is too restrained, which rarely happens. It's almost impossible to stay silent during the roars. I got involved in football through my daughter, who is an Arsenal supporter and brought me to some of the home games, which I imagined I would watch with my customary amused, silent and condescending detachment. Instead I shouted myself hoarse, discovering the pleasure of immersion and belonging in the exultant, protracted roar of *Arrrrrrrrrrrrrrrrsenal*.

Many traditional supporters deplore the commercialisation of the game and the exorbitant price of individual seat tickets, and are nostalgic for the lost authenticity of the terraces, where the densely packed standing crowd was more like a mosh pit – but less dangerous forms of communal togetherness have developed. The crowd can create its own synchrony in the Mexican wave, the overhead unison handclapping, the bearing aloft of giant banners or of large coloured rectangles that fit together to form the team colours, or the letters on individual T-shirts lined up to form words, or in the drumming, dancing, chanting and singing, often of popular songs given witty new words. Football chants are the choral singing of the rabble. One of my daughter's greatest ambitions was to come up with a song that Arsenal supporters would adopt – and she had a great contender when Arsenal signed a Belarusian player called Alexander Hleb, whose name leant itself to an adaptation of the Beatles song 'Help', as in 'Hleb ... we need somebody, Hleb ... not just anybody'. Unfortunately, Hleb was too good and quickly transferred to Barcelona.

The converse of supporting a team is the taunting of opponents with ritual insults that are not really insults but the verbal equivalent of play-fighting. In *A Season with Verona*,[6] his insightful and entertaining account of following the Hellas Verona football team, the English novelist Tim Parks records the constant insults shouted by the team's supporters, who warm up for an away game by taunting the driver on the coach with shouts of 'Your daughter's being fucked'. However, Parks suggests that the real target is the sanctimonious pieties of the liberal orthodoxy. The fun is in the joyous escape from contemporary righteousness – and the football crowd is a rare opportunity to enjoy group transgression in public. At a home game against a team from Naples in the despised South, a few of the fanatical Verona supporters place thousands of white surgical masks on seats before the game, and when it begins the supporters don these for the synchronous transgression of singing together, 10,000-strong, 'Get that smell, Even the dogs are running, The Neapolitans are coming'. Later, at the return fixture in Naples, the locals greet the Veronese with a banner describing them as pigs with foot and mouth, and, from the parapet of an upper stand, carry out the ritual hanging of an effigy in Verona colours.

'What delirium!' Parks marvels. 'What security in the close ties of an undying community!' This sense of community can even become an end in itself, with the group celebrating its own unity and abusing the owner, manager and players of the team they have come together to support, much as soldiers will vilify their officers and fight for each other rather than for their country or against an enemy. In the course of his season-long investigation, Parks travels by plane with the highly paid players, and by coach with the mostly penniless supporters and concludes that the supporters have much more fun.

But the most inventive abuse is reserved for traitors who leave the team to join rivals. When Ashley Cole left Arsenal for Chelsea, allegedly as a result of outrage at being offered a mere £50,000 a week instead of the £55,000 he was convinced he deserved, Arsenal fans began an energetic multimedia campaign, recording an entire album of abusive songs, setting up a chant, 'Ashley Cole is a fucking arsehole', wearing replica shirts with 'A. Hole' on the back, carrying posters of a photoshopped Cole in this shirt, and passing out banknotes for £55,000 bearing Cole's face. This campaign was sustained for months, and just when it began to run out of steam Cole gifted the fans dream material by suing two tabloid newspapers over allegations that he had taken part in a 'gay sex romp' and had a mobile phone inserted in his anus by a fellow footballer. When Chelsea next came to play Arsenal, the Arsenal fans had two new songs, an uptempo rap number, 'Why'd ya want to go and stick a phone up your arse?' and, to the tune of 'One man and his dog went to mow a meadow,' 'One man and his phone went to bed with Ashley'. Better still, the fans launched several giant inflated mobile phones and accompanied the songs by joyously batting these around the stands. This was performance art of the rabble, turning the stadium into a giant installation.

Needless to say, the football commentators – handsomely paid to analyse the minute details of games – ignored all of this.

Our age of demanding respect and taking offence cannot accept the concept of ritual insult, even though a good insult is like a good joke, simultaneously surprising and so accurate as to seem inevitable – and often a good insult *is* a good joke, as when Roy Keane described the new middle-class football fans as the prawn-sandwich people. Of course, as play-fighting can turn into real violence, ritual insult can become genuine cruelty and humiliation. Where is the dividing line? There is no abstract way to define lines and each instance has to be considered in the full complexity of its context and tone. Righteous condemnation is always easy but it does not require much sophistication to realise that a supporter is not entirely serious when he exhorts a player coming in for a tackle to 'tear his leg off and hit him with the soggy end'.

The transgressive abuse enjoyed by the largely working-class supporters is similar to the transgressive inversion of the lower orders in carnival, so it's not surprising that football fans adopted elements of carnival in the seventies, adding, to the flags and banners and drums, mascots, ridiculous costumes and face painting. All these are now so common that it's surprising to discover they were seventies fan innovations. According to the sports writer Alex Bellos, even the concept of the replica shirt, now an international multibillion-dollar industry, was originally the idea of a football fan, a low-level Brazilian government official called Jayme de Carvalho, who persuaded his wife to sew him costumes in his team's colours.[7] The origin of face painting has not been so precisely identified, with many also ascribing this to South American fans, though the anthropologist Desmond Morris noted it among English supporters in the seventies[8] while others have claimed it began in Europe. What is indisputable is that this, too, is internationally popular and the basis for another major industry in the manufacture and marketing of face paint. As with the general fondness for costuming and masking, the motivation is probably a complex and contradictory mix of the desire for a simple identity by immersing in a group and the desire for individual expression, as in the personal touches of brightly coloured cape, curly wig and hat with a pair of clapping hands on top.

The immersive delirium of the crowd experience is a key attraction of live sport, and digital gaming now provides this by staging tournaments in sports arenas, where exuberant supporters can watch the action on a giant screen, to a running commentary from professional 'casters', the equivalent of sports commentators. So League of Legends fans can follow the battle for control of a bridge over the Howling Abyss (a region in the Fields of Justice) between warriors led by Tryndamere, Cho'Gath, Gragas and Master Yi, and those of Blitzcrank, Kha'Zix, Gnar and Xin Zhao, each side armed with an array of weapons that includes Guinsoo's Rageblade, the Mercurial Scimitar, the Blasting Wand, the Blackfire Torch, Rabadon's Deathcap and the Elixir of Sorcery. Needless to say, gaming encourages cosplay, with supporters wearing the costumes of their champions (actually two teams of young men in separate soundproof booths) and roaring approval when they slay foe with Rageblades and Blasting Wands (actually mouse clicks).

The new phenomenon of esports is believed to have begun in South Korea where major matches bring crowds of up to 50,000 to football stadiums, and there is even an esports TV channel, but it soon spread to the USA and from there to Europe. In the UK there are plans to build dedicated esports arenas, and it is already big business, with professional gamers competing for major prize money in contests organised by professional leagues such as Major League Gaming in the USA and the European Esports League, with sponsorship from corporations such as Coca-Cola and American Express.

This is the latest development in the relentless rise of digital gaming, which has grown in popularity by shedding its inadequate-loner image and steadily becoming more social, first with multi-user online playing, then with websites, fan clubs and gaming conventions, and finally with the physical presence of a stadium crowd. Now games meet the contemporary demand for group involvement, as well as for fantasy, individual expression and emotionally engaging role play, while giving these a reassuring framework with the simplicity of a limited environment, the certainty of unambiguous goals, rules and outcomes, the security of repetition, like that provided by ritual, and the comfort of clear purpose, like that provided by religion. God returns as the game designer and his divine power is the algorithm. It's no wonder that young men become addicted and even game themselves to death, when these games provide so many apparently inconsistent satisfactions – the promise of freedom in a world not only circumscribed but with rigidly defined characters and precisely quantified actions involving levels, points and scores, the promise of fantasy and even magic in a world that is entirely rational and calculated, the promise of transgression in a world entirely bound by rules, and the promise of danger in a world entirely safe.

However, the quality that digital games can never have is authenticity, however ingenious the attempts to improve realism, and however medieval or pagan the goal of bringing the Blade of Drak'Mar to Jaelyne Evensong at the Argent Tournament Grounds by sunrise. I have always assumed that digital games would wipe out traditional board games – but it turns out that the opposite has happened. Board games have not only survived but actually *increased* in popularity, possibly due to the tactile authenticity of the physical board and pieces, and the physical proximity of a small group round a table.

Sales of board games are growing, more groups of board game enthusiasts meet more regularly to play and are becoming better organised. The latest development is the dedicated board-game café, initiated by Snakes and Lattes in Toronto, but now with similar venues in the UK – Thristy Meeples in Oxford and Draughts in London. When I visit Draughts in Hackney on a bright, sunny Saturday afternoon, which should have seen everyone strolling along the Regent Canal nearby, the café is packed, with not even a free seat, never mind a free table. There is a queue for seats and all the young game gurus in red T-shirts are advising people in the queue, which gives me an opportunity to browse the extensive library at the back, containing all the old favourites, Scrabble, Cluedo, Monopoly and so on (though there is now Monopoly Express for the age of the limited attention span), and many more new games. Intriguing titles include Blood in the Forest, Bonobo Beach, Nuns on the Run, Escape the Temple Curse, Kaosball, Hey That's My Fish, Xe Queo! and Cards Against Humanity ('as despicably awkward as you and your friends'). Next to me a portly middle-aged man utters a joyful exclamation and yanks out Survive: Escape from Atlantis, explaining, with gleeful enthusiasm, that treasure seekers have discovered the lost city of Atlantis, which has risen to the surface of the sea but is sinking once more, so the desperate looters have to escape in boats. 'Terrific game!' he cries, hugging the box to his chest and issuing a demented laugh. 'You can throw people overboard. Great fun.'

At last a Game Guru is free. Ben explains that the board game business is indeed booming and that Draughts is planning to open more cafes in London and also in Bristol and . . . *Dublin*. The cynical Irish adopting the very games they always despised most as the symbol of middle-class Englishness? The Irish playing *board games*? Something significant must be happening. But what?

'It's the social thing,' Ben confirms. 'You need to be face to face to enjoy the bluffing, conning and backstabbing . . . the *deceit*.' He leans close to me an expression contorted by low cunning, 'I like to look into people's eyes when I'm betraying them.'

And not only is the new technology failing to wipe out board games, it's actually helping them. Many check out games on their smart phones and tablets but then want to play them on boards face to face.

The new board games involve more complexity and collaboration and the European trend is towards team strategy, with many players balancing multiple factors and interacting in complicated ways, while the American games are heavy on theme and story, often based on films and TV series, with more emphasis on individual competition and – here Ben's face contorts again, this time in uncontrollable contempt – '*luck*'. He ponders, wondering if he has gone too far, and then goes even further, confidentially bringing his mouth to my ear, 'We call them Ameritrash.'

The most popular European games are Settlers of Catan, which involves Neolithic people trying to establish a farming community, and Carcassonne, which involves establishing a city in the Middle Ages. Once again the pagan and the medieval.

Ben is now in full flow. Who said that young people are apathetic? The world is full of youthful enthusiasts. 'It's like music,' he cries. 'There's only a few notes and you can't believe that there could be any more new songs ... until people go ahead and write them. It's the same with these games. They're all just a board and dice and a few rules. Same as it's been for thousands of years. You can't imagine that designers could come up with anything new – but then they do, they *do* ... all the time ... they keep coming up with these marvellous new games. They're ... they're ...' He pauses and I'm hoping he will confirm my theory by saying 'authentic' – but he goes one better, rapture lighting up his youthful features as he finally hits on the right word. 'They're *pure*.'

14

Fun Goes Spiritual

We always demand the impossible, which is why we have barefoot shoes, indoor sky diving, silent disco and Christian gangsta rap, and why, to satisfy our spiritual hunger, we now want religionless religion – or, to be more precise, the rituals of religion without the doctrines, the God or the solemnity, the meeting place without the traditional worship, the congregation without the divine faith, and the priest without the moralising sermon. It is why a new alternative to the orthodox Sunday church service is the Sunday Assembly, a movement that describes itself as 'a worldwide network of godless congregations that meet locally to hear great talks, sing songs and celebrate life', with the mission statement: 'Live better. Help often. Wonder more.' It may be an exaggeration to describe the reach as 'worldwide' but there are assemblies in seventy countries and the movement certainly seems to be growing rapidly.

The London Assembly is held in Conway Hall where arrivals are greeted by volunteers wearing large stickers asking HELP? on their sweaters and the beatific smile of the saved on their faces, though this suggestion of do-gooding evangelism is partly dispelled by the pounding rock music from the packed hall beyond and the animated excitement of the congregation, mainly young and all middle-class, white and conventionally dressed. No – in front of me is a girl with purple hair and behind me are two black guys leaning against the back wall, both looking as though they would like to disappear through it. What are they doing here? Child-minding for white partners? In general the congregation is similar to the audience at stand-up comedy, with women out-numbering men, though this may be an illusion due to the greater enthusiasm of the young women, many already boogying – a 'collective effervescence' even before the proceedings have started.

On stage is a six-piece band and a dozen or so singers, one of whom comes forward now, as the band hammer into 'Mustang Sally', and belts out in an authentically hoarse R&B voice, 'All you want to do is ride around, Sally.' It is impossible not to join the backing singers in the supportive exhortation, 'Ride, Sally, ride', especially as the words are displayed, karaoke style, on a giant screen at the back of the stage. Already the entire congregation is standing, clapping, swaying, grinning and air punching.

Then up springs the Assembly Leader, Sanderson Jones, with the classic look of the cult leader – tall, broad-shouldered, thin, with long, centre-parted hair and a full beard – but the manner of the stand-up comic, roaring, 'Good morning, London,' to thunderous applause and then, 'Who's in the mood to celebrate being alive?' which brings an even more thunderous affirmative. He chuckles happily, 'I've only started and already I've lost my voice.' Pause for another chuckle. 'Are you all right at the back?' A further noisy affirmative. 'How many of you are first timers?' Around a third of us raise our hands, and are enthusiastically cheered by the rest for having finally seen the light.

'CELEBRATE LIFE!' flashes the screen, as Sanderson tells us about his week, which included a visit to the Buddhist Meditation Centre where he tried Five-Rhythms Ecstatic Dance. Behind him the screen is now showing frenetic breakdancers spinning on their backs. 'It was pretty intense – a hell of a dance. I bonded with this guy called Tom who said *No one has ever manipulated my chi quite like that*.' But today Sanderson is overjoyed to welcome the leaders of new assemblies in Manchester, Norwich, Nottingham and Amsterdam, who will help us to appreciate the ay-may-zingness of local gatherings.

Gordon from Nottingham has a roguish air. 'I honour truth,' he begins, 'so believe it when I say that for forty years I have been with no woman except my wife.' There is a murmur of approval, especially from the women. 'That is absolutely true – but it doesn't mention the men.' This time there is a roar of laughing approval. Many even clap. We are thrilled by our tolerance.

Pippa from Amsterdam is wackier. 'Have you ever built a *massive* house of cards?' Many are glad to acknowledge this. 'To how many levels?' 'Two,' someone shouts, to uproarious laughter. 'Have you ever done a fart so loud that someone came running from another room?' Next she shares with us the advice she will be offering Amsterdam: 'Be yourself and be *proud* to be yourself. Do things that seem crazy. Be comfortable crying in public. Give yourself permission to meet and work with fantastic people. Start an international movement.'

Each piece of advice is roundly applauded, especially the last, and she takes her leave, well pleased: 'You're *amazing*,' she cries in valediction, nor does anyone dissent from this judgement.

Between the speakers there are songs, so the recipe is a mix of stand-up comedy, dance music ('Happy' by Pharrell Williams and 'Get Lucky' by Daft Punk are favourites) and feel-good T-shirt slogans. But halfway through, Sanderson announces a moment of reflection and heads bow in solemn contemplation of financial worries and health problems. 'Moment of Reflection' warns the screen. Emerging from reflection, we are exhorted to acknowledge our neighbours on either side, with the Catholic handshake of peace replaced by exuberant, palm-stinging high fives. Then round comes the collection basket – or rather, bag (a health-food-store bag). Followed by more speakers and songs.

At the end Sanderson returns to remind us that we are all on a journey, a message the screen helpfully supports by showing an express train tearing through countryside. This theme of the journey to find one's self seems to be as central as the theme of community. Now the screen is saying, 'You get more change by becoming more aware of what you are than by trying to become the thing you're not.' Sanderson finishes by announcing more exciting developments – a Sunday Assembly Festival in September, with the title *A Festival Called Wonder*, and in the meantime a barbecue called *Wow!* and a collaboration with the Morning Gloryville rave group to put on a Sunday Assembly Rave, which will be 'more fun than a barrel of monkeys'. Again the forms of fun have been recognised and combined. Sanderson's parting words: 'Work with people, be nice and have fun.'

These Wonder and Wow gigs reveal that the aim of spiritual fun is re-enchantment, via group ritual, to enjoy unity, community, belonging, transcendence and awe. And spiritual fun shares with secular spirituality in general the religious sense of a hidden power, something beyond, something more, though nothing sufficiently specific to impose any obligation other than wonder. This is a greed for the spiritual that is partly replacing the worldly version. The material more no longer works so we demand an immaterial more.

And the collaboration with a rave group is significant because communal dance is the obvious missing joy-and-wonder feature of Sunday Assembly, no doubt because the Assembly closely parallels modern pew-bound Christian services. Religious dance has always been accepted in the East, but the religions of the book, Judaism, Christianity and Islam, with their emphasis on scriptural doctrine and clerical authority, have been deeply suspicious of dance as an incitement to carnal thoughts, disobedience and heresy. Nevertheless, dancing has burst out in the rites of all three – most dramatically and persistently in the Whirling Dervishes of the Mevlevi Order, a branch of the Sufi tradition, itself a branch of Islam. This sect was founded by the poet Rumi in the thirteenth century in Konya (now in the Anatolian region of Turkey) and, according to legend, he discovered whirling when the rhythmic beat of a goldsmith's hammer made him turn to the beat and then go faster and faster until he experienced an ecstatic trance state. The fascinating aspect of the Whirling Dervish dance, properly known as *sema*, is that it is a fully conscious attempt to create what the archaic rituals experienced entirely unconsciously – a sense of personal transcendence through immersion in group dance. The key belief of the Sufi tradition is that the universe is in essence a unity, though it is experienced as a fragmented diversity, that this unity is God and that the manifold phenomena are all expressions of God. So the whirling is intended to dissolve ego in the oneness.

Like people, religious sects often begin with terrific enthusiasm and energy, dancing and singing, but with age become stiff, staid and solemn, disapproving of unruly behaviour and frequently banishing dance from their rites. So it is quite an achievement for the Mevlevi to be still whirling after more than 700 years, especially since their rite was banned by the secular Turkish government of Kemal Atatürk in the twenties. And what is even more surprising, astounding in fact, is that there is a branch of the sect in Hammersmith in West London, that its members still perform the *sema*, and that *the public are occasionally permitted to attend and watch.*

Naturally I get my aged ass down to Hammersmith at the earliest opportunity. Colet House, home of The Study Society, which hosts the *sema* on the first Friday evening of each month, is an unlikely survivor on a busy main road of office blocks, supermarkets and building sites. It is a big, dim Victorian building with an atmosphere of long-dead, nineteenth-century earnestness. A lecture hall on the first floor has been cleared for the whirling, which is a religious ceremony not a performance, with a few rows of chairs at one side for those who wish to watch – not called an audience but 'lovers'. This evening the lovers are mostly women, many of an Eastern Mediterranean appearance, expensively dressed and heavily bejewelled and made-up, with long, thick, black hair, in striking contrast to the English women who look like ageing humanists, with short grey hair, drab clothes and no make-up. As I take a seat, an alarming forty-something woman with burning eyes sits down in front of me, rips the tie from her hair, shakes it out and, opening both hands with spread fingers, drives them deeply and voluptuously into the black tresses, shaking them out even further, before deftly gathering them in one hand and replacing the tie. She is surely a reincarnation of the Sumerian goddess Inanna, or the Egyptian goddess Bastet.

By and by the dervishes enter slowly, led by their sheik, twenty-six of them, of all ages, at least half women, wearing floor-length black cloaks and tall chimney-pot hats, to walk slowly several times round the hall with eyes cast down, and then in turn kiss the floor and squat upon it, drawing their cloaks about them. One older man rises and begins a chant that lasts fifteen minutes. The pace is certainly that of a ceremony rather than a show.

But at last comes a solo on the *ney*, a Turkish reed flute, which, even played through a computer, has an eerily archaic, plangent sound. After a night of excess with his votaries, Dionysus, sated but melancholic, walks alone to the river, cuts a reed, fashions from it a flute and, squatting down on the green bank, idly plays to himself as the river flows. Then a drum starts to beat and the dervishes suddenly cast off their black cloaks to symbolise rebirth, revealing long, full-skirted, white robes that are the shrouds of their old, dead egos. They rise and, placing crossed hands on their shoulders to symbolise unity, form a line before the sheik.

Each in turn kisses his hand and, opening arms wide, the right lifted up to the heavens and the left pointing down, simultaneously one with the earth and transcending it, explodes into whirls that signify the harmonious cycles of all things and spread wide the full skirts – like a series of white flowers bursting into bloom and exuberantly dancing in a spring breeze. Soon the hall is full of swirling white figures that are dizzying to watch, though none lose their balance or stumble. Even one who looks to be in his late seventies whirls faultlessly, albeit more slowly than the others. The women are, of course, the most graceful but one man of at least sixty seems to be able to whirl without touching the floor. They continue whirling for fifteen minutes, even increasing the rhythm, their impassive expressions difficult to read but the sightless eyes suggesting a trance state. Then they return to squat at the front of the hall, drawing the black cloaks once again round their shoulders, while one recites a concluding prayer, and at the end of this all bow heads and release a prolonged *oooooohhhhhing* that is at once triumphant and sorrowful, like the groan and sigh after satisfying sex.

The ritual is the classic cycle of jubilant release, ecstatic personal transcendence and finally return to the group and sober reality (the black cloaks). As they rise to file slowly out, there is a powerful sense of something genuinely old and strange, profoundly other. And then strange, too, to descend the old staircase and emerge on to the main road, the red warning lights on tower cranes looking down on illuminated office buildings and the traffic roaring heedlessly by on the Great West Road.

The parallel in Judaism is the Hasidic sect, founded in the seventeenth century after the claim of an Eastern European Jew, Sabbatai Sevi, to be the Messiah, caused great excitement and celebration in the Jewish communities of Russia, Poland and the Baltic states. Belief in this Messiah soon faded but the singing and dancing were incorporated into the rituals of a new sect, Hasidism, with dance especially important in setting the heart on fire for God. Unlike the scholars of Torah, revered by mainstream Judaism, the Hasidic holy teachers were prized for their dancing skill, as in this description: 'His feet were as light as those of a four-year-old. And not a single one of those who saw the holy dance failed to turn to God in that very instance, and with his whole soul, for he stirred the hearts of all who beheld him to both tears and ecstasy.'[1]

But the authorities were right to suspect a link between dancing and more carnal pleasures. Another teacher compared prayer dance with sex in the T-shirt slogan, 'Prayer is copulation'. Not surprisingly, the Hasidim were soon in conflict with the Rabbinic authorities, one of whom denounced their behaviour as follows: 'They conduct themselves like madmen, and explain their behaviour by saying that in their thoughts they soar in the most far-off worlds ... Every day is for them a holiday. When they pray ... they raise such a din that the walls quake ... And they turn over like wheels, with the head below and the legs above.'[2]

Eventually Hasidism toned down the unruliness, while retaining the mysticism and emotional fervour, which enabled it to spread through Eastern and Central Europe in the nineteenth century and on to Western Europe, Canada, Australia and especially the USA, where there is currently a community of 100,000 in Brooklyn. As happens so often, the revolutionary movement hardened into conservatism, with Hasidic Jews living in close, patriarchal, authoritarian communities and bound by strict regulations on every aspect of daily behaviour, especially dress and diet, though the film maker Ben Zion Horowitz cites a Hasidic saying that Jewish Orthodoxy in general is as different from Hasidism as 'a stick from a caress. By them there's such strictness, but with Hasidim, the whole Jewishness comes with a happiness, with dancing and with singing.'[3]

The contemporary Hasidic communities are private and intensely secretive so there seems little chance of the public seeing cartwheeling Hasidim, if such a dance still exists – but Hasidism has given a gift to the world in *klezmer* dance music. This was the exuberant music for the Eastern European Hasidic rituals, especially weddings, adapted from the East European gypsy music of folk dancing (the dance inspired by the *vily*), and brought with the Hasidim to the USA but almost dying out in the mid-twentieth century when it was rejected by Jewish youth as boringly traditional – youth may not always reject its parents but it ALWAYS rejects the music of its parents. Then, as part of the seventies search for authenticity, *klezmer* was rediscovered by Jewish musicians, adapted and relaunched, and is now flourishing as an accepted world music genre with a flourishing subgenre of klezmer jazz.

There was an earlier but similar development in ecstatic Sufi music which spread through the Islamic world and influenced the rhythmic wailing of Moroccan music, which in turn was a crucial influence on the Spanish gypsy dance music of flamenco (in this case giving to gypsy music instead of taking from it). And as with *klezmer*, there has been renewed interest in recent years, leading to Sufi rock and Sufi jazz.

There are many parallels between Judaism and Islam, but it's good to remember that as well as fanatical fundamentalism, each has produced a sect devoted, at least in theory, to love and joy, and to celebration with song and dance. Imagine if the Hasidic and Sufi traditions could be brought together in a Hasufi Festival featuring *klezmer* and Sufi music, both traditional and jazz versions, and whirling dervishes and cartwheeling Hasidim. The musical finale would be a joint jam session to create an exciting new fusion genre, Hasufi jazz, which inspires the audience to respond in a new ecstatic Hasufi dance. Throw in a programme of talks on the Hasidic and Sufi traditions, a hip physicist on the cosmos as play, a deep guru on the philosophy of the cosmic dance, and a network theorist on the interconnectedness of all things, and you surely have the ingredients of a spiritual festival that would really rock.

There was nothing quite so ecstatic in the new Christian sects that formed after the Reformation, though the Diggers and Ranters had community singing with rhythmic body movement, swaying and clapping, if not actual dancing. From these descended the Baptists and the Quakers, so named because of the body movement. And then in the mid-eighteenth century the Quakers gave birth to the Shakers, and the Shaker leader Mother Ann Lee, after being imprisoned several times for dancing on the Sabbath, experienced a personal revelation and in 1774 sailed with eight of her followers to found a new Shaker community in North America. This prospered and in the nineteenth century other communities were set up throughout New England and further west and south, till there were twenty communities with around 6,000 members. Their financial success was largely due to their diligence in building, farming and manufacturing, especially of furniture, and their practical innovations have given to the world the concept of selling seeds in paper packets, as well as the clothes peg and the hernia truss. For the Shakers, making something well was 'an act of prayer' and one of Ann Lee's maxims is worthy of a T-shirt: 'Do your work as if you had a thousand years to live but also as if you were to die tomorrow.'

Their community ideals, especially of pacifism, gender equality and personal freedom, were also noble. Unlike many sects and cults, the Shakers did not attempt to retain members by coercion – anyone over twenty-one was free to leave at any time – and they were among the first groups to oppose slavery. Each community centred on a meeting house, and after the day's work the brothers and sisters gathered to hear the ritual exhortation of an elder: 'Go forth, old men, young men and maidens, and worship God with all your might in the dance.' Then they began with a circle dance, and after this the men and women separated into two facing groups for individual dancing that was emotional, unstructured and chaotic, with much shouting, twisting and jerking. When they eventually tired they fell silent and waited to see if anyone had 'received a gift', in which case this person would step forward and go into a silent, intense whirl for up to fifteen minutes.

Idealistic communities that set themselves apart from the world are notoriously unstable and short-lived but, as with the Hasidim sect, the community dancing of the Shakers seems to have been a major factor in sustaining the movement. Another practice shared with the Hasidim was speaking in tongues, glossolalia. When the ecstasy becomes intense it demands expression but cannot find it in conventional language and bursts out in unknown words and syllables. But the Shakers did not permit the natural consequence of men and women dancing together. Sexual intercourse is the source of all human woes, Ann Lee insisted, and while many would agree with her, few would be prepared to follow to the logical conclusion of celibacy. It was this rejection of sex that caused the Shaker communities to dwindle and die in the sex-obsessed twentieth century.

But as African Americans revitalised music and dance with an exuberant fun element at the beginning of the twentieth century, so too with religion. The Pentecostal movement in Protestantism began in Los Angeles in 1906, when a charismatic African-American preacher, William J. Seymour, set up a new church on

Azusa Street, whose chaotic, unstructured services with singing and dancing to a rhythmic accompaniment of hand clapping and foot stomping, and personal testifying and speaking in tongues, became wildly popular, not only with African Americans but Latinos and whites of all ages. As with the Hasidim, the source of the ecstasy was possession, in this case by the Holy Spirit – and it's significant that, where the Sufi immersed the self in God, for the modern transcenders, God immersed in the self. Even God has had to surrender to the primacy of the individual.

Such was the evangelical ardour of Azusa Street that missionaries went forth from it to spread the movement, first around the USA and then around the world, and within two years there were Pentecostal churches in more than fifty countries in Europe and Asia. The movement continued to grow throughout the century, especially in the third world, and received a major boost from the fun-loving mood of the sixties, which encouraged the spread of its enthusiastic style into mainstream Protestantism and even into Catholicism in the Charismatic Movement, reaching even into the heart of traditional Catholic Ireland.

As a boy I was vaguely aware of this development, dismissed with contempt by the older generation, and while I had no respect for trad Catholicism, I certainly shared its contempt for worship involving guitars and tambourines. In the twenty-first century, with most Christian congregations dwindling, at least in Europe, Pentecostalism has had another extraordinary growth spurt, with estimates of a 50 per cent increase in members in the last ten years and a worldwide membership of around 500 million. In London alone an astounding 550 new Pentecostal churches have opened in the last decade.

There are many possible reasons for the growth: the bottom-up development with no clerical hierarchy and no overall governing body, which suits the modern dislike of authority; the shift from believing in Christian doctrine to behaving like a Christian, which suits the modern experiential turn; the revivalist return to an original simplicity and purity, which meets the modern need for authenticity; the emphasis on rebirth through baptism in the Holy Spirit, which meets the modern need for renewal; the testimony of members of the congregation, which meets the need for participation; and of course the singing and dancing, which meets the modern taste for group fun.

The latest Pentecostal development is Hillsong, a branch of the movement which was founded in Australia thirty years ago and, with the effortless speed of its parent, has since spread round much of the world, with churches in New York, Paris, London, Amsterdam, Berlin, Barcelona, Copenhagen, Stockholm, Los Angeles and Cape Town. This success is based on attracting urban youth with fun. Hillsong services are held in theatres and concert halls with rock bands and state-of-the-art lighting to give the effect of a nightclub rather than a church – and the bands are of such a professional standard that many have had bestselling albums (over 16 million Hillsong albums have been sold). The church may even have the first tattooed cleric – Ben Houston, son of the founder Brian Houston – and the Los Angeles pastor, has F-A-I-T-H inked on his suntanned biceps. Another astute innovation is that Hillsong understands the contemporary importance of what it calls 'hang time with friends' and complements the community spirit of the mass services with regular meetings of groups of ten to twenty, which Robin Dunbar identified as the optimal bonding size for the small group. (The Sunday Assembly movement is now doing something similar by establishing small 'peer-to-peer' support groups.)

I have always had a vague awareness of 'holy rollers' worshipping in noisy services punctuated by jubilant shouts of amen and hallelujah, but believed these to be isolated independent churches dying out with an older generation imbued with traditional, and largely rural, values. It's surprising to discover that these churches are all part of the same movement, that, far from dying out, they are growing in strength, and that, far from appealing only to the rural elderly, they are increasingly popular with urban youth in many of the most sophisticated cities in the world. It turns out that, as with comedy clubs and tattoo parlours, there are several Pentecostal churches near where I live.

Everything splits and madly diverges – and then the divergent strands converge once more. While religion has become more fun, fun has become more religious, so that the two are now often difficult to distinguish. This religious aspect of fun is a development of the mystical spirituality of the sixties, which in the seventies produced many groups, organisations and networks, not so much churches or even cults, as a loose community which 'one does *not* join, which is *not* permanent and enduring, which is *not* exclusive, and which does *not* have clearly articulated beliefs'[14] but rejects Western orthodox religions for some combination of pagan and oriental myths and mysticism that has come to be known as occulture. While the mix varies and is never precisely defined, the common central idea is that the phenomenal world of everyday reality, which appears so fragmented, divided, chaotic and confusing, is merely the perceptible manifestation of a hidden deep unity and life force – an idea often accompanied by a belief in the dawn of a spiritual new age.

As a scientifically trained rationalist, for most of my life I have despised fuzzy, soft New Age spirituality as much as hard, clear Roman Catholic dogma, and the great joke is that science has brought me to much the same belief as the incense-burning hippies. One of the weirdest and most unlikely of all convergences is surely that between contemporary physics and ancient Eastern religion in their common understanding of matter and reality as basically some sort of mysterious unified force field (also a core belief of the Sufis, though for them the unifying force was God).

For those in the occulture, access to the life force is via dancing to electronic music – the technoccult – either indoors with psychedelic lighting effects or, better, outdoors or, better still, outdoors in the wilderness or at some sacred site, or, best of all, outdoors somewhere sacred during some significant celestial event or seasonal change – for instance the Full Moon Gatherings of Moontribe in the Mojave Desert, with dancing till dawn and 'massive group hugs, chain massages, mad group chanting and spontaneous gestures of creative spirituality: people sitting in prayer to the sun as it rises or screaming Energy from the top of a cliff'.[5] This trance dance has spawned its own subgenre of music, psychedelic trance or psytrance, which originated in Goa in the seventies and in turn spawned a further range of subgenres, including full-on, dark, progressive, Suomi, forest, ambient, morning and psybreaks.[6]

But the most interesting feature of psytrance is that, as explained by one of its founders, Goa Gil, it is a *self-conscious* attempt at 'recreating ancient tribal ritual for the twenty-first century'.[7] In particular, it strives for the oneness and transcendence of archaic ritual. The Consortium Of Collective Consciousness celebrates this 'rediscovery of ancient trance tradition' on its website: 'We dance for hours and hours, encountering aspects of our own personal karma, and the karma of humanity, transcending layer after layer like an onion, until the dancer disappears altogether and only the dance remains,' which represents a 'full-circle return of humanity to its primordial beginnings'.

Spiritual dance leads naturally to spiritual sex, which also uses physical activity to achieve an altered state that transcends the everyday and feels connected to, and part of, something cosmic and divine. In this field the market leader is Tantra, which combines the endorsement of a contemporary celebrity (the rock star Sting) with the authentic sanction of ancient Hindu origins involving a God, Shiva, and Goddess, Shakti, but is not burdened by doctrine and concentrates on practice. Serious Tantrists complain that there is much more to it than sex, but many are drawn by the hope of intensifying sexual pleasure through adding a sense of ecstatic union with the material world, so that the earth does not just move but joins in for a threesome. The first step is creating a sacred space in a room by removing domestic clutter, turning down lights, playing soft music and lighting incense or scented candles. Substitute Bombay mix for candles and this would be the preparation for my Ritual of the Aperitif, making me wonder if a combination would be possible in a Ritual of the Tantric Aperitif. After all, both Tantric sex and the apero are based on anticipation. In the sex ritual the next stage is for the couple to entwine in the yab/yum position and initiate mystic union by prolonged eye contact and synchronised breathing. In the combination ritual this could easily be extended to include spacing the synchronised breathing with synchronised sipping of chilled Pouilly Fumé, the sips held for as long as possible in the mouth and then exchanged, to symbolise the sharing of all things and especially fluids.

Another sexual approach is Spiritual BDSM which seeks a similar altered state but through pain rather than pleasure. This practice establishes a sacred connection with the past by flogging submissives strapped to a St Andrew's Cross, an X-shaped *crux decussata* like that said to have been used in the martyrdom of St Andrew. Or the submissive has hooks embedded in flesh and is hoisted aloft in a re-enactment of the Native American Sun Dance Ritual, a religious ceremony widely practised by the Plains tribes. These associations make spiritual the transcendent, loss-of-self state, known in BDSM as 'headspace'.

The same desire, to leave the contemporary quotidian and rediscover a lost spiritual intensity, is behind the neo-pagan movement, which began in the seventies with the emergence of new groups such as neo-Druids in Britain, Ásatrú in Germany and the Nordic countries and, in the USA, Dianic Wicca, a feminist organisation of witches devoted to the goddess Diana. This new paganism seems to be equally at home on the far left and far right. Many Nordic pagans are right-wing nationalists, while Dianic Wicca developed into Reclaiming, an international goddess movement organised on non-hierarchical anarchist consensus principles and devoted to anti-capitalist activism.

Accurate numbers are difficult to obtain because many neo-pagans do not wish to advertise their allegiance and many national censuses do not specifically count pagans, but the numbers seem to be increasing. For instance, the Icelandic branch of Ásatrú has grown sixfold in the last decade, with over half of its 3,000 members in their twenties, and is now so popular that it is building its own temple, thought to be the contemporary world's first dedicated pagan temple. One of the new young members has explained the attraction: 'In a world that is quite artificial, here there is an interest in the real, the authentic.'[8] In the UK the census began to include pagan as a religious category only in 2001, and between this census and that of 2011 the numbers self-reporting as pagan doubled from 7 per 10,000 to 14.3. The profile of neo-pagans is also difficult to establish, but there seems to be general agreement that most are citizens of northern countries and are white, middle-class and educated.

When I mention this phenomenon to a friend who wants to know what I am writing about at the moment, the reaction is unexpected. This woman is an executive in a multinational corporation, a food and wine connoisseur with a savagely sceptical sense of humour, and we are enjoying an aperitif, so I expect her to laugh along with me – but instead there is a lengthy, fraught silence. Is she offended at even the mention of paganism?

At last she says, quietly, '*I'm* a pagan.'

There is another, longer, and even more fraught silence. This update takes a while to configure. For support we each take deep, thoughtful sips of our Viognier.

Hesitantly she begins to explain how, in reaction to a Catholic upbringing, she developed a love of occult horror literature and Xena Warrior Princess. Fortified by Viognier, she gets into her stride and leans across the table. 'I loved the idea of women ruling the roost . . . buxom, bare-breasted women whipping men. It was liberating, empowering, transporting. Secret powers and potions that save you from a fate worse than death.' Now she can laugh, in her unique style, which is first to sit back upright, then slowly lean to the left until almost horizontal, and finally to shake and shake and shake.

Restored to the upright, she continues: 'From that I got into paganism ... the British Pagan Federation, pagan gatherings, pagan conventions ... *pagan camp.*' A significant pause.

'Ah.'

'No, it was deeply disappointing ... half-arsed and mimsy, sad, no fun at all. I wanted something radically different – wildness, transcendence, flaming ritual, Satan in the woods, the horns and cloven hoof ...'

'Dionysus and his maenads?'

'But it was just these sweaty, unkempt, greasy men hoping for sex, and obese women in crushed velvet with bad teeth.' Abruptly she adopts a high-pitched, querulous tone. '*Baphomet, you're supposed to have the van keys. No, I gave them to Taleisin.* More Women's Institute than Warrior Goddess.' Remembering, grim-acing. 'I got so fed up I left and went into Nuneaton to do the shops.' This time the laughter leans so far over that it seems sure to end in collapse – but she recovers. 'And the music was terrible. Almost happy-clappy. Singing with recorders.'

'Whereas you prefer?' Something bluesy and jazzy, no doubt. Wrong again.

'Dark Wave,' she declares, brightening. 'Doom Ambient.'

Now it's my turn to shake, though in an upright position.

'Sun O>>> or even bands like Electric Wizard, who are very tongue-in-cheek with their satanic imagery.'

Much of this neo-paganism does indeed seem to be ironic,

simultaneously serious and aware of being absurd. Not just neo-but postmodern paganism.

Here there is a pleasant break to accommodate the arrival of her char-grilled liver with tangled greens and my venison burger with hand-cut chips, and we discuss the relative merits of skinny and chunky chips, and order another bottle of Viognier.

'I thought you'd be a red wine man,' she remarks.

'And I thought a pagan would prefer chunky chips.'

We eat in silence, musing, and then, trying to probe to the heart of the matter, I resume. 'But what do you actually *believe in*? Surely not gods and goddesses?'

She ponders for a time. 'There's stuff we don't understand. Something that goes way, way back. Something connected to nature. I want to be initiated by a Finnish shaman into Finnish tree magic.'

I wonder if this is a joke but she appears to be serious. There is always something more and it's always somewhere else, and the more remote the elsewhere in place and time the more sacred the something more. Part of the attraction of paganism is that its beliefs are conveniently vague. It is all ritual and no doctrine.

She too has been thinking. 'I've always felt connected to ancient history. Often I feel as though I'm a million years old.'

At last something to share. 'I often feel like that, too. Especially in the company of young women.'

This time we shake together.

'Ah,' she sighs, after more liver and Viognier, 'I had photos on my laptop but lost them all. Me in my horns and ram's head headdress.'

This gives me the crucial connection. I suddenly see that, not only is neo-paganism all about ritual, but this ritual is essentially cosplay, a fancier form of fancy dress, offering a great range of dramatic capes, tunics, robes and headgear, and great accessorising with swords, axes, horns, amulets, bracelets and rings. And shamans and goddesses are a fancier version of superheroes and superheroines. I wonder if suggesting this will be insulting but she readily accepts the comparison.

'Of course role playing is part of it. But the best role play I've been involved in was the zebra hunt.'

'?????'

'You strip to your pants, get body-painted all over in zebra stripes . . . really professional make-up, takes two hours . . . and then get pursued through the woods by hunters. When they catch up, you can lick sugar lumps out of their hands,' leaning over the table two hands held together in docile paw position, 'or you can be skittish.'

'How do you know zebras are skittish?'

For the first time she is irritated. 'It's an *interpretation* of a zebra.' And she draws back, tossing her head skittishly.

During the week this woman sits in meetings in the upper level of a corporate building, wearing a business suit and spouting corpobabble about powering the brand – and at weekends she runs through the woods nearly naked painted with zebra stripes. Though perhaps the two roles are not as different as they seem. I have a sudden acute awareness of my own experience poverty. This executive zebra has certainly lived.

'But being hunted . . . eating sugar lumps . . . how does this fit with Xena Warrior Princess making men subservient . . . with wanting to *whip men*?'

This attempt to be logical sends her into her lowest-leaning and most dangerous laughing fit. And I remember Peter Birch explaining that most submissives are highly successful people, and that most BDSM practitioners can switch between dom and sub. As paganism can go left or right, the role in the playing can be dominant or submissive. What matters is the escape to extremity itself and not the direction or position of the extreme.

'Was it fun being a zebra?'

'The best.'

15

Fun Goes Political

Carnival is probably now the last place to find the carnivalesque, in Bakhtin's sense of transgressive inversion – though the carnivalesque is still very much alive and high kicking elsewhere. For instance, the Notting Hill Carnival in London,[1] advertised as the largest street party in Europe, is now largely a commercialised spectacle, with the costumes bearing no relation to real life, past or present, the participating groups funded by government grants or commercial sponsorship, the parade routes lined by stalls selling worthless items like balloons, flags and whistles at outrageous prices, and householders offering toilet facilities for £1. Last year I noticed a sign for a Community Centre and assumed that here at least there would be free facilities. Not a bit of it. The charge was £1.50, on the grounds that the Centre's grant had been cut. Later, an experienced reveller explained how to avoid this expense – drink vodka jellies instead of liquid alcohol.

I suspect that most contemporary carnivals have become like this – empty spectacles whose main purpose is to attract and fleece tourists. In 1980 the Venice carnival was revived as a tourist attraction and has been spectacularly successful in generating revenue.

When the traditional carnival died, it was individual writers, many French, who took on the duty of public transgression. Gérard de Nerval walked with a lobster on a lead, Baudelaire dyed his hair bright green, Rimbaud cultivated lice in his hair to throw at priests on the street, and J. K. Huysmans included in one of his novels a character who has Christ tattooed on his feet so that he can be always tramping on him. The most extreme, surpassing even Rimbaud, was a young Frenchman from Uruguay, Isidore Ducasse, who wrote, under the name of Comte de Lautréamont, *Les Chants de Maldoror*, a sort of book-length prose poem without structure or plot but a masterpiece of cosmic transgression, screaming at God and the entire human race ('Stupid and idiotic species! You will regret your conduct, I tell you! You will regret it, yes, regret it! My poetry shall consist of attacks, by every means, upon that wild beast, Man, and the Creator, who should never have begotten such vermin! Volume shall pile upon volume until the end of my life.'[2]) Unfortunately, Ducasse reached the end of his life all too soon, dying in mysterious circumstances during the siege of Paris in 1870 at the age of twenty-four. He could have gone on to rival Nietzsche, with a similarly complex style of delirious excess tempered by irony. The words are aggressive but the tone suggests play-fighting.

At the end of the nineteenth century the bohemian writers and artists took to congregating in cafés in informal groups and in due course one such group became the Dada movement. In March 1916 the anarchist German poet Hugo Ball and his wife Emmy Hennings opened the Cabaret Voltaire in a small back room in a disreputable area of Zurich, otherwise a virtuous Protestant town but now teeming with a motley crew of war refugees, including revolutionary writers and artists and real revolutionaries. Joyce was there, planning to shock the literary world with his work in progress, *Ulysses*, and a few streets away Lenin was planning to shock the entire world with a Russian revolution. Cabaret Voltaire was one of the first attempts to have fun combining artistic and political transgression, and featured artists in home-made costumes and masks who performed readings and skits to percussion music played on drums, pot lids and frying pans. The unifying concept was provocation, with audience baiting a prominent feature (it sounds much like a contemporary comedy club in a shabby room above an old pub), so one of the most successful evenings was when an infuriated audience stormed the stage, possibly after hearing Ball recite his poem, *gagji beri bimba*, which begins:

> gadji beri bimba glandrich laula lonni cadori
> gadjama gramma berida bimbala glandri
> galassassa laulitalomini
> gadji beri bin blassa glassala laula lonni
> cadorsu sassala bim
> gadjama tuffm i zimballa binban gligla
> wowolimai bin beri ban[3]

The Dadaists were among the first to recognise that in the twentieth century meaninglessness was the new meaning (but not sophisticated enough to understand that the meaninglessness has to be meaningful) and a month later Ball suggested a meaningless name for this new movement – Dada. A year later the Romanian Tristan Tzara provided a Dada Manifesto: 'I write a manifesto and I want nothing, yet I say certain things, and in principle I am against manifestos, as I am also against principles … I write this manifesto to show that people can perform contrary actions together while taking a fresh gulp of air; I am against action; for continuous contradiction, for affirmation too, I am neither for nor against and I do not explain because I hate common sense.[4] In so far as Dada had any coherent purpose, something Tzara vehemently denied ('DADA DOES NOT MEAN ANYTHING'), it was to rebel against the rational logic of the modern age and replace it with Ducassian raving (though in Tzara's case without Ducasse's literary talent): 'We have experienced the trembling and the awakening. Drunk with energy, we are revenants thrusting the trident into heedless flesh. We are streams of curses in the tropical abundance of vertiginous vegetation, resin and rain are our sweat, we bleed and burn with thirst, our blood is strength.'

The Surrealists, influenced by Ducasse and Dada, continued the assault on sense by championing automatic writing and random association (inspired by the Ducasse image, 'beautiful as the chance encounter on an operating table of a sewing machine and an umbrella'[5]) but they were largely solemn and humourless. The joker in the pack was Salvador Dali, an egotistical showman obsessed with self-promotion and money but also a major contributor to fun. His most famous performance was delivering a lecture in a deep-sea diver's suit, including helmet, though this almost went badly wrong when he began to suffocate and his desperate flailing was applauded as a hilarious part of the act. Other stunts included walking a giant ant-eater on a lead and arriving at the Sorbonne in a Rolls-Royce full of cauliflowers to deliver a lecture on 'Phenomenological Aspects of the Paranoiac Critical Method', in which, leaning his elbows on a table scattered with breadcrumbs, he explained that 'all emotion comes to me through the elbow'.

After the Second World War the assault on conformity was

resumed in Paris by the Letterists, whose leader was another Romanian, Isidore Isou, a twenty-year-old with a startling similarity to Elvis – the same dark quiff and delinquent-baby look of surly resentment embedded in puppy fat. Isou also had the new contempt for forebears and began his public career by disrupting a performance of Tristan Tzara's play, *La Fuit*, storming the stage with his friends to shout, 'Dada is dead! Letterism has taken its place!'

The Letterists introduced the idea of the city as a source of resistance and renewal (their manifesto was titled 'A Formula for a New City') and pioneered the use of graffiti with slogans such as 'Never work', 'Long live the ephemeral', and 'Everyone will live in his own cathedral'. But they are mostly remembered for their coup on Easter Sunday 1950 when Michel Mourre joined the congregation in Notre Dame dressed as a Dominican monk and, just before Mass began, gravely mounted the pulpit and, after a reverent pause, in priestly language and intonation (Mourre had been in a seminary), began, 'I accuse the Catholic Church of infecting the world with its funereal morality, of being the running sore on the decomposed body of the West. Verily I say unto you, *God is dead.*' It took a while for the congregation to catch on and when they did they were not amused but chased Mourre out of the cathedral and along the quais where they quickly caught up (Mourre was young and fit but a monk's robes are designed for solemn pacing not sprinting) and would have lynched him but for the intervention of the police. Mourre was a problem for the authorities, who wanted him symbolically lynched but feared the publicity of a trial, and persuaded a psychiatrist to recommend locking him away in a lunatic asylum. Luckily for Mourre, this too provoked a public outcry and he was eventually released.

As is usual with such groups, the Letterists split up (over a disagreement about disrupting Charlie Chaplin's press conference for *Limelight* in the Ritz) and one of them, Guy Debord, became a founder of Situationism, a movement pretty much indistinguishable from its predecessor, vehemently opposed to materialism and believing in the city. Debord would go on to write its manifesto, *The Society of the Spectacle*, in the sixties but began with a book whose covers were made of sandpaper and a film with twenty-four minutes of black screen. Situationism was remarkably successful, with a magazine appearing regularly, affiliated groups springing up all over Europe and a Situationist International in Italy in 1957. However, it is also remarkably difficult to define. This is because, like fun, part of its definition was a refusal of definition. It was never a single thing because it wished to combine many ideas and attitudes, and never fixed because it rejected fixity for continual reinvention. Whatever Situationism was, it made itself up as it went along, though it had no direction or destination. One of Debord's key techniques was the *dérive*, which involved random groups randomly drifting round cities in search of a Situation, whatever that was.

Again like fun, Situationism is best defined by what it opposed, which included individualism (particularly artistic), ideology (particularly Marxist), specialism (particularly academic), and the commodification, spectacle and work ethic of contemporary society (one of Debord's first slogans was the Letterists' 'never work'). This negative orientation could explain why Debord spent much of his time and energy expelling members, especially artists who became successful. As he wrote to the painter Giuseppe Gallizio, 'The tumult over your glory grows great, despite the discretion we maintain.' Later Debord declared that 'the Situationist International knew how to fight its own glory.'[6]

However, Situationism also had positives. Above all, it was for collective activity (often on an international scale), but also for play (Huizinga was an influence), for gifting in general and sharing of all cultural productions in particular, and for intimate engagement with the city rather than disdainful detachment. Debord was a process philosopher who believed that it was futile to resist the basic truth that everything is interconnected and constantly changing. Hence his opposition to individualism and specialism and his concept of a 'unitary urbanism', where architecture, planning and aesthetics combined to create cities conducive to play. For Debord it was necessary to change everything to change anything: 'Everything being connected, it was necessary to change it by a unitary struggle, or nothing.'[7] He could as easily have argued that changing anything changes everything. The butterfly flapping its wings in Brazil is the cause of a tornado in Texas.

Situationism was just such a butterfly. It had little effect at the time, but its ideas diffused into the culture and its influence is everywhere – in the sixties' hippies, the seventies' punks, the new political protestors of the eighties and after, in conceptual, playful and participative art, intertextuality in literature, sampling in music, Internet hacking and piracy, culture jamming, the rise of festivals and the emergence of the city as playground (the most famous Situationist slogan was 'beneath the street the beach'). But its most important legacy was its rejection of the individualism of the Surrealists and their predecessors in favour of a new kind of communal activity that combines artistic and political action but imposes no doctrine or authority ('divided we stand').

Another key Situationist technique was *détournement*, a term as difficult to define as the movement itself, but including the use of stunts, hoaxes and pranks as a form of social criticism. Debord himself seems to have done little in this line but other groups around Europe, and especially in the USA, became enthusiastic practitioners.

The novelist Terry Southern was a crucial link between Europe and America. He spent four years in Paris from 1948 to 1952, was close friends with the Scottish novelist and subsequent Situationist Alexander Trocchi and, after moving back to the USA, wrote a novel of Situationist *détournement* (though probably without that conscious intention). In *The Magic Christian*, Guy Grand is a fabulously wealthy financier who decides to use his wealth to disrupt the system ('make it hot for them') with a series of increasingly elaborate stunts. This is a ridiculously limited plot for a novel but, unlike much satirical writing of the period, *The Magic Christian* is still sharp, fresh and above all funny, thanks to Southern's exquisitely fastidious style – the equivalent in writing of a deadpan expression.[8]

Prankster Grand begins modestly by offering people $6,000 to eat his parking tickets, but quickly moves on to more ambitious schemes, like buying a thriving company, Vanity Cosmetics, and launching a new shampoo, Downy, that is advertised as Cleopatra's Secret – which allowed a woman of 'only average prettiness (*which one must never, never underestimate*)' to win a throne and many illustrious men. In fact, Grand's Downy makes hair as stiff as barbed wire. Then he acquires a Madison Avenue advertising agency and installs as president a pygmy instructed to 'scurry about the offices like a squirrel and to chatter raucously in his native tongue'. Next Grand takes to dining in the most exclusive and expensive gourmet restaurants and when the food arrives, first writhes in ecstasy, then scoops it up with his hands in a wild urgency that splatters all of his top half, and finally charges to the kitchen, knocking over tables, to shout at the top of his voice, 'MES COMPLIMENTS AU CHEF!'

Southern was remarkably prescient in identifying, back in the fifties, cosmetics, advertising and gourmet dining as key forms of modern pretension, and even more prescient in identifying the exclusive luxury cruise as the key symbol of the age. In Grand's final and most extravagant coup, his chef d'oeuvre, he buys a cruise liner, has it refurbished in fabulous luxury, renames it *The Magic Christian*, and announces that applications for the maiden voyage will be carefully screened, which of course makes the wealthy elite desperate for places, though when a famous Italian socialite submits an application Grand scrawls moronically across it with a blunt pencil, 'Are *you* kidding?!? No wops!'

To captain the *Magic Christian*, Grand has engaged a silver-haired actor with 'a manner both authoritative and pleasingly genial' who appears on screens in cabins to welcome and reassure passengers. But once at sea odd things begin to happen. The few passengers watching their screens in the early hours see a sinister figure creep up behind the captain, hit him over the head and seize the wheel, though their stories are discounted when the captain reappears next morning as jovial as ever. Then the ladies who visit the ship's doctor for aspirin and sea-sickness pills are informed that they look 'rather queer' and require examination, which reveals 'latent abrasions' requiring gigantic dressings a foot wide and several inches thick, attached by adhesive flaps almost impossible to remove. During the afternoon tea dance a gigantic, stark-naked bearded woman rushes madly on to the floor and has to be forcibly removed. Strange crudely scrawled posters appear, saying DEATH TO RICH or SUPPORT MENTAL HEALTH LET'S KEEP THE CLAP OUT OF CHAPPAQUIDDICK. And when the passengers are called out for an emergency drill their life jackets inflate hugely, causing them to roll around in open space or become jammed in corridors. Grand himself is of course a passenger, complaining bitterly and leading assaults on the bridge to find out 'What the devil's going on?'

Southern's novella was either prescient or influential, or possibly both, because the sixties became a golden age of US pranksterism. In 1964 the novelist Ken Kesey actually made pranking a full-time profession when he and his Merry Pranksters took to the road in an old school bus painted in swirls of bright colour, bearing on the back a sign 'Caution: Weird Load' and, on the destination board at the front, simply 'Further'. Prankish underground magazines sprang up, like Ed Sanders's *Fuck You: A Magazine of the Arts* and Paul Krassner's *Realist*, which featured writing by Terry Southern, Ken Kesey, Lenny Bruce and Kurt Vonnegut, and had its greatest success with a red, white and blue poster bearing an apparently simple but actually complex message in which two bad-magic words fought it out: FUCK COMMUNISM.[9]

In 1967 Krassner founded the Youth International Party, the Yippies, with Abbie Hoffman, one of the most prominent of the counter-cultural activists, who made what may well be the first explicit connection between fun and political action with his claim that 'revolution is a game that's just more fun'.[10] Looking back on his long subversive career twenty years later, Hoffman explained, 'I really did it because it was fun'[11] and the fun included pretending to have dropped LSD in the New York City water supply, organising public fuck-ins, attempting to levitate the Pentagon, releasing white rats at a dinner for President Nixon's wife Pat, and nominating a pig to run for president. (When the Yippie Stew Albert was arrested he told the police, 'I got bad news for you boys, the pig squealed on you.'[12]) To publicise an anti-Vietnam War rally, the Yippies invented a drug called Lace which produced an uncontrollable urge to strip naked and have sexual intercourse, and during a press conference accidentally spilled some on two 'reporters', actually Yippies, who proceeded to demonstrate its effect. However, it is acknowledged that the greatest Yippie coup was bringing the New York Stock Exchange to a standstill by getting on to a balcony and showering the floor with dollar bills.[13] This was similar to a stunt in *The Magic Christian* (except that Grand put 10,000 $100 bills in a vat of liquid manure and blood in central Chicago), hardly surprising because Hoffman was a good friend of Terry Southern.

The glory days of Situationism and the Yippies were in 1968, with the May riots in Paris, which featured Situationist graffiti like, 'Be Reasonable, Demand the Impossible', and the riot at the Democratic Convention in Chicago, where the Yippie pig was nominated to run for president. Arrested and charged with inciting a riot, Hoffman and other Yippies appeared in court in judicial robes and, when ordered to remove these, complied, revealing Chicago police uniforms beneath. Throughout the trial Hoffman referred to Judge Julius Hoffman as 'Uncle Julie' and attempted to change his first name to Fuck so that Uncle Julie would have to refer to him as Fuck Hoffman – and was rewarded with an eight-month prison sentence for contempt of court.[14]

It was certainly fun while it lasted – but when it became obvious that the revolution was not going to happen, the sixties fun protest movements fizzled out (and both Debord and Hoffman eventually committed suicide). The torch of transgression was passed back to the arts and taken up by the punk bands of the seventies, as, after exactly a century, the snarls and screams of Rimbaud and Lautréamont worked through to popular culture. But this punk rebellion also fizzled out and the eighties were a low point for organised subversion, as capitalism seemed to have become stronger than ever, with a new idol to worship – the free market. Protest continued, but feebly and ineffectively, and activists became increasingly bored by the tedious routine of meetings, marches, placards and garbled clichés and insults shouted into loudhailers from the backs of trucks. It was apparent to many that, not only was all this having no effect, it might even be counterproductive. Screaming insults is more likely to bolster than undermine, often wins sympathy for the insulted, and always makes the screamers unattractive. Who would wish to live in a new world run by aggressive, self-righteous fanatics?

Many remembered the comment of philosopher Herbert Marcuse on the late sixties upheavals, 'Our goals, our values, our morality, must be visible already in our actions.'[15] This was the concept of prefiguration, which requires that the nature of the protest itself must be an example of the society it desires to create. And after the sixties everyone wanted to have fun. Where was the fun? And everyone also wanted individual expressiveness. Where was the opportunity to do your own thing? The protesters themselves would like to be original and to have fun, the fun would be more likely to win support and it would break the cycle of aggression and counter-aggression. It's easy to suppress fanaticism but difficult to attack fun.

The first evidence of change was a collection of interviews called *Pranks!* published in San Francisco in 1987, which advocated imaginative but benign political pranking as an effective form of protest, and became the manual for a new wave of cultural sabotage groups like The Barbie Liberation Front, who in 1993 purchased Barbie and G.I. Joe dolls, switched their voice boxes and 'reverse shoplifted' them back on to the shelves, so that Christmas shoppers bought Barbies which growled, 'Dead men tell no lies,' and G. I. Joes who cooed, 'I'd like to go shopping with you.' Later, Front founder Mike Bonanno joined Andy Bichlbaum and computer specialist Zack Exley to form the Yes Men who specialised in parody websites that had convincing domain names and looked like the real thing but were subtly different. They began with a George W. Bush campaign site that had slogans like 'Hypocrisy with Bravado' and graduated to a site for Dow Chemical, who had purchased Union Carbide, the company responsible for killing thousands with poisonous chemicals in Bhopal. This lookalike site promised that Dow would sell Union Carbide and use the money to compensate Bhopal. BBC World believed the site to be genuine and interviewed a 'Dow spokesperson', in fact Andy Bichlbaum, posing as Jude Finisterra, a hoax that wiped $2 billion off Dow stock before the company had time to expose it.

In the UK, public fun protest got going in 1995, when the activist John Jordan, inspired by Dada, Surrealism and the Situationists, wanted to bring artistic transgression into politics and found his opportunity with anti-road-building protest groups. 'To me the question was always how to have space to connect the transformation of politics and the poetics and imaginary space of the arts.'[16] Jordan developed anti-road protest into the Reclaim The Streets movement, which blocked busy roads and intersections with parties of dancers boogying to EDM from mobile sound systems (tactical dancing, or dance with a stance) and dug up roads to plant saplings (guerrilla gardening by 'avant gardeners'). Naomi Klein has described a 1996 RTS action on London's M41: 'Two people dressed in elaborate carnival costumes sat thirty feet above the roadway, perched on scaffolding contraptions that were covered by huge hoop skirts. The police standing by had no idea that underneath the skirts were guerrilla gardeners with jackhammers, drilling holes in the highway and planting saplings in the asphalt. The RTSers – diehard Situationist fans – had made their point: "Beneath the tarmac . . . a forest," a reference to the Paris 68 slogan, "Beneath the cobblestones . . . a beach."'[17]

The movement was successful in its immediate aim of reducing road building in the UK and even more as an example of fun protest. 'The magical collision of carnival and rebellion, play and politics is such a potent recipe and relatively easy to pull off that anyone can do it. Even you.'[18] And so was born the phenomenon of the 'artivist' creating and participating in the 'protestival'. RTS groups sprang up around the world and were followed by a legion of other protest groups with names like Carnival Against Capitalism, Billionaires for Bush, Reverend Billy and the Church of Stop Shopping, The Society for Creative Anachronism and The Clandestine Insurgent Rebel Clown Army.

Tactics were as diverse as the groups and included new techniques of disruption (in New York the Lower East Side Collective broke up an auction of communal gardens by releasing 10,000 crickets and causing cartoon pandemonium, with people standing on chairs screaming) and of confrontation – tickling police officers with feather dusters, attacking them with balloons or water pistols, disconcerting them with Rockette-style kick-line dancing and ridiculing them by blaring the Death Star theme from *Star Wars* at full volume on mobile sound systems. The Billionaires for Bush dressed in tuxedos and evening gowns, carried bottles of champagne and handed police officers wads of fake dollar bills as a reward for suppressing protest. In New York the Ya Basta! Collective looked deliberately ridiculous in elaborate foam padding, gas masks, helmets and white chemical-protective jumpsuits. At the Québec City protest against the Free Trade Area of the Americas, The Society for Creative Anachronism constructed a giant medieval siege engine to lob teddy bears over the police line. At the G8 protest in Edinburgh in 2005 The Clandestine Insurgent Rebel Clown Army confused the police by appearing to fight with each other. During the Occupy Wall Street protest in 2011 a group of activists drew on the new fascination with the undead by dressing as corporate zombies and staggering about spewing dollar bills from bloodstained mouths.

The tactics have to keep changing, both to engage the activists themselves and to disconcert the authorities who learn to deal with the familiar. In fact, the Occupy actions, and sit-ins in general, are regarded as ineffective by some recent activists, for instance Srdja Popovic, leader of Otpor! (Serbo-Croat for 'Resistance'), founder of The Centre for Applied Non-Violent Action and Strategies, and author of *Blueprint for Revolution: How to Use Rice Pudding, Lego Men and Other Non-Violent Techniques to Galvanise Communities, Overthrow Dictators or Simply Change the World*. According to

Popovic, 'Occupy is a high-risk, divisive tactic of concentration: getting everyone in one place, fighting with the police, and pissing off the people, like shopkeepers, you need to win over.' It's too predictable and all the authorities have to do is wait for the protesters to become bored and drift away. 'What you want in a campaign are what we call low-risk, inclusive tactics of dispersal.' Humour is also a crucial feature in what Popovic calls 'laughtivism': 'In Chile, against Pinochet, they drove at half speed: not illegal, very low risk, pretty funny, nothing the cops can do. It's about doing something neat, and living to tell everyone.' This is transgressionism raised to the level of political strategy, a resistance that undermines dignity in ways that minimise risk. In Popovic's native Serbia, one of Otpor!'s tactic's in the struggle to oust the dictator, Milosevic, was to paint his face on barrels and leave these on streets with sticks propped against them so that passers-by were encouraged to drum on, or just whack, the face. If you want to depose a dictator at no personal risk and have fun in the process, Popovic is your man.

One of the most unlikely tactics, which Popovic would surely endorse, must be guerrilla knitting, established in Calgary in 2001 by The Revolutionary Knitting Circle and subsequently practised by New York's Activist Knitting Troupe, London's Cast Off, and other groups round Europe and North America, in a movement coordinated by the Viral Knitting Project. Cast Off stages 'knit-ins' on the London Underground and the more radical groups join street protest action, as when members of Weaving the Web sat serenely knitting in the midst of the Québec City mayhem in 2001.

One of the most successful tactics is using giant papier-mâché puppets, which seem to infuriate the authorities more than anything else. Many reports of protest action describe police officers spending inordinate amounts of time and energy destroying these puppets in visceral fury. For instance, after a protest against the Free Trade Areas of the Americas Summit in Miami in 2003 police officers first forced the abandonment of the puppets and then 'spent the next half hour or so systematically attacking and destroying them: shooting, kicking and ripping the remains; one even putting a giant puppet in his squad car with the head sticking out and driving so as to smash it against every sign and street post available'.[19] The anthropologist David Graeber, a veteran of protest action, quotes this eye-witness report and has himself witnessed and pondered this phenomenon: 'Giant papier-mâché puppets are created by taking the most ephemeral of material – ideas, paper, wire mesh – and transforming it into something very like a monument, even if they are, at the same time, somewhat ridiculous. A giant puppet is the mockery of the idea of a monument, and of everything monuments represent: the inapproachability, monochrome solemnity, above all, the implication of permanence, the state's (itself ultimately somewhat ridiculous) attempt to turn its principle and history into eternal verities.'[20] It is also possible that, as eventually happened with the giants in medieval carnivals, giant puppets are hated by the authorities not just because they ridicule the very idea of solemn importance but also because they reject the very concept of official control.

But the most constant tactic in contemporary protest is drumming. The groups usually have at least one drummer, often many, and sometimes a full band, such as Seattle's Infernal Noise Brigade, Toronto's Guerilla Rhythm Squad, New York's Hungry March Band, France's *Front Musicale d'Intervention*, London's Rhythms of Resistance Samba Band and Edinburgh's Pink and Silver

Samba Band, which enlivened the Carnival for Full Enjoyment at the Edinburgh G8. According to its website, the Infernal Noise Brigade 'is a marching drum orchestra and street performance crew activated by massive political and cultural uprisings. We are a tactical mobile rhythmic unit consisting of a majorette, medics, tactical advisors, rifle-twirling contingent, flag corps, and percussionists . . . The INB provides subliminal disruption of time, using drums to divide it into disorienting rhythmic patterns which are disturbing to the linear sequence.'[21] Drumming, the inspiration for collective effervescence, seems to be equally effective at inspiring collective protest. There is even a theory that drumming set off the French Revolution, when on 5 October 1789, a young woman took a drum to the central market of Paris and led the market women on a march to Versailles, where they occupied the palace and forced the king to return to the city, an action many historians believe to have been more significant than the storming of the Bastille.

For the activists themselves, one of the main pleasures of protest is discovering the solidarity of the group, in the manufacture of costumes, puppets, equipment, banners and so on, and in the discussions on tactics. David Graeber: 'If one talks to someone fresh from a major mobilization and asks what she found most new and exciting about the experience, one is most likely to hear long descriptions of the organization of affinity groups, clusters, blockades, flying squads, spokes-councils, and network structures, or about the apparent miracle of consensus decision making in which one can see thousands of people coordinate their actions without any formal leadership structure.'[22]

At the same time Graeber is acutely aware that the lengthy, rambling meetings are themselves often as laughable as the objects of protest, and he seems happy to reveal this in often hilarious detail. His book *Direct Action: an Ethnography*[23] includes diary accounts of wildly disparate groups and individuals attempting to agree protest plans. In New York's Little Italy, round a table in a pastry shop bearing a map of Québec City drawn on a napkin in felt-tip pen and salt cellars and sugar bowls representing activist and police units, he and fellow members of Ya Basta! listen to a Canadian activist called Jaggi Singh explain a plan to re-enact the battle of Québec: 'That was the battle in 1759 in which the British conquered the city in the first place. They surprised the French garrison by climbing up these cliffs . . . near the old fort. So here's my idea. You guys can suit up in your Ya Basta! outfits, and climb the exact same cliff, except – no, wait, listen! This part is important – over all the padding and the chemical jumpsuits, you'll all be wearing Québec Nordiques hockey jerseys.' Later, in Québec City, Graeber listens to Starhawk, a practising witch who believes in a 'Magical Activism' that uses 'magic as a way of reshaping consciousness, to add a spiritual dimension' but also has a practical plan to 'pull sources of strength out of apparent weakness, to show how little homely things like yarn can, if woven together – sort of like a spell – stop even military machinery'. Later still, he listens to a man from the Pagan Cluster in Vermont submit 'a proposal for an action based on the Cochabamba statement, about access to water as a basic human right. We want to create a Living River of People that can flow through different zones in the city, trying to cause as much disruption as possible.'

This ability to self-mock is an appealing feature of the new anarchism espoused by many of the protest groups, and is often incorporated in the protest itself, as when The Tranny Brigade

chant, 'We're queer! We're cute! We're anti-war to boot!' or The
Glamericans display a banner saying, 'War is just so *Tacky*,
Darling.'

Such behaviour is a long way from the anarchist stereotypes,
first the cartoon traditional anarchist in a black cloak, demoni-
cally grinning as he prepares to throw a fizzing bomb, and now
the contemporary version, also dressed in black but concealing the
demonic grin beneath a black hood and bandana, as he smashes
in corporate windows with a crowbar and booted feet. The early
stereotype persists via the ruthless anarchists in Joseph Conrad's
novel *The Secret Agent*, which is revered as the first novel to deal
with terrorism but seems to me one of Conrad's least successful
works, absurdly implausible in every way. Though it has to be
acknowledged that early anarchists did succeed in assassinating
two kings (of Italy and Greece), two presidents (of France and the
USA) and three prime ministers (of Spain, Russia and Spain again).
And the later variety in the black bandanna has certainly smashed
many windows. But it's a lazy mistake, which I have made myself,
to equate anarchism with irresponsibility, fecklessness, violence
and destruction.

In fact, anarchism has as much in common with fun as with
violence. There is the obvious affinity with humour in the shared
scepticism about power, the powerful, and self-importance in general, and even an affinity with dancing in the remark attributed
to the early anarchist, Emma Goldman, 'If I can't dance, it's not
my revolution.' It's a shame that Goldman never said anything
so quotably pithy, though she did mount a spirited defence of
fun when scolded for dancing by a puritanical young comrade:
'I did not believe that a cause which stood for a beautiful ideal,

for anarchism, for release and freedom from conventions and prejudice, should demand the denial of life and joy. I insisted that our cause could not expect me to become a nun and that the movement should not be turned into a cloister.'[24] David Graeber says something similar about anarchism, 'It is not an ideology, a theory of history. It tends, rather, towards a kind of inspirational, creative play.'[25] And anarchism is like fun in being largely rejected by thinkers as unworthy of serious consideration – despite the fact that hedonism has been as important a factor in contemporary personal life as anarchism has been in the social and political.

One reason for the academic neglect is that anarchism is more interested in practice than in ideology, though it is not so much against theory as against theorists, in particular the idea of vanguardism, the belief in an intellectual elite who will lead the ignorant to the promised land. Similarly, it is not so much against organisation as against hierarchy (the top-down structures with a boss at the top and many levels of power descending to the powerless at the bottom), not so much against authority as against authoritarianism (the authority that believes itself *entitled*, and even *obliged*, to tell everyone else what to do, and to coerce those who resist), not so much against individuality as against individualism (which considers *only* the interests of the individual), and not so much for freedom as for autonomy (having control over one's life, which does not mean rejecting responsibility in favour of infinite choice).

Histories of anarchism usually begin with Proudhon, who coined the term in the nineteenth century, and then move on to Bakunin and Kropotkin, who developed Proudhon's ideas, and on again to twentieth-century anarchists like Emma Goldman and Murray Bookchin – but many anarchists insist that these writers merely gave a name and description to something that has existed as long as history itself, in the practices that evolved in egalitarian tribal communities, then among Chinese peasants, medieval European peasants, the Diggers, Ranters and Levellers of seventeenth century England, Swiss watchmakers, American Quakers, the Paris Commune of 1871, the Spanish revolutionaries of 1936, the Zapatista rebellion in Mexico in 1994, and now among contemporary protest groups. It is 'a certain kind of insurgent common sense'[26] based on rejection of leaders, hierarchy and coercive authority in favour of voluntary association, self-organisation, cooperation, mutual aid and consensus decision making. So it does not seek to win arguments, or even to change people's minds, but only to arrive at a course of action that everyone involved can live with, if not wholly endorse.

According to this way of thinking, many contemporary groups are following anarchist principles without being aware of it – for instance the leaderless urban tribes and fluid affinity groups so common in cities. And it occurs to me that marriage is an anarchist group of two, with each partner going along with some of the beliefs and practices of the other without really sharing them, and in some cases actually detesting them. The secret is not to condemn or attempt to convert, and above all not to display contempt.

This form of anarchism fits neatly with the contemporary idea of freedom as absence of coercion. It has gradually come to me over the years that what I dislike most is people telling me what to do, especially in a righteous tone, and even more especially righteousness backed by threats. I have come to detest bullies above all – and I am sure that many others have arrived at the same conclusion, as demonstrated by recent concern about bullying in schools and other institutions (though the self-righteous, superior bullies, supported by group dogma, are much more dangerous than the merely violent individuals).

The new anarchism also jives with the contemporary demands for fun, self-expression, group participation and authenticity, in the sense of something valuable and ethical that has been lost and must be recovered from the past. However, Graeber is scathing about what he defines as 'primitivism', the belief that technology, and in the extreme case, all of modern civilisation, has been a terrible mistake and that the only solution is to return to the Stone Age and start again (the Paleo lifestyle fad is Primitivism Lite). At the other end of the scale, he is equally dismissive of pretentious postmodern intellectuals who peddle an obscurantist nihilism that rejects all forms of social organisation as hopelessly corrupted by power. There is no going back and there is also no giving up. There is only the difficult, frustrating, exhausting, uncertain and often absurd struggling forward.

The new anarchism even fits developments in contemporary science, though neither anarchists nor scientists seem to be aware of this. The new scientific paradigm of emergence, which claims that the order, organisation and complexity of the material world developed bottom-up from a chaos of simple components, with no guiding hand or principle, is analogous to the anarchist belief in a bottom-up social organisation without theory or leaders. In biology the emphasis has moved from the neo-Darwinist belief in strength, power and ruthlessness as the key to survival, to an understanding that cooperation and interdependence may be more effective. In neuroscience there is the hypothesis that there is no unitary self, no boss of all bosses controlling a top-down structure of dedicated brain modules. According to this approach, the brain is not a rigid hierarchy but is organised bottom-up in a flexible anarchist federation of affinity groups. Also, the new discipline of network theory, which claims to show how interlocking networks facilitate structure and organisation, is analogous to the anarchist belief in a network of affinity groups.

Strangest of all is the correspondence with religion, between the Pentecostal and neo-pagan preference for ritual over doctrine and the anarchist preference for action over ideology. While, in politics, the increasing demand for regional and local autonomy matches the anarchist belief in federations of local and regional communities. And the anarchist emphasis on provisional forms of organisation that do not ossify but change to meet changing circumstances is a perfect example of the twentieth-century process philosophy that claims there is no solidity or finality in the material or social worlds and that all is fluidity, flux and change. Even the development of technology has suited anarchism, with the Internet and cell phones perfect for group coordination.

All this makes anarchism seem much more acceptable. It has the potential to be more authentic than capitalism or socialism, more representative than democracy and more moral than religion – and it's always good to feel virtuous (providing of course that this does not inspire superiority). The problem comes with envisaging how it would work on a large-scale, macro level. The examples are all of small-scale local groups. Many anarchists argue that living in nation states for so long has made us incapable of imagining the anarchist alternative of federated communities and regions. The state presents itself as the natural, permanent and only feasible form of political organisation, just as capitalism does for economic organisation. But many have come to see capitalism as neither inevitable, desirable nor permanent, so why should the nation state seem eternal?

It could be that I have too much of a top-down, controlling mentality to surrender to bottom-up development, even in theory. But one lesson from the study of networks is that there is an inherent tendency for some nodes to become hubs and dominate the network activity (as has happened with the Internet, which began as an egalitarian free-for-all but is increasingly controlled by a few powerful companies). And at the individual level there will always be a hunger for power over others. The bullies, alas, we always have with us. So it's difficult to avoid the development of hierarchy (and even more difficult to dismantle existing hierarchies). Another lesson from network theory is that the most successful systems combine a measure of top-down control and bottom-up spontaneity, with the two contending in fruitful tension. A good example is the contemporary city, which derives its energy and creativity from bottom-up activity but needs top-down control in areas like public transport – and a good example of the two combining is the success of the Reclaim the Streets resistance to the automobile and demand for public commons, which has resulted in city authorities creating more pedestrianised streets and removing many of the barriers between pedestrians and vehicles.

It may be that anarchism works best as a political corrective, as fun is a social corrective, because a society organised solely on anarchist principles could be as disastrous as a personal life devoted entirely to fun. However, when anarchism and fun get together, the combination can certainly be liberating, and a good example of a successful combination is the week-long Burning Man Festival in the Black Rock Desert of Nevada, a radical elsewhere several hours' journey from the nearest city, so that the Festival first requires an arduous pilgrimage through a wilderness, and then goes on to combine playful, artistic, comical, sexual and spiritual fun. It is almost as though the Festival was designed to offer the entire range of contemporary fun, which is no doubt why it grows every year (now attracting over 70,000 to a site of 5.7 square miles) and is producing affiliated offshoots round the world (in South Africa, Australia, Israel, Spain and Wales).

The political aspect is the rejection of capitalism and commerce. Nothing can be bought or sold, advertised or sponsored, and only gifting is permitted. All those who attend must bring their own supplies, which encourages clubbing together in camps with a policy of fierce egalitarianism like that of hunter-gatherers or contemporary anarchist groups. Nor are there paid performers or paying spectators. Everyone participates and freely.

The spiritual fun includes workshops on yoni massage, ashtanga yoga, shamanism, paganism and Tantra, and the building from junk materials of a secular temple, a sacred space where revellers may go for quiet contemplation. As art attempts to re-enchant the world, spirituality attempts to re-sacralise it – and as anything, even junk, can be art if someone says so and others agree, so anything, even junk, can be sacred if it is consecrated and heads bow in reverence.

The artistic fun includes giant art installations involving play and games (with names like Hayam Sun Temple, Cosmic Praise, Lost Nomads of Vulcania, Tree of Impermanence and Infinite Infant and the Trail of Toys), and art cars known as Mutant

Vehicles, often converted to look like animals – polar bears, ducks, unicorns or snails (the essential condition for an MV is that it is mutated not decorated, i.e. the base vehicle cannot be recognised). Needless to say, personal artistic transformation is also encouraged, with all sorts of elaborate costumes and body painting (for both sexes there is a Tutu Tuesday and a Fishnet Friday), though minimal or no clothing is also common, with male 'shirtcockers' wearing only shirts, and female 'yoga bunnies' conducting workshops in the nude.

For participative sexual fun there are petting zoos, cuddle puddles, spanking classes, pornographic puppet shows, naked foam parties, group masturbation, a Hot Sex Fire Jam (sex and fire-eating) and a twenty-four-hour air-conditioned Orgy Dome for spiritual swingers ('a sex-positive consensual space for couples and moresomes to play'). However, despite its name, the Dome is not a free-for-all but has stringent entry screening and a code of conduct, just as in the swinger clubs.

A unique feature of the Festival is its celebration of the transience of fun, and indeed of all things. At the end of the week, the art installations, junk temple and, of course, the giant Man are all burned, and everything non-flammable is removed. The fabulous city in the desert, at once pre- and post-everything, a combination of *Arabian Nights* and *Mad Max*, appears briefly and then disappears again like a shimmering mirage, obeying its own maxim of 'Leave no trace'.

PART IV

Assessing Fun

The Post-Postmodern is the Pre-Premodern

Many would claim that the rise of fun is a sign of a decadent culture, frivolous, narcissistic, passive and self-indulgent, and there is plenty of evidence for this in the likes of binge drinking for the indigent and luxury cruises for the affluent. But there is also plenty of evidence for fun that is none of these things. Increasingly, fun activities are not passive but active, seeking experience as much as pleasure, and may even involve learning and effort. Far from being narcissistic, most fun rejects individualism and seeks belonging in a group. It's not so much that there are groups in order to enjoy fun as that there is fun in order to enjoy groups. As for the charge of frivolity, much fun is indeed play, but many philosophers and even theologians now regard play as profoundly serious, even essential, and fun is an increasingly important part of the serious endeavours of education, art, religious evangelism and political protest.

Rather than being dismissed as mere hedonism, fun can be interpreted as a response to a failure of the modern age, accentuated in the postmodern period, to live up to its promise, resulting in a general and inchoate but intense feeling that something has gone wrong, that we have been led astray by false gods and lost something crucial. What exactly this was is not clear, much less how to regain it, but it is certainly clear that life is short and that during the wait for an authentic messiah the best way to evade the false gods is to reject their authority in the group rituals of fun.

This feeling of failure and loss has many overlapping and interconnecting negative manifestations – including a refusal to accept Western culture as the ultimate, superior form of civilisation, a loss of faith in the traditional Western monoliths (the nations, established religions and political parties), an abhorrence of the growing inequality of Western societies, a reluctance to accept the traditional models of centralised control and hierarchical power structures, a distrust of all ideologies and doctrines, and a bracing scepticism about all that presents itself as important (often dismissed as cynicism and apathy by those who regard themselves as important). On the positive side, there is a search for new sources of meaning, and for fun that offers some combination of play, transgression, transcendence, belonging, oneness, re-enchantment and authenticity.

This is why so much fun is a rediscovery of early beliefs and practices. The rise of the festival is a return to the earliest form of celebration (as is the trend to active participation rather than passive spectating); raving is a return to the trance dance of archaic ritual; secular spirituality is a return to early enchantment and oneness; group sex and sexual fluidity are a return to early openness; holidays are a return to pilgrimage (and now often *are* pilgrimages); carnivalesque protest is a return to the transgression of inversion rituals; the reverence for DJs and comedians is a return to the appeal of the shaman and trickster; the popularity of play and games is a return to the spirit of mythology and pre-Socratic philosophy; and the emergence of urban tribes is a return to the egalitarianism of the hunter-gatherers.

This return to the distant past is not restricted to fun. Contemporary physics sees the cosmos as a flux of forces, much as did the ancient world. Philosophy understands consciousness and the self as a similar flux, much as did Buddhism, not a separate entity but a process formed in reaction to others. Neuroscience now proposes a theory of distributed mind, claiming that the mind is not separate, or even entirely embodied, but is partly *in* its environment, actually *in* the world, a notion remarkably similar to the extended self of the traditional world.[1]

Everywhere there is evidence that the way forward involves a return, a development predicted by T.S. Eliot:

> We shall not cease from exploration
> And the end of all our exploring
> Will be to arrive where we started
> And know the place for the first time.[2]

We seem to be experiencing just such a journey and recognition. The post-postmodern is the pre-premodern.

This is the source of the hunger for authenticity, for anything that seems old and therefore genuine. But the only way to regain authenticity would be to annihilate it, to return to a time before the concept existed and became an issue, which is not possible. The very existence of the term means that the thing itself is no longer attainable. There is no way back to the primal, unconscious embedding in oneness. There is only the way forward into self-conscious detachment and fragmentation. There are only the forms and degrees of inauthenticity. So, as meaninglessness can become the new meaning, the thoroughly inauthentic can be the new authenticity.

This is the solution of irony, which seems entirely modern, even the modern disease, some would say, but is also a return to the ancient ability to live in contradiction, to be serious and non-serious at the same time. Irony is the adult form of the play philosophy of the child, a refusal of seriousness that is wholly serious – or, rather, a replacement of traditional seriousness with a new form. It is a way of making self-conscious detachment no longer alienating but a pleasure, even a delight. Irony is an effervescent, an aerator of life, imbuing it with bubble and sparkle, making detachment into a buoyancy and self-consciousness into a burnish.

The ironic solution was discovered by modern writers and thinkers but has long since passed into common practice, as shown by the rise in popularity of subversive comedy. Even a football crowd is ironic now, as Tim Parks has noted: 'For years now I've had the suspicion that there is something emblematically modern about the football crowd. They are truly fanatical . . . but simultaneously ironic, even comic. A sticky film of self-parody clings to every gesture of fandom. We cannot take ourselves entirely seriously. Or perhaps this *is* the serious thing, this mixture of delirium and irony, this indulgence in strong emotions without being burned up by them. When the Haaaayllas chant ends everybody claps in self-congratulation and lots of them burst out laughing. *Forza Hellas!* We know we're ridiculous.'[3]

This is similar to the attitude of many neo-pagans, who go to great lengths to recreate accurately ancient costumes and rituals but do so with a strong sense of irony, to many cosplayers who take similar pains but are aware of being laughable fantasists (Ethan Watters boasts that his urban tribe's themed costume evenings have 'so much more irony' than those of other tribes), to many tourists who understand the inherent absurdity of package tours to 'undiscovered' places, and to many anarchists who are profoundly serious in their desire to change the world but understand that the process of consensus making is often absurd. And role playing of every kind is increasingly common because it is another consequence of uncertainty and self-consciousness. We are all performance artists now and might as well enjoy the show. Fun with a dash of astringent irony may be the new seriousness.

A good example of serious fun, where entirely serious purpose combines with acute awareness of absurdity, is the secular church/temple created by the artist Grayson Perry, as famous for his public cross-dressing as his art, and the architect Charles Holland, renowned for the playfulness of his buildings and often described as a prankster. This building, with elements of the Russian Orthodox Church and Hindu Temple, is a memorial to a fictional everywoman, Julie May Cope, a shrine supposedly erected by her second husband Rob as a 'Taj Mahal on the River Stour' to honour his 'all-knowing pagan goddess', also described by Perry as 'a shopping mall Madonna . . . with a kick-ass spirit'. The exterior has tiles showing a naked near-Eastern fertility goddess and the interior has a ceramic statue of Julie pregnant and a tapestry of episodes from her life, including evidence of the breakdown of her first marriage to Dave, i.e. the hairbrush of Dave's mistress Pam, which Julie found in Dave's Cortina. Suspended overhead, like a chandelier, is the cause of Julie's early demise – the moped delivery bike that in its haste to deliver a pizza knocked her down.

Every detail of this building, both inside and outside, has been lovingly crafted, with the most demanding task the fitting by hand of Julie's nipples on 1,925 individual tiles. Charles Holland:

'We were concerned that it wasn't pure fairy tale but something where certain ideas of authenticity and materials rub up against fantasy.'[4] Yet the building is also a functioning home that, in line with Julie's love of holidays, is available to rent by holiday-makers. Perry, however, is also hoping for more spiritual interest and would like the shrine to become the destination of a secular pilgrimage that follows Julie's life in Essex from her birthplace in Canvey Island to her final resting place in Wrabness. This could be a new ironic ritual, the Pilgrimage to the Temple of the Goddess Julie.

And this temple project could be an example of a new form of irony or, rather, a maturing of the old form. Postmodern irony had an elitist, narcissistic, show-off quality, enamoured of its cleverness at being so knowingly detached in finding everything a game. But post-postmodern irony is often egalitarian and sincere, a caring irony. Above all, it wants not to detach but to engage, not to be a superior observer but to belong in a group. In a documentary about his temple Perry brings six real-life Essex Julies to see it, and when they are moved to tears he, too, is deeply moved.[5]

The most important revelation from investigating fun is that group activity of every kind seems to be on the increase, though many individualists continue to hold out. At one of those tradi-tional group meetings, the dinner party, my wife and I are invited to the exciting new variation ('it's great fun') – the murder mystery dinner party where one of the guests is mysteriously murdered and the others have to identify the murderer.[6] Needless to say, all guests are in fancy dress. I explain that attending such a dinner would be too dangerous.

'Why so?'

'I might genuinely murder someone,' I tell this enthusiast, 'possibly you.'

Another couple try to bully us into renting an allotment next to theirs. Here many couples meet at weekends to chat, drink craft beer and nurture their authentic, organically grown vegetables. 'It's great fun.' We allow ourselves to be dragged along for a look and I am rewarded with a back covered in giant insect bites and a bag of some unidentifiable giant coarse ragged leaves full of giant ragged holes.

It occurs to me that it is not the young, urban singletons but older people from the traditional, 'tightly knit' communities of nuclear families who are more likely to be reclusive and to reject contact and refuse to join groups. My wife and I recently had parallel traumas. The enthusiastic young manager of the local bookshop discovered that I read poetry and began inviting me to poetry readings (a ritual I find almost as boring as church services), while my wife's enthusiastic young hairdresser actually invited her to her wedding (a ritual my wife finds wasteful and boring). And while we were still trying to recover, an enthusiastic neighbour called to invite us to a 'hooley' he had organised in the local hall, where we could bring our own drink and dance to a rock band. If it continues like this we may have to move house.

Holed up at home, I open my Saturday paper and discover a new monthly supplement, 'Do Something', dedicated to fun activities, mostly involving groups, such as making your own toothpaste or building a bicycle of bamboo. I open my emails and find a message from the Idler Academy, a London institution founded to promote the joys of doing nothing, but now advertising courses on Scottish country dancing, ukulele playing, bookmaking, sequinification (working with sequins), mosaic tile-making, taxidermy, calligraphy, crochet, gin and knit (learning to knit a beanie while drinking gin cocktails), embroidery and appliqué ('Come and learn to make an appliqué heart pincushion. Price includes your own pin cushion made with vintage and Liberty fabrics to take away and gin cocktails').

Much of this new fun activity is in service to serious causes, because fun is increasingly recognised as the key to group solidarity and commitment. It is no accident that fun is used by both the conservative right (in Pentecostal evangelism) and the radical left (in anarchist protest), and that these groups are among the most dynamic in religion and politics. And much of the new fun is itself a serious cause, a quest for the spiritual comfort of re-enchantment. My wife forwards an email she has just received from a new group called The London Joy Club. Always a diligent researcher, she has answered and received this response: 'Yay! So excited you want to join in the fun and frolics as we explore together how to live a richer, more joyful life! As a member you'll learn loads of techniques to get in your body, feel your joy and make sure it stays around for good. We'll have experts in to share tools and techniques that you can take away to create more joyful lives right now. Things like pleasure, mindfulness, desires, values, feminine power, improv, dance, laughter, yoga and finding beauty in your everyday. Love to get to know you before the next meet up so please drop a note and say "Hi" :) Big Hugs, Lynn.'

Note the keywords – fun, body, tools, improv, dance, laughter – and the excitable tone and feel-good, joy-and-wonder language of the new re-enchantment spirituality, just like that of the Sunday Assembly. The time is right for a new comic-book superheroine called Sensa Wunda. In everyday life this is a drably dressed, earnest young woman, but when she discovers people who are passive, inattentive, querulous and depressed, she utters the magic incantation, 'Gaia, bring wonder,' which reveals her true self, an Earth Goddess in a costume made of green plants from each continent, who now illuminates the myriad interconnections of planet and cosmos, so that the peevish complainers gasp in awe.

And Sensa Wunda accompanies me when I go out for a walk and discover that within the local area there are several Pentecostal churches, a secular choir who meet weekly in a local church, several stand-up comedy clubs, an Art 4 Fun shop where groups meet to make and paint pots, a wide range of dance evenings in every available hall, as wide a range of fitness and sporting activities, an even wider range of spiritual and therapeutic practices, oriental martial arts training (another local church has just hung out a giant banner inviting participation in Fujian White Crane Tai Chi) and literary evenings in the local bookshop (this may sound like passive spectating but the real purpose of such events is not to listen to the writer but to use the so-called question period for impassioned personal speeches). Even the quintessentially solitary activity of reading has become a communal endeavour, with reading groups meeting in bookshops, bars, cafés and private homes.

And a short journey on public transport will access a further astounding range of groups, some offering new activities (urban foraging for food, scavenging in skips for junk sculpture materials), others reviving activities that appeared to be hopelessly out of fashion (sewing, crocheting and knitting for women, repairing gadgets for men), others offering familiar activities in unfamiliar places or at unfamiliar times (urban hide-and-seek for adults, winter camping, midnight hiking, Vinyasa Flow Yoga on the new glass floor on top of Tower Bridge). Still others are new combinations of familiar activities (dodgeball disco, trapeze fitness exercising, football on roller skates, go-karting on ice, paragliding on skis, stand-up paddleboarding – a cross between punting and rowing – and slacklining – a cross between trampolining and tightrope walking. Most bizarre of all is chess boxing, where, in a symbolic union of mind and body, intellectual trickery and brute force, players first deploy cunning strategies on the board and then don boxing gloves to beat the crap out of each other.

It is the time of the gatherings of the active fun tribes. All over the world festivals proliferate like Japanese knotweed, from the techno festivals, teknivals, beloved of the youthful dance tribes, in disused quarries and abandoned airfields, to the literary festivals beloved of senior citizens in Arts Centres in National Heritage beauty spots. Many inner cities, which only a few decades ago were in apparently terminal decline, places of decay and crime, from which the affluent fled in panic, are increasingly used as festival sites, offering urban beaches in summer and skating rinks in winter, and making Sunday, when people traditionally stayed at home and the city centres were deserted, into a day of communal activity, with major areas closed to traffic and given over to farmers' markets, craft fairs, food stalls, marches, parades, street performance and music.

The urban crowd, once generally feared as a threat, now often seems more like a source of comfort, the loosest and most transient group of strangers. As well as the proliferation of special festivities there has been a steady proliferation of public spaces where people can see and be seen – the communal open-plan eating areas of malls, the outdoor tables colonising pavements and squares, and the continuing spread of coffee shops (as in the music industry, authentic indies competing with the corporate chains). In the past I have interpreted this as evidence of narcissistic attention-seeking, but it is also possible to see it as a new form of togetherness and belonging, a new form of community – a paradoxical community of strangers. There is something oddly fulfilling in looking on as people, mysterious, unknowable and seething with deep forces and passions, go about their urgent but inscrutable business. It is the urban equivalent of watching the sea.

Many would angrily reject the suggestion that casual group involvement and, even more absurd, wandering the streets and sitting in cafes, could constitute any kind of meaningful community. What possible relation could there be between people who do not meet, do not want to meet, never speak, avoid even eye contact, see each other only once and briefly and have no wish to see each other ever again? But the relation is in the mutually enjoyed proximity itself, and the pleasure is in the very lack of communication, which would inevitably involve assuming a boring role and exchanging clichés and platitudes – the inauthenticity of the social rather than the mystery of the restless sea.

Certainly these new ways of connecting have little in common with the close, tight, long-term bonding assumed to be necessary for meaningful relations. But it is pointless to lament the death of the traditional community. It may well have been much less congenial than the romanticised memory, and may never have existed at all. It is significant that the ideal community is always in the past. Even in the past it was in the past, as in the Roman nostalgia for a lost, bucolic harmony, and before that the Jewish nostalgia for a Garden of Eden. And even if there once was a community as fulfilling as its mourners claim, there is no possibility of a miraculous resurrection. The fragmentation and fluidity of contemporary life were inevitable developments, and seem likely to accelerate. The monolithic structures were themselves once new and were never as stable as they liked to pretend. Everything changes, including community. And it may be that the new pick 'n' mix approach of membership in many transient, informal groups is a way of enjoying fragmentation and fluidity. It may even be that this approach accords better with human nature. There is nothing monolithic or stable in the human organism, and personal identity, including sexuality, is increasingly uncertain. Just as irony can make self-consciousness a pleasure, the obsession with dressing up and role-play can be seen as a way to make a game of the fragmentation and fluidity of the self.

So the contemporary city can be a community with no rules, binding obligations or enforced identities, where overlapping groups form and dissolve and members join and leave according to choice, and all the groups are embedded in and connected to the rest of the city. This is the crucial distinction between a community and a commune. The commune attempts to cut itself off and remain enclosed, which tends to raise issues of dogma, rules and leadership that lead to acrimonious break up. Few if any such communes have enjoyed long-term flourishing. But the fluid, organic, structureless and ruleless new communities can avoid these conflicts.

Of course restrictions remain. Only those at a certain level of affluence can afford to live in such a way – and probably only while they are childless. Children require dedicated carers who will watch over them for twenty years and provide the affection, support and guidance they need to feel entirely secure and become properly independent. Belligerent demands for rights are common nowadays but unfortunately those with the most absolute rights are also those least able to make demands.

The needs of children always override the need for fun. But fun is not entirely feckless. And thinking about fun raises many serious issues. This is not surprising. Investigating anything illuminates everything, including the investigator. You discover that there is much more going on, that it is all more complex, interconnected and subject to change than you thought, and that your thought was a mixture of lazy assumptions, prejudices and so-called convictions, believed to be objective truth, but based mostly on cultural fashion and personal temperament. The suspicion that much of my aversion to fun was intellectual snobbery has been confirmed. I understand now that the individualism I believed to be the terminus of Western civilisation may be merely a short-term aberration, though this is unlikely to change my behaviour at this stage.

I have not become a born-again Funist, and will not trance dance till dawn at a Full Moon Gathering, learn axe throwing at The Good Experience Festival, or join a protest against capitalism dressed as Coco the Clown. I am Mr High Windows rather than Mr Fun2BWith – but I can look down from the window with understanding rather than contempt, which is significant and surprising. If anyone had told me years ago that I would be sympathetic to ravers, swingers, gamers and anarchists, I would have laughed myself into a double hernia.

And I am certainly coming down from the window for this

year's World Naked Bike Ride, to observe a combination of comedy, sexuality, play, transgression, neo-pagan spirituality (in its celebration of the body) and fun political protest (in its opposition to the automobile). However, the June day turns out to be profoundly unpropitious, overcast and chilly, with a petulant, moody drizzle that can't be bothered to develop, as though the jaded sky is saying, 'I would rain on your parade if I had the energy, but you are not even worth pissing on.'

Then there are the problems of location and timing. It's important to see as many riders as possible and in full flow.

Piccadilly Circus is the meeting point for three streams from North London – but shows no sign of unusual traffic. It would be just my luck if I missed the riders or the route had changed. But suddenly there is a shrill whistle and my God here it comes, a tsunami of bare flesh on wheels pouring down Piccadilly. Astounded tourists and shoppers stop to watch this bizarre flow on every form of pedal-driven transportation, including every model of bicycle and unicycles, tricycles, tandems, three- and four-seaters and rickshaws. The men are mostly naked as promised, and while many of the women are merely topless, a few confirm the welcome news that, after decades of trimming, plucking, shaving and waxing, the quest for authenticity has brought back into fashion luxuriant female pubic hair. Every size, colour, shape, age and condition of body is on display. With every imperfection, surplus and deficit – shrimp dicks and jellyfish tits, whale-blubber bellies and asses like acid-corroded reefs, straggly hair white as gull feathers, and long, broken veins resembling, as William Burroughs memorably once put it, 'little red poisonous sea snakes swimming for dear life in sewage'. Flesh decorated in every way – wrapped in cling film, tattooed, glitter-sprinkled, painted, dyed, daubed with symbols and slogans ('It's Oil Over', 'Carfree is Carefree', 'Less Gas and More Ass'). Sporting every kind of non-concealing accessory – scarfs, boas, chains, necklaces, garlands, a genital padlock – and every kind of headgear – fluorescent wigs, rabbit ears, bowlers, mitres, crowns, turbans, Roman helmets, sailor caps, Dionysian coronals of leaves and a rubber mask of Munch's 'Scream'.

Commotion – an accident! A girl has fallen off her unicycle but is unhurt, laughs and remounts, arms raised in triumph, to a round of applause from the onlookers. A sound system on wheels goes by, pounding out manic techno and surrounded by boogying riders. A man, naked but for a miner's helmet with lamp, suddenly stands up on his pedals to flaunt a micro dick as though it is worthy to be the figurehead of a galleon. A girl, naked but for a jaunty Tom-of-Finland police hat in black vinyl, and bearing the word POLICE in black paint on her back, cycles close to the pavement squirting liquid into the upheld camera phones. Good for her. We should be content just to watch. I have no phone or camera but she squirts me in the face even so, which is all right, too.

This is a serious fun ritual fit for the times, symbolising the fight back of play against purpose, absurdity against self-importance, the city against the car, the ordinary body against flawless models, and pubic hair against scissors, razor and wax. Better still, it symbolises a new awareness that the long pretence is over at last, for everyone now understands that all the emperors are not only naked but have big bellies overhanging minuscule dicks.

This must be how human life looks to God – or Dionysus – an endless river of flesh, ridiculous, vulnerable, ageing, flawed, flowing towards its dissolution in the unforgiving sea. But how blithe, how wanton, how glad the doomed flesh! As though intrigued at last by such defiance, the sun suddenly appears and irradiates the Circus and the statue of Eros. A ragged cheer goes up from the riders and fists salute the relenting sky. This river is bound for oblivion but can make its own beguiling music, frolic, sparkle, dance and laugh along the way.

Acknowledgements

I would like to thank Jennifer Christie, Kerri Sharp, Frank Carney, Jo Roberts-Miller and my wife Martina for many valuable suggestions; Jo Whitford for scrupulously careful editing and Marie Lorimer for compiling such a detailed and well-organised index.

I would also like to thank the many enthusiasts who generously gave me so much of their time – especially Dan Gold, Jamie Cunningham, Peter Birch, Jill from Mad World, Ben from Draughts, and several cosplayers, including Lux from League of Legends, Bambi, her hunter and the zombie princess.

Notes

Chapter 1 – Isn't this Fun?

1   *Evening Standard*, 10.10.2014
2   Aris Roussinous *Rebels: my life behind enemy lines with Warlords, Fanatics and Not-So-Friendly Fire*, Cornerstone 2014

Chapter 2 – Fun and Ritual

1   Quoted in the *Daily Telegraph* 23.12.2004
2   The Irish version of this ritual demanded a separate visit to church to pray for each soul, so arrivals at the church door would see a solemn file of people apparently leaving but then abruptly turning back in for a new visit. Needless to say, no one found this bizarre.
3   The French created a Festival of Reason – but this celebration of the modern was obliged to ransack the rituals of antiquity, and featured goddesses of Reason dressed as shepherdesses and riding in chariots distributing flowers, and banners featuring temples, obelisks and pyramids and the symbols of freemasonry, always useful for contributing occult heft (the Orange Order later appropriated many of these for the same reason).

Similarly, the Soviet authorities realised that ideological lecturing was a waste of time and set up commissions to invent new appropriately socialist rituals. The most spectacular was the 'initiation into the working class', which was celebrated in the workplace 'palace of culture'. Senior workers and communist dignitaries sat on a raised platform, with a giant red flag at their backs and below them an audience of lesser workers and relatives and friends of the initiates, and all rose as bugles sounded a fanfare, chandeliers were suddenly illuminated, an orchestra struck up and a dramatic drum roll announced the entry of the new workers surrounded by an honour guard bearing a great torch lit in the furnace of a factory and paraded through the streets the evening before. Taking turns to face the torch, each initiate would recite the labour oath: 'We swear to follow always the traditions of the proletariat. We swear to carry forward with honour the baton of our fathers.' This certainly beats the West's feeble Induction Day.

4   'The Context, Performance and Meaning of Ritual: The British Monarchy and the Invention of Tradition', by David Cannadine, in *The Invention of Tradition*, ed. Eric Hobsbawm and Terence Ranger, Cambridge University Press 1983

5   'The Highland Tradition of Scotland' by Hugh Trevor-Roper (in *The Invention of Tradition*) gives a full account of the evidence: 'We may thus conclude that the kilt is a purely modern costume, first designed, and first worn, by an English Quaker industrialist, and that it was bestowed by him on the Highlanders in order not to preserve their traditional way of life but to ease its transformation: to bring them out of the heather and into the factory.'

Chapter 3 – Fun and Transcendence

1   For instance the Sumerian Inanna, the Canaanite Asherah, the Egyptian Isis, the Greek Artemis, Goddess of Childbirth, and Demeter, Goddess of the Harvest, and the Roman Cybele, The Great Mother.

2   In *The God of Ecstasy: Sex Roles and the Madness of Dionysus*, St Martin's Press 1988, the archaeologist Arthur Evans identified Dionysian gods in cultures across Europe, Africa and India – 'Bakkhos, Pan, Eleutherus, Minotaur, Sabazios, Inuus, Faunus, Priapus, Liber, Ammon, Osiris, Shiva, Cerenunnus'

3   Emile Durkheim, *The Elementary Forms of Religious Life*, Free Press 1915

4   Aniruddh Patel, *Music, Language and the Brain*, Oxford University Press 2008

5   Merlin Donald, *Origins of the Modern Mind*, Harvard University Press 1991

6   This therapy, claimed to be effective for relief of anxiety, stress and pain, as well as losing weight, growing your finances, and much more, is explained in a book, *The Tapping Solution*, by Nick Ortner, Hay House 2013, which shrewdly taps into ancient oriental medicine by claiming connections between tapping and acupoints, energy meridians and Bonghan channels. There is also an annual Tapping World Summit, which claims to have more than 500,000 attending.

7   James Wood, *The Fun Stuff*, Jonathan Cape 2013

8   Aniruddh Patel and John Iversen, 'A non-human animal can drum a steady beat on a musical instrument', Proceedings of the 9th International Conference on Music Perception and Cognition, ed. M. Baroni, A.R. Addressi, Bologna 2006

9   Research results presented at a meeting of the American Association for the Advancement of Science, February 2014

10   Layne Redmond, *DRUM! Magazine*, December 2000

11   Exodus 15:20

12   Steven Strogatz, *Sync: The Emerging Science of Spontaneous Order*, Hyperion 2003

13   Nick Stewart, Oxford Brookes University website, www.brookes.ac.uk

14   William McNeill, *Keeping Together in Time: Dance and Drill in Human History*,
      Harvard University Press 1995

15   Thaddeus Russell, *A Renegade History of the United States*, Free Press 2010

16   Mircea Eliade, *Shamanism: Archaic Techniques of Ecstasy*, Routledge and Kegan
      Paul 1964

17   I. M. Lewis, *Ecstatic Religion*, 3rd edition, Routledge 2003

18   Johan Huizinga, *Homo Ludens*, Roy 1950

19   Mac Linscott Ricketts, 'The Shaman and the Trickster', in *Mythical Trickster
      Figures*, ed. William J. Hynes and William G. Doty, University of Alabama Press
      1993

20   *Trickster Makes This World*, by Lewis Hyde, Canongate 2008, has an extensive
      selection of trickster tales masterfully analysed.

21   Robin Dunbar, *How Many Friends Does One Person Need?*, Faber 2010

22   Ibid

23   Robin Dunbar, *Human Evolution*, Penguin 2014

24   A young woman who is a scholar and lecturer at Oxford University confided to me
      that she naively agreed to be a bridesmaid for a school friend and was horrified to
      discover that she would have to get a fake tan. When she objected, she was told that
      if she continued to complain they would go for the Jamaican Five, and she would
      have to lecture on Mallarmé in the darkest fake tan available.

25   Don DeLillo, *Underworld*, Scribner 1997

26   Jon Henley, 'The Rise and Rise of the Tattoo', *Guardian* 20.07.2010

Chapter 4 – Fun and the Group

1   A more recent example is *The Hangover* (2009), where the three amigos are
     Bradley Cooper (leader), Zach Galifianakis (shaman) and Ed Helms (insignif-
     icant third).

2   Ethan Watters, *Urban Tribes: Are Friends the New Family?*, Bloomsbury 2004

3   It is obviously difficult to reconstruct Palaeolithic social life but those who have
     studied the foraging groups that persisted into the modern era agree on their ethos.
     In a paper collating research from many areas, a multi-disciplinary team came to
     this conclusion: 'A core characteristic of documented nomadic foragers is their
     political egalitarianism. Nomadic foragers have no hierarchical social stratification

and decisions are reached through deliberation and consensus; leaders (if they exist) have little authority over group members; rotation of roles and functions occurs regularly; people come and go as they please; and no person can command or subject group members ... The connection between political egalitarianism and nomadic foragers is robust.' D. Shultziner, T. Stevens, M. Stevens, B. A. Stuart, R. J. Hannagan, G. Saltini-Semerari, 'The causes and scope of political egalitarianism during the Last Glacial: a multi-disciplinary perspective', *Biology and Philosophy* 25, Springer 2010

4   Ibid

5   For a full account of developments in friendship in the West from the classical period to the present, see *Friendship: a History*, ed. Barbara Caine, Equinox 2009

6   The evidence is presented by complexity theorist Scott Page in *The Difference: How the Power of Diversity Creates Better Groups, Firms and Societies*, Princeton University Press 2007. Page even expresses his conclusion as the diversity prediction theorem, where the term 'prediction diversity' is the range of individual predictions:

$$\text{collective error} = \text{average individual error} - \text{prediction diversity}$$

7   The evidence for this is in Richard Crisp, *The Social Brain*, Robinson 2015

8   Robin Dunbar, *How Many Friends Does One Person Need?*, Faber 2010

9   More on religious and political affinity groups in Chapters 14 and 15

10   *How Many Friends Does One Person Need?*

11   Robin Dunbar, *Human Evolution*, Pelican 2014

12   Many have speculated on how successive All Blacks teams from a small country like New Zealand have managed to dominate international rugby for decades. One theory is that these teams are bound by a fierce egalitarianism that suppresses any manifestation of egotism and rejects even the most talented players if they put themselves before the team. This philosophy is succinctly summarised as 'no dickheads'.

13   Mark S. Granovetter, 'The Strength of Weak Ties', *American Journal of Sociology* 78, 1973

14   Apparently this is a character from *Adventure Time*, a TV cartoon series about the adventures of a boy called Finn and his magical dog Jake in The Land of Ooo.

15   Seth Grahame-Smith and Jane Austen, *Pride and Prejudice and Zombies: The Classic Regency Romance now with Ultraviolent Zombie Mayhem*, Quirk Classics 2009, which begins, 'It is a truth universally acknowledged that a zombie in possession of brains must be in want of more brains.'

16   Broadcast on Channel 4, 06.01.2014

Chapter 5 – Fun, Boredom, Anxiety and Authenticity

1 Søren Kierkegaard, *Either/Or: A Fragment of Life*, Penguin 2004

2 Charles Baudelaire, '*Au Lecteur*', translated by Michael Foley

3 J.G. Ballard, *Extreme Metaphors: Interviews with J.G Ballard 1967–2008*, Fourth Estate 2012

4 Many may be sceptical about this claim – but it is supported by Natsal, the National Survey of Sexual Attitudes and Lifestyles, which shows a steady drop in frequency of sexual intercourse over the last few decades. A survey in the Observer (28.09.2014) confirmed this. 'Britain is losing its libido. That is the striking conclusion of an Observer survey ... which reveals that the average British adult has sex only four times a month ... Our previous survey recorded a figure of seven times a month.' This survey also revealed that, where in 2008 76% were satisfied by their sex lives this had shrunk to 63% by 2014.

5 Guy Debord, *The Society of the Spectacle*, Zone Books 1994

6 Jean-Paul Sartre, *Existentialism is a Humanism*, Methuen 1948

7 *Inventing the Individual: The Origins of Western Liberalism* by Larry Siedentop, Allen Lane 2014, is especially good on the religious, material and social factors. *Sources of the Self* by Charles Taylor, Cambridge University Press 1989, is equally good on the intellectual and literary factors.

8 From *Dockery and Son*, in *Collected Poems*, Faber 1988

9 From *Aubade*, in *Collected Poems*

10 Jean-Paul Sartre, *Being and Nothingness: An Essay on Phenomenological Ontology*, Routledge 2003

11 Placenta eating seems to be especially fashionable with celebrities. When the actor Tom Cruise was about to have a daughter, he told *GQ* magazine, 'I'm going to eat the cord and the placenta right there.' For the squeamish, there is a less Paleo but more palatable option, as explained by the reality TV celebrity Kim Kardashian on her website: 'I'm having it freeze-dried and made into pill form. Not actually fry it like a steak and eat it (which some people do BTW).' In the UK this service is available from a company known as Placenta Plus.

12 Quoted in the *Evening Standard*, 08.01.2015

13 One of the most extreme is *Being a Beast* (Profile 2016) by Charles Foster, a former barrister desperate to reconnect with the wild and dissatisfied by running ultra-marathons over the deserts of Africa, who applied the technique of method acting to nature exploration and attempted to live like a deer, a fox and a badger, crawling on all fours, eating worms and sleeping in a sett in the woods, where he 'wriggled inside and tried to be a bit more authentic'.

14 The critic David Shields has expressed this view in a passionate and influential polemic, *Reality Hunger*, and his demand for raw, undistorted, authentic experience in writing was immediately met by the Norwegian writer, Karl Ove Knausgard, whose huge and hugely successful 'novel' *My Struggle* is an alarmingly honest and minutely detailed account of his own life, with not even the names of the people changed.

15 Charles Taylor, *The Ethics of Authenticity*, Harvard University Press 1991. Taylor also addresses the issue at length in *Sources of the Self* and *A Secular Age*.

16 Following Heidegger and Sartre there was Adorno's *The Jargon of Authenticity*, and, more recently, the American philosophers Marshall Berman with *The Politics of Authenticity* and Charles Guignon with *On Being Authentic*, the Israeli philosopher Jacob Golomb with *In Search of Authenticity*, and the critic Lionel Trilling with *Sincerity and Authenticity*. While Matthew Crawford, a philosopher who also runs a motorcycle repair shop, shares the literary hunger for reality in his book, *The Case for Working with Your Hands*, and says of a later book, *The World Beyond Your Head*, that 'The philosophical project of this book is to *reclaim the real*.'

17 Related to this is the Dead Writers Fragrance Line with scents inspired by such famous literary figures as Henry VIII and Marie Antoinette.

Chapter 6 – Fun and Play

1 Philip Wheelwright, *Heraclitus*, Atheneum 1964

2 Herbert Giles, *Chuang Tzu: Musings of a Chinese Mystic*, London 1920

3 Swami Prabhavananda and Christopher Isherwood, *The Bhagavad Gita*, Los Angeles 1944

4 Friedrich Schiller, *Letters On the Aesthetic Education of Man*, Clarendon Press 1967

5 Friedrich Nietzsche *Beyond Good and Evil*, Oxford 2008

6 Friedrich Nietzsche *Human, All Too Human*, Penguin 1994

7 Johan Huizinga, *Homo Ludens: A Study of the Play Element in Culture*, Roy 1950

8 Ibid

9 Jurgen Moltmann, *Theology of Play*, and David L. Miller, *God and Games: Towards a Theology of Play*, World Publishing Company 1970

10 V. Barabanov, V. Gulimova, R. Berdiev, S. Savelier, 'Object Play in Thick-toed Geckos During a Space Experiment', *Journal of Ethology*, May 2015

11 Robert Fagen, *Animal Play Behaviour*, Oxford University Press 1981

12 Sergio Pellis, Andrew Iwaniuk and John Nelson (Monash University), 'Do big-brained animals play more? Comparative analyses of play and relative brain size in mammals', *Journal of Comparative Psychology* 115 2001

13   *Basic Writings of Nietzsche*, Modern Library 2000

14   Brian Sutton-Smith, *The Ambiguity of Play*, Harvard University Press 2001

15   David Graeber, 'What's The Point If We Can't Have Fun?', *The Baffler*, February 2014

16   Ibid

17   Quoted in the *Daily Telegraph*, 17.07.2012. I am thinking of trying for the Turner myself with a work called *Castles of Sand*. This will involve turning the floor of a large gallery into a sandpit strewn with buckets and spades, and encouraging art lovers to knock down existing castles and build new ones. The work will be a metaphor for transience and precariousness overcome by the indomitable human spirit.

18   For instance The Lego Architecture Series which aims to 'celebrate the past, present and future of architecture through the Lego Brick' and includes Lego sets for constructing the White House, Burj Khalifa, Taj Mahal, Sydney Opera House, Big Ben and the Leaning Tower of Pisa.

19   Zoe Williams, 'Meet the couples who click together like Lego', *Guardian* 12.12.2015

Chapter 7 – Fun and Transgression

1   *The Selected Letters of Gustave Flaubert*, Hamish Hamilton 1954

2   Louis E. Backman, *Religious Dances in the Christian Church and in Popular Medicine*, Allen and Unwin 1952

3   Ibid

4   Horace, *The Satires of Horace and Perseus*, Penguin 1973

5   It would be fun to have a corporate Saturnalia, when, on one of the days after Christmas, senior managers change places with the catering staff, who solemnly lecture them on mission statements, targets, synergy and blue-sky thinking, and cast angry looks at the CEO, as with bowed head and cautious tread, he tries unsuccessfully to push in the coffee trolley without rattling cups. Afterwards the caterers in suits retire to the atrium and refuse to acknowledge, or even make eye contact with, managers in waistcoats obsequiously offering trays of prosecco and canapés. This would surely dispel the post-Christmas depression and have workers rushing back to the office with joyous cries of '*Io Saturnalia!*'

6   *The Complete Tacitus Collection*, Karpathos 2015

7   Mikhail Bakhtin, *Rabelais and His World*, Massachusetts Institute of Technology 1968

8   Ibid

9   *Gargantua and Pantagruel*, Penguin 1955. This is the excellent J. M. Cohen translation. The free online version by Thomas Urquhart is dreadful.

10 Johan Huizinga, *Homo Ludens: A Study of the Play Element in Culture*, Roy 1950

11 Milan Kundera, *The Art of the Novel*, Faber 1988

12 *Rabelais and His World*

13 Quoted in ibid

14 'Shite' is a key word in the Irish vocabulary, so it is fitting that Rabelais himself connected it to Ireland. When a character on a ship discharges a cannon for a laugh and the cowardly Panurge, cowering below deck, shits himself, he denies that this is what has stained his shirt tail: 'Not a bit of it. Do you call it shit, turds, crots, ordure, deposit, faecal matter, excrement, droppings, fumets, mation, dung, stronts, scybale, or spyrathe? It's saffron from Ireland, that's what I think it is. Ho ho, saffron from Ireland.'

15 Renee Descartes, 'Discourse on Method of Rightly Conducting the Reason and Seeking Truth in the Field of Science', in *Philosophical Essays*, Bobbs-Merrill 1964

16 Two notable exceptions to this trend were Laurence Sterne and William Blake. Both explicitly distanced themselves from satire. Swift, said Sterne, 'keeps a due distance from Rabelais; I keep a due distance from him'. And Blake: 'Mock on, Mock on Voltaire, Rousseau: Mock on, Mock on: 'tis all in vain.' Sterne's favourite writer was Rabelais, and *Tristram Shandy* has a ribald extravagance bursting to get out of its eighteenth-century waistcoat. Blake's work is full of invocations to mirth, laughter and joy: 'Exuberance is beauty'. And I see now that his aphorism, 'The road of excess leads to the palace of wisdom', which I have always disliked, can be read as an acceptance of the excessiveness of life rather than an incitement to personal self-indulgence.

17 In *Carnival* (Scolar Press 1980) the historian Emmanuel Le Roy Ladurie gives a detailed account of one especially brutal bourgeois suppression – the 1580 carnival in the southern French town of Romans. A group of the bourgeois elite, led by a judge, murdered the leader of the carnival organised by artisans and farm workers, the Bear King (a French version of the Lord of Misrule) and imprisoned the other organisers. The judge then sealed off the town, set up an illegal council and condemned the prisoners to torture and hanging. Le Roy Ladurie estimates that the judge, Antoine Guérin, had only sixty men, whereas the Bear King carnival had a force of 600, but the bourgeoisie prevailed through ruthlessness and the belief, often repeated by Guérin, that their actions had been inspired and guided by God.

18 Friedrich Nietzsche, *The Birth of Tragedy*, Dover 2012

19 Friedrich Nietzsche, *Thus Spoke Zarathustra*, Penguin 1969

20 *Selected Letters of Friedrich Nietzsche*, Hackett 1997

21 *The Birth of Tragedy*

22 I. M. Lewis, *Ecstatic Religion*, 3rd edition, Routledge 2003

Chapter 8 – Fun and Hedonism

1   Epicurus, *The Art of Happiness*, Penguin 2012

2   Ibid

3   Ibid

4   Ibid

5   Ibid

6   John Stuart Mill, *Utilitarianism*, Start Publishing 2012

7   Ibid

8   Ibid

9   One is *Pleasure and the Good Life: Concerning the Nature, Varieties, and Plausibility of Hedonism*, Oxford University Press 2004, by the American Professor of Philosophy Fred Feldman. It is significant that Feldman feels it necessary to 'try' to 'defend' hedonism, and to beg for a charitable interpretation. The first two sentences of his introduction: 'The central aim of this book is to defend hedonism as a substantive theory about The Good Life. I try to show that, when carefully and charitably interpreted, certain forms of hedonism are plausible and defensible.'

10 Eric Klinenberg, *Going Solo: The Extraordinary Rise and Surprising Appeal of Living Alone*, Penguin 2012

11 *The Selected Letters of Gustave Flaubert*, Hamish Hamilton 1954

12 Friedrich Nietzsche, *Human, All Too Human*, Penguin 1994

13 Ibid

14 Friedrich Nietzsche, *Will to Power*, Vintage 1967

15 Friedrich Nietzsche, *Thus Spoke Zarathustra*, Penguin 1969

16 Ibid

17 Ibid

18 Friedrich Nietzsche, *The Birth of Tragedy*, Dover 2012

19 Milan Kundera, *The Unbearable Lightness of Being*, Harper and Row 1984

20 Lesley Chamberlain, *Nietzsche in Turin*, Picador 1996

21 I had this fantasy myself for several years in my early twenties. Becoming a lighthouse keeper was the only satisfying job I could imagine – but the Commission for Irish Lights wrote to say that there were no current vacancies, and that the lighthouses were becoming automated.

22 Quoted in Klinenberg, *Going Solo: The Extraordinary Rise and Surprising Appeal of Living Alone*

23 Jean Jacques Rousseau, *Emile, or On Education*, Penguin 1991

24 Charles Taylor, *The Ethics of Authenticity*, Harvard University Press 1992. 'We are expected to develop our own opinions, outlook, stances to things, to a considerable

degree through solitary reflection. But this is not how things work with important issues, such as the definition of our identity. We define this always in dialogue with, sometimes in struggle against, the identities our significant others want to recognize in us. And even when we outgrow some of the latter – our parents, for instance – and they disappear from our lives, the conversation with them continues within us as long as we live.'

25   Larry Siedentop, *Inventing the Individual: The Origins of Western Liberalism*, Allen Lane 2014, gives the full story of the development, which he summarises elegantly as: 'Secularism is Christianity's gift to the world.'

26   It would be interesting to trace this trend. My feeling is that it began in the sixties with movies like *Ocean's Eleven*, *The Magnificent Seven*, *The Dirty Dozen* and *The Wild Bunch*, and that the buddy movie took off with *Butch Cassidy and the Sundance Kid* in 1969. The continuing popularity of James Bond is the exception that proves the rule.

27   It should also be acknowledged that he was not always right. His estimate of the sun's diameter as two feet was slightly out.

28   Rabelais also believed in a community of fun-loving individuals. In *Gargantua and Pantagruel* several delightful chapters describe Gargantua's plans to establish on his land in Thélème an abbey unlike any other. For a start it would not be enclosed behind walls but remain open to the world because enclosure encourages envy, malice and conspiracy. And it would not be restricted to one sex but include both equally, though only women who are 'sweet-natured' and men who are 'of pleasant nature also', with all required to be 'keen-witted and serene', all welcome to apply and admittance refused only to bankers, lawyers and judges. Unlike religious institutions, this abbey would impose no binding oath. 'It was decreed that both men and women, once accepted, could depart from there whenever they pleased, without let or hindrance.' Nor are there vows of 'chastity, poverty and obedience', nor even any 'laws, statutes or rules', with life regulated only by 'free will and pleasure'. Even the tyranny of time will be rejected here. 'And because in the religious foundations of this world everything is encompassed, limited, and regulated by hours, it was decreed that there should be no clock or dial at all, but that affairs should be conducted according to chance and opportunity.'

The facilities in this new abbey would include swimming baths, tennis and ball courts, archery ranges, a horse-riding ring, and for walks an orchard and gardens with a 'neat maze'. For the pleasures of the mind, the main building will house not just one but a series of 'fine, great libraries of Greek, Latin, Hebrew, French, Italian and Spanish books, divided storey by storey according to their languages'. There would also be 9,332 spacious and well-appointed personal apartments, each giving on a great central hall for communal activities and with access to a roof terrace. Here even human vanity would not only be accepted but indulged. 'In each retiring room was a crystal mirror, set in a fine gold frame embellished all round with pearls, and it was large enough to give a true reflection of the whole figure.'

Nothing better illustrates Rabelais's understanding of human nature than this provision not only of mirrors but *full-length* mirrors. His abbey sounds like the ideal apartment complex for urban singletons.

Chapter 9 – Fun Goes Dancing

1   Jane Goodall, *My Friends, the Wild Chimpanzees*, Washington 1967
2   Aniruddh Patel, *Music, Language and the Brain*, Oxford University Press 2008
3   Oliver Sacks, *Musicophilia*, Knopf 2011
4   Merlin Donald, *Origins of the Modern Mind*, Harvard University Press 1991
5   Everyone should celebrate a *Rite of Spring*, so I have created a new ritual for couples on the last Sunday in April. While Man the Hunter ventures forth to track down venison steaks in Waitrose, Woman the Fertility Goddess goes to the Garden Centre for bedding plants and solemnly reunites these with Mother Earth in her back garden. Then she performs a pagan *vily* dance to Stravinsky's wild rhythms, before bearing to her consort the sacred flame to light the first barbecue of the season. Finally they each drink a glass of Coonawarra Shiraz and have sexual intercourse on the La-Z-Boy Recliner, with the woman on top shaking out her hair and chanting the ancient Sumerian hymn of the Goddess Inanna, 'My vulva, the horn, the Boat of Heaven, is full of eagerness like the young moon.'
6   Quoted in E. L. Blackman, *Religious Dances in the Christian Church and in Popular Medicine*, London 1952
7   Quoted in ibid
8   Elizabeth Wayland Barber, in *The Dancing Goddesses: Folklore, Archaeology, and the Origins of European Dance*, Norton 2013, reconstructs some of the ancient dances, as well as giving a full account of the *vily* tradition.
9   Maurice Louis, *Le Folklore et La Danse*, Maisonneuve et Larose 1963
10 *The Times*, summer 1816
11 Quoted in Sheryl Garratt, *Adventures in Wonderland: A Decade of Club Culture*, Headline 1998
12 Ibid
13 Quoted in Graham St John, *Technomad: Global Raving Countercultures*, Equinox 2009
14 Quoted in *Adventures in Wonderland: A Decade of Club Culture*

15 The splendidly named English duo *Shut Up and Dance* satirised the plagiarism frenzy with a dance record called '£10 to get in' (with its remix '£20 to get in').

16 David Foster Wallace and Mark Costello, *Signifying Rappers*, Ecco Press 1990

17 The theme song of the age should be *In My Tribe* by 10,000 Maniacs, one of my favourite group names (in fact second only to Throbbing Gristle). My beloved was a great fan of this group and I enjoyed answering family phone calls with the apology, 'I'm sorry but my wife has ten thousand maniacs performing in the living room.'

18 Sally Sommer, 'C'mon to my House: Underground-House Dancing', *Dance Research Journal* 33, 2001

19 Quoted in *Technomad*

Chapter 10 – Fun Goes Comical

1 Ben Jonson, 'Volpone: or the Fox', in *Five Plays*, Oxford University Press 1981

2 Quoted in Andrew McConnell Stott, *The Pantomime Life of Joseph Grimaldi: laughter, madness and the story of Britain's greatest comedian*, Canongate 2009

3 *Basic Writings of Nietzsche*, Modern Library 2000

4 Quoted in Oliver Double, *Getting the Joke: the inner workings of stand-up comedy*, Methuen 2005

5 Zadie Smith, *Changing My Mind*, Penguin 2009

6 Richard Pryor, *Live in Concert*

7 Quoted in the *Guardian*, 30.11.2014

8 Harry Thompson, *Peter Cook: a Biography*, Hodder & Stoughton 1997

9 In his book on stand-up, *How I Escaped My Certain Fate: the Life and Deaths of a Stand-up Comic*, Faber 2010, the English comedian Stewart Lee puts the ideal audience size at between 100 and 200 and reveals that his two favourite venues are 150-seaters. This book includes transcripts of his stand-up routines, with interesting analysis of what worked and what failed.

10 John Berryman, *The Dream Songs*, Farrar, Strauss and Giroux 2014

Chapter 11 – Fun Goes Sexual

1 Several species once believed to be sexually monogamous for life, for instance the gibbon and penguin, have been revealed as only temporarily, or socially, monogamous. Even the stately swan screws around.

2 *Sex on Earth* by Jules Howard, Bloomsbury 2014, gives a full account of monogamy among animals.

3 And bonobo sex is not just for fun, or, rather, the fun has a serious social purpose

in avoiding or resolving violent conflict within and between groups. As the prima-
tologist Franz de Waal neatly summarised, 'the chimpanzee resolves sexual issues
with power; the bonobo resolves power issues with sex.' When one bonobo provokes
another, say by accidentally knocking it off a branch, one will offer sex to prevent a
fight, and when bonobo groups meet in the forest they are more likely to have sex
than to start a fight. The bonobo really has put into practice the old hippy maxim
of 'Make Love Not War'.

4   *Sex at Dawn* by Christopher Ryan and Cacilda Jetha, Harper Perennial 2012, gives
a full account of this.

5   *The Poems of Catullus*, translated by Peter Whigham, Penguin 1966

In Ovid's *Metamorphoses* Tiresias is a man who was transformed into a woman
by the gods for seven years and had both the male and female experience of sex.
Asked by Zeus to say which gender experienced more pleasure, Tiresias answered
women, and was immediately struck blind by Hera, wife of Zeus, as a punishment
for revealing women's secret.

The Greek poet Herondas wrote about a leather dildo made by the cobbler
Kerdon and passed around middle-class wives who prefer it to their husbands. A
woman called Koritto rhapsodises about it to another woman called Metro:

> The workmanship! What workmanship! You would say
> it's Athena's work, not Kerdon's when you see it.
> And I – for he came bringing two of them, Metro –
> when I saw them my eyes went wide.
> Men don't make their cocks so –
> it's just here – straight. And not just this, but it's soft as sleep, and the straps
> are wool, not leather. You could search,
> but you'd not find a cobbler more kindly disposed to women.

Metro's response is to ask why Koritto did not acquire both dildos. Koritto
explains that it was difficult enough to get one from Kerdon ('I kissed him, I rubbed
his bald head, I poured out sweet drinks, I teased him – the only thing I didn't give
him was my body'). Metro complains that Korritto should indeed have given her
body and leaves to find Kerdon herself.

This is not an isolated mention of dildos, which appear on pottery from
the fourth century BCE on, and archaeologists have found numerous 'phallic
objects' from the Palaeolithic period that look like dildos and have come to be
acknowledged as such, though, despite the obvious penis heads, they were originally
identified as sculptures of women, batons for orchestrating rituals and even arrow

and spear straighteners. This is as credible as interpreting *The Song of Songs* in the bible, blatantly erotic, as an expression of Yaweh's divine love for his people. There is even a double dildo, two phalluses at an angle of 120 degrees, perfect for two women. If Koritto and Metro had seen this they might well have commissioned a version in leather from Kerdon.

6   Gauter Le Leu, *Fabliaux: Ribald Tales from the old French*, New York 1965

7   Ibid

8   Ibid

9   Rabelais, *Gargantua and Pantagruel,* Penguin 1955

10   Geoffrey Chaucer, *The Canterbury Tales*, translated by David Wright, Oxford University Press 1985. Most translations of Chaucer are in clunky rhyming couplets full of inversions and padding to get rhyme words. David Wright was a poet and translates in strong free verse.

11   There were other similarities. Both writers were learned, embracing a variety of disciplines (Chaucer knew enough astronomy to invent an astrolabe for his son and write *A Treatise on the Astrolabe*), both were widely travelled and had been to Italy, both were men of the world who had to operate in tricky, dangerous milieus, and both were publicly denounced – Rabelais by the Church and Chaucer in Parliament. When they had roused the anger of the powerful, both went into prudent, self-imposed exile – Rabelais in north-east France and Chaucer in Kent. Chaucer's employment does not sound dangerous. He was a collector of duties on wool shipments going out of London docks, which in the contemporary world would be an undemanding administrative post – but in the 14th century wool brought in a third of the country's revenue, and the wool shippers Chaucer was supposed to regulate were powerful men making fortunes and giving much of it in bribes to the king and others.

12   The Inquisition persisted as an institution within the Catholic Church until 1904 when, in an early example of imaginative rebranding, it was renamed the 'Supreme Sacred Congregation of the Holy Office'.

13   Quoted in *Sex at Dawn*

14   As a result, men were often shocked, and even disgusted, by the revelation of desire in supposedly well-bred women. The most well-known example is the wedding night of John Ruskin, when his bride Effie stripped naked for him and he fled in horror. Time did nothing to mitigate this disgust and eventually Effie got a divorce on the grounds of non-consummation. Revelations of sexual desire in older women were of course even more shocking. When the sixty-year-old George Eliot married a fervent admirer of her novels who was twenty years younger, and the couple went to a hotel in Venice on their honeymoon, the new husband jumped out of the room

into the Grand Canal. No clear explanation for this has emerged but I have often wondered if the husband, expecting a soul mate, was terrified by a sexual approach and would rather have drowned than engage physically.

15 Rachel Maines, *The Technology of Orgasm: Hysteria, the Vibrator and Women's Sexual Satisfaction,* Johns Hopkins University Press 1999

16 There were even a few daring advocates of free love. One of these, the editor and publisher of *The Adult: A Journal for the Advancement of Freedom in Sexual Relationships*, was actually called John Badcock.

17 Philip Larkin, *Collected Poems*, Faber 1988

18 Erica Jong, *Fear of Flying*, Martin Secker and Warburg 1974

19 John Updike, *Picked-Up Pieces*, Random House 1975

20 John Updike, *Self-Consciousness*, André Deutsch 1989

21 Adam Begley, *Updike*, Harper Perennial 2014

22 An isolated swinger ranch would be a great setting for a murder mystery. At Christmas the ranch is full but cut off by a major snowfall, and a woman is found hanging from a suspension hook in the Bondage Suite. At first this is thought to be a suicide based on sexual shame but when many stress the dead woman's joy in swinging the detective who is one of the swingers begins to suspect murder. The novel would of course be called *The Swinging Corpse*.

23 Antoinette Kelly, 'Swingers Groups in Ireland Are Growing at a Massive Rate', www.irishcentral.com/news 14.09.2010

24 Quoted in William Jankowiak and Laura Mixson, 'I have his heart, swinging is just sex: the ritualisation of sex and the rejuvenation of the love bond in an American exchange community', in *Intimacies*, Columbia University Press 2008

25 Katherine Frank, *Plays Well In Groups: A Journey Through the World of Group Sex*, Rowman and Littlefield 2013

26 Robin Baker and Mark Bellis, *Human Sperm Competition: Copulation, Masturbation and Infidelity*, Springer 1994

27 For a full account see Carin Bondar, *The Nature of Sex: the ins and outs of mating in the animal kingdom*, Weidenfeld and Nicolson 2015.

28 *Dogging Tales*, Channel 4, broadcast 04.04.2013

29 William Blake, 'The Crystal Cabinet', in *The Complete Poems*, Penguin 2004

30 YouGov survey August 2015

31 Just like Halloween, circus was revived in the seventies by being associated with fear. Before this there was Batman's foe, The Joker, but the fashion for evil clowns really got underway with Stephen King's novel, *It*, which was followed by films such as *S.I.C.K. Serial Insane Clown Killer*, *The Clown at Midnight*, *Sloppy the Psychotic* and *Bongo: Killer Clown*. Fans of these movies might like to consider a stay in The

Nevada Creepy Clown Motel, where all public areas and rooms are sinisterly clown themed.

Chapter 12 – Fun Goes on Holiday

1   The UK was slow to cash in on Chinese tourism but in 2013 British Airways put on a direct flight to Heathrow from the central Chinese city of Chengdu and advertised this in a Chengdu shopping mall by staging a 'Chinese panda flashmob dance' with fifty people in panda suits but also, to remind the shoppers of Britain's major achievements, a few dressed as the Duke and Duchess of Cambridge, Sherlock Holmes, David Beckham and Harry Potter. And the Yorkshire town of Barnsley, birthplace of James Taylor Hudson, the missionary who converted many Chinese to Christianity in the nineteenth century, hoped for a piece of the action by selling itself as the Chinese Bethlehem – but the Chinese who came to assess the town were not impressed. The Chinese preferred Thailand, which not only offered a satisfying mix of spirituality, entertainment and sex – Buddhist temples in the morning, theme parks in the afternoon and ladyboys in the evening – but was also much warmer than Barnsley.

2   In France the Cathedral of Vézelay in Burgundy was doing well as a pilgrimage destination, until it was blown away by the Monastery of St Maximin La Sainte Baume in Provence that claimed to have the body of Mary Magdalen, on the grounds that the 'suave odour' emanating from an ancient sarcophagus meant it must hold the remains of someone seriously holy.

3   Quoted in Maxine Feifer, *Tourism in History:from Imperial Rome to the Present*, Stein and Day 1986

4   Geoffrey Chaucer, *The Canterbury Tales*, translated by David Wright, Oxford University Press 1985

5   Kim M. Phillips and Barry Reay, *Sex Before Sexuality: A Premodern History*, Polity 2013, has more on these badges.

6   Quoted in Victor Turner, *Process, Performance and Pilgrimage*, Concept 1979

7   Maxine Feifer, *Tourism in History: from Imperial Rome to the Present*, Stein and Day 1986

8   *The Gentleman's Pocket Companion for Travelling into Foreign Parts*, London 1722

9   Mark Twain, *The Innocents Abroad*, Harper and Row 1966

10   Don DeLillo, *White Noise*, Viking Penguin 1984

11   James Howell, *Instructions for Forraine Travel*, Humphrey Mosley 1642

12   Flaubert travelled with his fellow writer Maxime Du Camp and enjoyed seeing a young man being publicly buggered by a monkey, a donkey being jacked off by

another monkey, and a marabout (an idiot saint) religiously masturbated by Moslem women until he died of exhaustion ('from morning to night it was a perpetual jacking off'). Du Camp had himself jacked off by a tour guide behind some ruins, pronouncing it very good, and Flaubert, hoping to 'skewer' an attractive young masseur in the baths, was disappointed to discover that it was the young man's day off, and had to settle for being masturbated by an ugly male attendant in his fifties. 'Travelling as we are for educational purposes, and charged with a mission by the government, we have considered it our duty to indulge in this form of ejaculation.'

For hetero sex, Flaubert journeyed up the Nile to Esna and the house of the famous prostitute Kuchuk Hanem. First Flaubert, Kuchuk and her musicians drank several glasses of *raki*, then the musicians were blindfolded before they played for Kuchuk's dance in an archaic style described by Flaubert as 'brutal' and like the 'dance on old Greek vases'. A colleague of Kuchuk's, Safiah Zugairah, arrived. '*Coup* with Safia Zugairah – I stain the divan. She is very corrupt and writhing, extremely voluptuous. But the best was the second copulation with Kuchuk. Effect of her necklace between my teeth. Her cunt was like rolls of velvet as she made me come. I felt like a tiger.' Flaubert persuaded Kuchuk to let him spend the night with her. Between *coups* she snored and he amused himself by killing bedbugs on the wall. What he enjoyed most about the whores was the mingled aroma of bedbugs and sandalwood.

Flaubert in Egypt by Francis Steegmuller, Michael Haag 1983, gives an entertaining account of all this and much more.

13 Or *Yankee Doodle Dandy*, if appropriate.
14 *Guardian* 10.01.2015
15 David Foster Wallace, *A supposedly fun thing I'll never do again*, Little Brown 1997
16 Many seem to believe in this cruise promise of eternal life. At the London Cruise Show there were queues of the silver-haired everywhere waiting to book but no one within even twenty yards of the Write a Will Stand.

Chapter 13 – Fun Goes to the Game

1 Kendall Blanchard, *The Anthropology of Sport*, Greenwood 1995
2 In 1968 Frederick Exley got the ball rolling, as it were, with *A Fan's Notes*, a 'fictional memoir' about his obsession with the New York Giants, followed in 1969 by B. S. Johnson's *The Unfortunates*, a novel about a sports reporter covering a football match. In the seventies John Updike made his everyman hero Harry Angstrom a former basketball player, and more or less claimed golf, not that there was much competition for this most suburban of games, making it a

feature of many of his novels and stories and producing enough non-fiction golf writing to make a book. Later, David Foster Wallace claimed tennis by making a tennis academy the subject of his most famous novel, *Infinite Jest*, and writing several long essays about tennis. Other sports books by prominent novelists include Bernard Malamud's baseball novel, *The Natural*, Don DeLillo's American football novel, *Endzone*, Nick Hornby's memoir, *Fever Pitch*, about his obsession with Arsenal, and Tim Parks's non-fiction account of following an Italian team, *A Season with Verona*.

3   Aristotle, *On Rhetoric*, Oxford 2007
4   Jean-Paul Sartre, *Critique of Dialectical Reason*, Verso 2006
5   Jacques Derrida, *Society Matters*, Autumn-Winter 1998
6   Tim Parks, *A Season with Verona*, Vintage 2012
7   Alex Bellos, *Futebol: Soccer, the Brazilian Way*, Bloomsbury 2002
8   Desmond Morris, *The Soccer Tribe*, Jonathan Cape 1981

Chapter 14 – Fun Goes Spiritual

1   Quoted in William McNeill, *Keeping Together in Time: Dance and Drill in Human History*, Harvard University Press 1995
2   Quoted in *A Brief Introduction to Hasidism*, Public Broadcasting Service website, www.pbs.org
3   Ibid
4   Christopher Partridge, *The Re-Enchantment of the West: Alternative Spiritualities, Sacralization and Popular Culture and Occulture*, T & T Clark International 2004
5   Linda Woodhead, 'The World's Parliament of Religions and the Rise of Alternative Spirituality', in *Reinventing Christianity*, Ashgate 2001
6   Apparently, psybreaks can be easily mistaken for nu skool breaks, but where nu skool favours heavily distorted bass and frequent glitch edits, psybreaks is more inclined to arpeggiated synths. I have no idea what this means but I love the authoritative sound of it.
7   Quoted in Graham St John, *Technomad: Global Raving Countercultures*, Equinox 2009
8   Quoted in the *Guardian*, 07.02.2015

Chapter 15 – Fun Goes Political

1   Like Halloween, this was a reimportation to Europe, in this case of the carnival tradition that travelled to Trinidad with French plantation owners and was taken

up by the natives, who introduced many inversion features to mock their masters. These included men dressed as French ladies in caricatured frilly outfits, with exaggerated busts and bottoms, a sailor mocking the naval authorities, a Pierrot dressed in the European style but insulting prominent officials and onlookers, and self-mockery with a group pretending to be slaves, dressed in loin clothes, covered in a mixture of soot and molasses to look blacker, attached to a chain drawn along by an overseer who occasionally knocked one down and delivered a mock beating with a big stick. Some of these characters featured in the early London version of the sixties and seventies, but have not appeared since the turn of the millennium.

2   Comte de Lautréamont, *Maldoror*, Apollo 1973

3   'Poem of the Week', *Guardian* 31.08.2009

4   Tristan Tzara, 'The Dada Manifesto', in *The Dada Reader: a Critical Anthology*, edited by Dawn Ades, Tate Publishing 2006

5   Comte de Lautréamont, *Maldoror and Poems*, Penguin 1978

6   Quoted in McKenzie Wark, *The Beach Beneath the Street: The Everyday Life and Glorious Times of the Situationist International*, Verso 2015

7   Quoted in *The Beach Beneath the Street*

8   The actor Peter Sellers was so taken by *The Magic Christian* that he bought 100 copies and distributed these to everyone he met, including Stanley Kubrick, who then hired Southern to write the script for *Dr Strangelove*. Sellers eventually appeared in a film of *The Magic Christian* (with Ringo Starr) but this, alas, was woefully bad, another example of the folly of trying to film a novel whose excellence is in its prose style rather than its characters or action (*The Great Gatsby* has suffered several times from the same mistake).

9   This apparently new development was also a return. The first literary pranks may well have been perpetrated by Rabelais, who published two spoofs on astrology, *Almanac for 1532* and *Pantagrueline Prognostification*, which predicted that, 'This year the blind will see very little' and 'In winter wise men will not sell their fur coats to buy firewood.' Rabelais made fun of solemn prose right to the end, when he suggested for his will, 'I have nothing; I owe a great deal; the rest I leave to the poor.'

10 Quoted in Benjamin Shepard, *Play, Creativity and Social Movements*, Routledge 2011

11 Abbie Hoffman, *The Best of Abbie Hoffman*, Four Walls and Eight Windows 1989

12 Quoted in *Play, Creativity and Social Movements*

13 A feminist offshoot of the Yippies was the Women's International Terrorist Conspiracy from Hell (WITCH), who specialised in disrupting beauty pageants, though their most carnivalesque action was at a Bridal Fair in Madison Square

Garden where a Coven performed an Un-Wedding Ceremony with the vows, 'We promise to smash the alienated family unit. We promise not to obey,' and celebrated the un-union by releasing white mice into the crowd. It was expected that the brides-to-be would scream and jump on chairs – but instead they rushed to save the mice. The WITCH stunts provoked a significant reaction from the religious right who interpreted them as evidence of genuine Satanism, and Andrew Greeley, a Catholic priest employed by the University of Chicago's Sociology Department, published a solemn warning article, 'WITCH is only one manifestation – though a spectacular one – of a resurgence of interest in the occult.'

14   Terry Southern was with Hoffman during the Chicago disturbances and testified in his defence. Later, in an obituary on Hoffman (collected in *Now Dig This,* Methuen 2002), Southern described how 'Abs' had saved the French writer Jean Genet from being clubbed by a crazed police officer, and how he, Southern, had congratulated him afterwards:

"'Abs," I said, "that was great." You went the distance for the fab frog poet."

'He tried to deprecate the incident by explaining it away.

"'Man," he said, "didn't you see his *gourd*?" referring to Genet's bald head. "Nobody with a gourd like that can take the kind of whacks these guys are laying out." He flashed his extraordinary smile.

"'Me?" and he touched his Afro-bouf. "I've got some *padding* for it. No problem."'

15   Quoted in *Play, Creativity and Social Movements*

16   Ibid

17   Naomi Klein, *No Logo*, Flamingo 2000

18   Notes from Nowhere, *We are Everywhere: The Irresistible Rise of Global Anti-Capitalism*, Verso 2003

19   Protestor quoted in *Possibilities: Essays on Hierarchy, Rebellion, and Desire*, by David Graeber, AK Press 2007

20   Ibid

21   www.infernalnoise.org

22   David Graeber, *Possibilities: Essays on Hierarchy, Rebellion, and Desire*

23   David Graeber, *Direct Action: An Ethnography*, AK Press 2009

24   Liz Highleyman, 'Emma Goldman', in *The Encyclopedia of Social Movements*, ME Sharpe 2004

25   *Direct Action: An Ethnography*

26   Ibid

Chapter 16 – The Post-Postmodern is the Pre-Premodern

1 This theory is known as 'externalism' or 'extended mind' and is explained by the philosopher Mark Rowlands in *Externalism*, Routledge 2003. For a full account of contemporary theories of mind, see *The New Science of the Mind: From extended mind to embodied phenomenology*, also by Rowlands, MIT Press 2010

2 T. S. Eliot, 'Four Quartets', in *Collected Poems 1909–1962*, Faber 1963

3 Tim Parks, *A Season with Verona*, Vintage 2012

4 Quoted in the *Observer*, 10.05.2015

5 *Grayson Perry's Dream House*, Channel 4, first broadcast on 17.05.2015

6 This form of role playing has become so popular that it is often extended from an evening to a murder mystery weekend, usually organised by a hotel.

Index